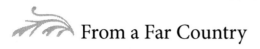 From a Far Country

From a Far Country

Camisards and Huguenots

in the Atlantic World

CATHARINE RANDALL

The University of Georgia Press • Athens and London

Paperback edition, 2011

© 2009 by the University of Georgia Press

Athens, Georgia 30602

www.ugapress.org

Set in 10/13 Minion Pro by BookComp, Inc.

Printed digitally in the United States of America

The Library of Congress has cataloged the hardcover
edition of this book as follows:

Randall, Catharine, 1957–

From a far country : Camisards and Huguenots in the
Atlantic world / Catharine Randall.

    176 p. ; 24 cm.

    Includes bibliographical references and index.

    ISBN-13: 978-0-8203-3390-8 (hardcover : alk. paper)

    ISBN-10: 0-8203-3390-5 (hardcover : alk. paper)

    1. Huguenots—United States—History.

2. Camisards—United States—History.

3. Protestantism—United States—History.

4. Protestantism—France—History.

5. United States—Civilization—French influences.

6. United States—Religion—To 1800.

7. United States—History—Colonial period, ca. 1600–1775. I. Title.

    E184.H9R36 2009

    973.2—dc22   2009009153

Paperback ISBN-13: 978-0-8203-3820-0

        ISBN-10: 0-8203-3820-6

British Library Cataloging-in-Publication Data available

For my father, E. V. Randall, Jr., genealogist extraordinaire, and my mother, Sally Shaw Randall, who is a direct descendant of Gabriel Bernon and whose story, therefore, this is in part.

CONTENTS

Camisards and Huguenots

Old and New World

> Ce qui fait à la fois la force et la faiblesse des gentilshommes de la
> Religion, c'est le grand nombre de fugitifs passé à l'étranger.
> —Ducasse, *La guerre des Camisards, la résistance huguenote sous
> Louis XIV*

George and Martha Washington, Alexander Hamilton, and John Jay are just a few of the numerous historical figures who felt the influence of the Huguenots, a religious and ethnic minority whose ideas informed American culture in important ways. Until fairly recently, however, other than Charles Baird's documentation of the history of Huguenot immigration to the New World, the only study specifically to explore the significance of this phenomenon was Jon Butler's *The Huguenots in America*. Butler organized his exploration regionally, and unlike the emphasis in this book, theological stance was not one of his primary considerations.[1] His thesis of "rapid assimilation" has been contested by the work of scholars such as Robin Gwynn (*Huguenot Heritage*, 1985), who maintained that the Huguenots formed a distinct minority element, perhaps for several generations, before being "slowly assimilated."[2] My research indicates that the French immigrants underwent a lengthy period of adaptation without assimilation, characterized by both a clinging to distinctive religious traits and an overt intention to conform to, and not to contest, the prevailing mind-set of the Puritan New World.

The past few years have seen a dramatic growth of interest in French Protestantism as a marginalized ethnic and religious subculture representing coping mechanisms of minority groups. In particular, the way for further scholarship has been opened by Neil Kamil's encyclopedic investigation of material culture and the artisanal production of Huguenots in the New York and Long Island areas, as well as in other parts of the colonies; Georgia Cosmos's monograph, the only one of its kind, on the testimonials of the Camisard prophets; Randy Sparks and Bertrand Van Ruymbeke's edited collection of essays on religious distinction and integration, including those on the furtherance of the Calvinist polity in London (by Raymond Mentzer) and the transmission of the faith generationally (by Caroline Lougee Chappell); and Randolph Vigne and Charles Littleton's edited collection of papers on the assimilation of immigrant communities in colonial America and elsewhere.[3]

In a conversation with Jon Butler a couple of years ago, when I was beginning research on this project, Butler concurred that "the whole subject—pious literature about the afflictions of French Protestant exiles—could use much more explication." Delighted to get this green light for my project, I plunged in. Then, about a year ago, at a Religion in America seminar at Columbia University, I presented some of the material from this book. I was astounded at how few of the scholars present had heard anything about the Camisards and how little they knew of the Huguenot experience. However, the seminar served as a wonderful laboratory, for the scholars participating immediately began to make connections, especially with the context of colonial America, and to articulate affiliations.

It was clear from our conversations that many different strands of French religious experience became stitched into the "patchwork quilt" of religious diversity in the American colonies. Thus, I hope in these pages not only to provide the fuller "explication" for which Butler called but also to suggest new avenues for scholarly exploration, particularly in relation to colonial America, along the lines of those sparked in discussions at the seminar. I hope also to engage in a dialogue with those scholars now working in the field—some writing so recently that their work entailed a second round of revisions on this manuscript, as they were not available to comment on it the first time I thought it was complete.

The stories recounted in these pages have been, to date, essentially unknown.[4] This is especially true in the case of the Camisards, whose voices might have been lost for all time had not history preserved them through the medium of François Misson, a paradoxical Enlightenment crusader on behalf of the *inspiré* and the oppressed, or through the autobiographies of the handful of Camisards who lived to tell the tale—among them, Bonbonnoux's *Mémoires* and Antoine Court's eyewitness history, both little known to American scholars and little worked on outside of confessional circles in France.[5] History has also retained the impress of the wild and wonderful French Prophets, crying out over the impending Apocalypse, which, they believed, could not fail to ensue in the face of genocidal attacks on loyal French citizens and ecclesial abuses by corrupt Catholic priests, wolves to their flock of Camisard shepherds.[6]

The formerly untold story of the Camisards and Huguenots is a quintessentially American story. Because the antecedents have been little worked on, it seemed vital not to tell this tale in isolation. It was necessary to establish the European context, the transcontinental connection, so that conflicts over ethnicity and identity in the New World could be more deeply understood as resulting from Old World precedents. What could be more American than this rugged rope tying Old to New World experience? The perennial questions of identity are posed: Where do we come from? How did we get here? How can we survive? What does it take to make it in this new land? In addition, issues of appropriating or relinquishing ethnicity and other forms of self-definition are experienced at a very deep level by all Americans of every generation and in every day and age.

The French Protestant subculture did not survive in an externally recognizable form. The only persistence is that of "genealogical memory," such as the Huguenot Society of America, or what Van Ruymbeke calls Huguenot "myth-making," the passing down of stories about one's Huguenot ancestors and their courage in the face of adversity. This may be due to the fact that the French Protestant subculture in the New World lacked the institutional framework that had originally bolstered it.[7]

So what faith did persist may have been fostered by a sort of pietistic reformulation of Reformed theology, along the lines of the Camisards' survival strategy.[8] Once that piety went "underground" or, more accurately, became situated within the space of the individual believer's heart, its surface manifestations became both rare and untraceable to scholars. Many valuable stories were oral testimonies, which died off with their storytellers. Extant sources include the archives of the Musées du désert; the confessional multivolume history of Camisard minister Antoine Court; the supportive and sympathetic polemic of Calvinist preacher Pierre Jurieu; the testimonies collected in London by François Misson; the occasional biography, such as the life of the Baron de Salgas; and some correspondence, such as that between the Walloon churches and a former galley slave, the Huguenot Elie Neau. No overarching or complete perspective or documentation survives to fully flesh out the tale of tribulation, triumph, and testimony.

The themes of self-reinvention, another quintessential American leitmotif, and self-help, the metaphor of "pulling oneself up by one's bootstraps," typically Puritan but also characteristic of both the Camisard and Huguenot strategies for survival, are also present here. For instance, in the absence of their ministers, all slain or fled, the Camisards raised up from their midst lay prophets as leaders: a protodemocratic impulse in the Old World that found a greater realization in the context of the American colonies. To take another example, Gabriel Bernon, self-reinventor extraordinaire, was an entrepreneur par excellence. Once he had escaped imprisonment for his Protestant faith, he fled to Canada, where this former merchant mariner traded in furs, then left for Massachusetts, where he set up a model colony and a distillery and plied numerous other trades, becoming extremely wealthy in the process, before turning to an extensive program of church building. His at times aggressive behavior comported uneasily with his reverent professions of faith; in 1716, the General Assembly of Providence Plantation met at Newport to censure Bernon for "contemptuous and disorderly" conduct, for which he, ever with an eye to self-interest and profit, heartily apologized.[9] Bernon represented a way of being in the world that combined religious fervor with self-interested financial gain, in the best American frontier tradition. In sociolinguistic terms, he was a consummate code shifter, adroit at manipulating the vernacular of two cultures to his best advantage. The life of this charming Reformed rogue epitomizes the sort of American story we love to hear, indeed expect to hear, but the antecedents to his tale have been largely unknown to scholars.

This book supplies a missing component, the French Protestant piece of the puzzle, of the body of ethnographic studies in early American history. It complements Randall Balmer's work on the Dutch in the Middle Colonies, Ned C. Landsman's study of the Scots presence in colonial America, A. G. Roebber's monograph on German immigration patterns to the New World, and Jon Butler and Bertrand Van Ruymbeke's sociological studies of Huguenots in selected cities to help form a more well-rounded ethnographic picture. The discussion of the derivation of Reformed piety coming from the Old World to the New enlarges the complex picture of the significance of ethnic identity and religious conviction during the period, a variegated portrait that adds to the work of Janice Night, *Orthodoxies in Massachusetts*, to take just one recent study given nuance by the exposition of the Camisard and Huguenot plight.

My focus on religious identity, both individual and communal, adds an explicitly theological aspect to other interdisciplinary treatments of the Huguenots and Camisards, such as Kamil's concentration on material culture; differentiates between Camisards and Huguenots in ways that complement the findings of studies like those in Sparks and Van Ruymbeke's *Memory and Identity*; and constructs a more comprehensive narrative than that provided by a focused emphasis on one or two of the more controversial Camisard leaders, such as Walter Utt and Brian Strayer's study of Claude Brousson, *The Bellicose Dove*.

The picture of colonial religion is enhanced, too, by the inclusion of the little-studied Camisards, and the present study recognizes the distinctive characteristics of their subculture and that of the Huguenots.[10] Its fleshed-out discussion of the French Protestant experience in the New World uses the lens of Reformed Christianity to shed additional light on the very important role, already much studied in other respects, played by the Jesuits in the New World. We see the direct clash between these two religious systems, two different styles of converting and evangelizing, and the political machinations that occurred as each responded to the other. Ezéchiel Carré's screed against the Jesuits, published by Cotton Mather (whose writings contributed a substantial body of original source material for this project), provides a cogent illustration of the conflict.

A much-studied historical occurrence such as the uprising of slaves in New York in the early 1700s, for which Elie Neau was blamed, now comes into greater focus as we discern the theological principles, in addition to the personal experience of enslavement and suffering, undergirding Neau's socially radical stance.[11] Sources for the study of Huguenot and Camisard ways of self-expression include, among other documents, Cotton Mather's publications of Neau's spiritual poetry and Carré's sermons, and offer material for the exploration of other colonial connections, such as those explored by Amanda Porterfield in her work on female piety in the colonies.[12] For instance, the Camisards began with women *inspiré* prophets, and early Huguenots had female preachers, such as Marie Dentières. My explication of the influence of Camisard piety on Puritan mysticism, such as the flowery descriptions of spiritual phenomena recorded by John Cotton and by Increase Mather, further develops the work of scholars such as Richard Godbeer.[13] In addition, the present study encourages a fresh look at the role and significance of the Salem witch trials upon Cotton Mather's thought. Could it be that scholars have not talked about Cotton Mather's French connection because the Salem witch trials are so controversial and quirkily compelling, overshadowing the other very important matter that was on Mather's mind at precisely the same time: the status and importance of the French Protestant refugees with whom he was entering into conversation and for whose cause he wished to advocate? And what might scholars make of the fact that the very tortures that Mather—at least in the early stages of the trials—condoned to be employed against the alleged witches were markedly similar to the sorts of depredations he criticized Louis XIV for using against the Camisards? Both "witches" and Camisards were condemned for being involved in highly controversial manifestations of the supernatural. Yet nothing short of a strong sense of religious affiliation between Puritans and French Protestants, an espousal of identity between them and Mather himself, can be suggested by the vehemence of Mather's reaction to the Camisards' extremity. Henricus Selyns of New York City may have eventually persuaded Mather to discard his reliance on "spectral evidence"; however, this study illuminates a historical moment when Mather was not yet ready to do so. Mather was at the nexus of Protestant variations in piety in the New England and Middle Colonies, an unexpected position in which to find a man generally portrayed as a Puritan party-liner. Mather's French connection, heretofore untouched by scholars, now invites exploration from colonialists.

Mather's early, more affective piety was described by Richard Lovelace in his 1979 study as having been profoundly affected by German Pietism.[14] However, Lovelace's study, while seemingly definitive, overlooks the fact that the German Pietists themselves claimed to have been influenced by the Camisards. To argue that Cotton Mather's piety was influenced by German Pietism is not inaccurate, but incomplete; such an argument does, to some extent, put the theological cart before the horse. Consequently, an exploration of the influence of Camisard piety on Mather's hybrid faith, combining both Puritanism and Pietism, adds a significant, formerly missing detail to the theological landscape in the colonies.[15]

The pan-Reformed connection is crucial to a full understanding of the role that religious identity played in the colonies. With respect to the French component, this study extends and deepens Butler's contributions. While he claims that the Huguenots assimilated extremely rapidly by intermarrying with other ethnic groups and confessions and jettisoning their own religious identity, it is now clear that the particulars of Camisard and Huguenot religious self-perception remained crucial, but were operative in a new, more private, and more individual way that nonetheless significantly informed their public accomplishments: Gabriel Bernon, for instance, who helped found three Anglican churches in Rhode Island, was venerated by his contemporaries as a man of solid Reformed faith. Bernon's attendance at an Anglican rather than a French Reformed church might be interpreted not as Butler has suggested—that is, as evidence of assimilation, effectively a diminution of faith—but rather as the reasoned selection of an inoffensive alternative. This option was made possible by England, whose government Bernon admired for its Enlightenment principles of freedom of conscience and rationalism, and whose citizenship he accepted. This enabled him to retain his core beliefs intact.

While it might superficially appear that French Protestants in the New World assimilated rapidly and almost completely, in fact a unified core of beliefs, ideologies, and ways of life deriving from Huguenot and Camisard experiences persisted, informing some very important decisions, both personal and social, that these personalities made in the New World.

Assimilation, no; adaptation, yes. But this adaptation occurred paradoxically: by the Huguenots imitating the Camisards' survival tactics, thereby reincorporating their "enthusiastic" cousins—who had often been cast out, at least in the Old World, by their more staid coreligionists—into the Reformed family fold in the New World. The family relationship between Camisards and Huguenots, coupled with a mutual distrust born of faiths experienced in different idioms, complicated the picture for them. So, too, did the social and religious scene that confronted Camisard and Huguenot survivors when they immigrated to the New World.

Despite the predominant Puritanism of the New England colonies, there was a variegated tapestry of fringe faiths seeking to maintain their standing and theological integrity in this new space. The reception the Camisards and the Huguenots received, varying from distrust of the French to assistance offered to fellow Protestants; their sponsors and interlocutors, such as Cotton Mather and the Boston church; the institutions with which they affiliated, like the Society for the Propagation of the Gospel and the Society for the Propagation of Christian Knowledge, or those which they themselves established, such as Bernon's churches or Neau's school for African Americans—these all became venues for the working out of their salvation in the realm of the here and now.

The story of French Protestantism is both Continental and American in that the Camisards and Huguenots created connections and cross-pollinations among the varieties of religious expressions they encountered or fostered, both in America and abroad. The Philadelphia movement in London responded directly to Camisard apocalypticism; the Shakers acknowledged the Camisards as their progenitors in faith; George Whitefield, John Wesley, and the Moravian Pietists all had contact with them and were moved by their plight, persuaded by their ecstasy, and awakened by their prophecies. Again, the story stretches across the Atlantic. Like the Camisards in France, the Quakers both in England and in the New World placed primary importance on the working of the Holy Spirit, spoke of imminent apocalypticism, as did the Camisard *inspirés* and the French Prophets, and appealed to the lower and working classes, consistent with the Camisards' origins in a poor, disenfranchised peasantry. In England, the Shakers of Manchester derived "inspiration and nurture from the French Prophets," and once in America, they acknowledged direct descent from the Camisards on the very first page of *Shakerism: Its Meaning and Message*, their institutional autobiography.[16] Both groups had female preachers who experienced "Ecstatick Fits." Again, similar to the analphabetic Camisards, the Shakers, in the first "Opening of the Shaker Gospel" (May 19, 1789), professed distrust for the written word and stated a preference for oral testimony and "witnessing." Further work on how the little-recognized Camisards' faith became interwoven with the motley fabric of religions in colonial America now seems in order.

Further, the story stretches a narrative thread from France, Switzerland, England, Germany, and the Low Countries over to the American colonies by virtue of the common theme of freedom of conscience. Camisard beliefs included "the light of conscience," the action of the Holy Spirit within, and freedom of conscience in regard to matters without; in important and admirable ways, these convictions conformed to Enlightenment notions of freedom of conscience, despite the rather paradoxical vehicle for it that the Camisards, often unlettered, glossolalic peasants, presented.

In the face of dire persecution, torture, and royal antipathy, this small subculture asserted its right both to be loyal citizens and to dissent religiously. All of Europe—and the colonies—heard their message loud and clear. Pierre Jurieu, in exile on the Continent, became their mouthpiece, providing theory to legitimize the prophetic Camisard praxis; François Misson risked his reputation to prepare their legal dossier; William of Orange and Voltaire upbraided Louis XIV; Cotton Mather preached their plight and penned their first history; and the Continent and the colonies, convulsed over this cause célèbre, awaited the end-times.

What they got instead was change: social, political, and theological change of a magnitude hard to comprehend given the small minority that was its agency. But as the Camisards contended, miracles still could and did happen. As they understood it, revelation was not closed; God was still working out his purposes through his chosen people in the world.

An essentially untold story, a quintessentially American story, a tale of two continents, this is also a contemporary story. Huguenots throughout the world still form a minority community, but a community that, despite its small size, has had, and continues to have, a significant impact. Another contemporary motif is the repugnant notion of a program of "ethnic cleansing," so present to us from the horrors of Nazi Germany, Bosnia, and Rwanda. This theme resounds throughout the Camisard story: Louis XIV turned against his own people with a deliberate strategy to eliminate French Protestantism in France. The Abbé Basville, commissioned to oversee this project, even used the term "cleansing" in his report on the Camisard "exterminations" when he boasted, "There is no parish which has not been thoroughly cleansed."[17]

The Camisard story in particular also resonates with the contemporary American notion of an implicit political theocracy; the religious Right, for example, increasingly draws on the historical American (and, we now see, European) experience of a Protestant minority sect or "subculture," as Randall Balmer has termed it.[18] The experiences of "circling the wagons," of needing to devise institutional structures to protect a subculture from the larger world, of finding guidance and a mandate in a literal reading of scripture—all of these are also Camisard experiences. Since America increasingly finds itself under the aegis of a political system in which church and state are not separate—a notion that would have troubled the Camisards, who claimed, under freedom of conscience, the right to worship as they chose while still professing loyalty to the king—it may be helpful to discover how such a subculture developed, evolved, and now seems largely to steer the helm of the ship of state.[19] Perhaps had the history of religious persecutions gone another way, this development would not have transpired.

What seeds of the present-day predicament may we discern in the early travails of an imperiled cluster of ranting farmers huddled around a fire on a mountaintop, chanting psalms to defy the king? In the case of the Camisards, their subculture never exercised influence in the political sphere such as that displayed by the American evangelical subculture. In the case of the Huguenots, however, there may be some similarities. The influence that Huguenots wielded in the New World was pervasive, and while it was, for the most part, benign, such involvement as Bernon's diplomatic intervention with Lord Bellomont attests to an overweening political leverage in the American colonies. Bernon's intervention derived primarily from the commendable goal of protecting his ethnic and confessional community; however, the degree—though not the kind—of power he possessed seems akin to that currently wielded by certain powerful religious persuasions in American politics.[20]

It is for other historians to ascertain these affiliations, similarities, differences, and their long-term effects. But we know ourselves best when we turn back to look at whence we have come. We are also most fully in touch with the texture of history when we approach it from an interdisciplinary angle, weaving together text and theology, politics and personality.

The contributions of French Protestants to America survive in many forms. Their memory may remain in genealogical records attesting, for example, to the political importance of figures descended from Huguenot stock, like Martha Washington, Alexander Hamilton, Paul Revere, and John Jay, men and women who helped craft the American legend. Their inheritance may survive through a theological commitment to integrity seemingly transmitted both by genetic makeup and by historical memory, as in the case of the entire village of Le Chambon, willing to sacrifice itself utterly during World War II in order to hide and protect Jewish children from the Nazis. The Camisard tradition of social dissent persists in the small but pronounced vocal presence of descendants of French Protestants in the left wing of the French government today (many in François Mitterand's socialist cabinet were of Huguenot descent, as is Lionel Jospin). The Huguenot heritage persists in the work of artists who filter their creative projects through a remembrance of their French Protestant ancestry, such as director Jean-Luc Godard, so proud of his Huguenot heritage that he explored themes of marginalization and oppression in reference to it; filmmaker René Allio, who made a powerful film called *Les Camisards*; or the novelist Tracy Chevalier, who recalled her Huguenot bloodline in several novels of historical fiction. Further, the French Protestant legacy is cultivated by special societies organized to retain a collective memory of the Camisard and Huguenot travails and contributions, such as the Huguenot Society of America, based in New York City. Whatever the medium this recollection takes, the Camisard and Huguenot experience does not fade.

The historical context for the shift from the Old World to the New World now established, the voices of several figures representative of the French Protestant contribution to the New World can be heard. Ezéchiel Carré's role in protecting the fledgling colony of Huguenot refugees transplanted to Boston, Elie Neau's school for slaves in New Amsterdam, and Gabriel de Bernon's church-building campaigns as well as his career as a political diplomat are told in these pages. They are in good colonial company: Neau's and Carré's history of publication with Cotton Mather, who acted as their interpreter and intercessor, attests to a significant and formerly unrecognized French connection between Continental and American Protestantism. Now that the narrative scaffolding on which to reconstitute the lives of these figures is in place, they can tell their formerly untold tale.

CHAPTER ONE

Crisis in the Cévennes

> I will pour out My Spirit on all flesh; your sons and your daughters shall
> prophesy, your old men shall dream dreams, your young men will see
> visions . . . I will show wonders in the heavens and on the earth.
> —Joel 2:28–30 (New International Version)

A letter dated June 30, 1705, paints a portrait of Camisard piety.
Written by Commandant Bâville of the dragoons, a Catholic, it recounts how
the king's troops surprised some Camisards along the bank of a river: "The day
before yesterday, we came upon ten or twelve men assembled together. One
was reading the Bible and several were washing in the stream. Our men shot
at them from a bit too far away . . . wounding two of them, [including the] one
holding the Bible; they ran off and escaped into the woods."[1]

The Camisard military leader and, later, pastor Jacques Bonbonnoux, described walking at night for miles in the snow to reach the mountaintop designated for worship, singing psalms with over a thousand believers, the words of
the spirit-filled preacher shouted over the wind; Bonbonnoux recalled seeing a
man nearby who remained in ecstasy for four hours on his knees, beseeching a
star to fall into one outstretched palm, praying for a dove to alight on the other.[2]

The Camisard story is the stuff of legend. And yet at least some of the legend
is rooted in reality. The Protestant community in France resisted all assaults—
those coming from Versailles and those of the provincial delegates. Even if the
Revocation of the Edict of Nantes (1685) put the Protestants in peril, it was
not able to eliminate them or their beliefs. Louis XIV, intending to wipe out
with one stroke of his pen this irritating religious anomaly in his kingdom, succeeded only in creating serious internal and external political problems.[3]

An Overview of the Camisards

The Revocation arose from Louis XIV's determination to extirpate Protestantism from France forever ("il n'y aura qu'une seule religion en son royaume")
and particularly to eradicate the Huguenot remnant clinging to its creed
in rural outposts against all odds, even after systematic persecution in the
early years of the seventeenth century. The Revocation, though shattering to

Protestants in France, on the Continent, and elsewhere, especially devastated a small, persecuted, and marginalized community in the mountainous southeastern region of France called the Cévennes. Repression of the Camisards led to years of strife, destruction, and horror—"through the depredations of the dragoons, their churches had been burned or demolished, martyrs hanged or thrown into the fire"—resulting in an "enormous gap, a lack in their religious system, the deprivation of identity of an entire people for whom Protestantism was culture, ethnic identity, social and political organization . . . All this constituted a . . . trauma that truncated their history."[4] Moreover, the crisis in the Cévennes raised questions of confessional allegiance, issues that were to influence the Western world in developing the concept of the freedom of the individual conscience before God, the right to uncoerced worship, and the notion that limits might be set on royal or state power when it impinged on religious observance.[5] In the "Avertissement pastoral à ceux de la religion prétendue réformée, pour les porter à se convertir et se réconcilier avec l'Eglise" (July 1, 1682), Louis XIV and his ministers declared that French Protestants, formerly treated as heretics, were now to be regarded as "schismatics." As such, they became enemies of the state.[6]

The Camisards were seventeenth-century French Protestants. They were Huguenots, but their location and unique historical circumstances set them apart from their confrères in southwest France. Initially identical doctrinally and ecclesiastically to Huguenots in their Reformed emphases, the Camisards formed a distinct confessional subculture because of particular constraints and specific experiences of persecution. Consequently, they developed forms of worship and expressions of belief that were more enthusiastic and ecstatic than those of their Huguenot coreligionists, yet were, in tenor and vocabulary, much like those of other persecuted Protestant sects: the Camisards relied on a sort of inspired prophecy to inform their everyday activities in the midst of crisis and chaos.

Camisard prophecy was ardent preaching initiated by a formulaic preface ("I say to you, my children")[7] and apocalyptic in tone; it was always based on a biblical passage that inspired its auditors to action (they were "sent" on their mission "by God").[8] Worship services could last up to twelve hours. Eyewitnesses spoke of "changed lives" at such assemblies. Abraham Mazel, for example, observed that "wherever God's Holy Spirit was present, those who received it and those who associated with them suddenly became really good people, even those who had formerly led dissolute lives."[9]

Driven by their spiritual needs, the Camisards carried on their religious traditions even without the guidance of ministers. Hounded by the authorities, they practiced their religion in secret nocturnal gatherings. Confined within the Cévennes mountains and cut off from their fellow Huguenots, the Camisards were, especially in the years immediately following the Revocation, terrorized by Louis XIV's massive campaigns of *dragonnades*—the quartering of troops in Protestant households, compulsory conversions to Catholicism, the forced removal of Camisard children so that they could be raised as Catholics, and the banishing of Huguenot pastors.[10] A royal edict further mandated the demolition of all Huguenot *temples* throughout France.[11]

The Camisards—poor, generally illiterate shepherds and farmers—were hit particularly hard by these measures.[12] Unlike the wealthier Huguenots in La Rochelle, who sometimes fled across the English Channel (even when the king ordered that no such emigration occur), the Camisards could not escape.[13] A few did, but most attempts were unsuccessful. Finding passive resistance unavailing, they decided to stand and fight. Attired in tattered shirtsleeves (*camisas*), these farmers stood against uniformed royal troops. Against all odds, for several years the Camisards won many battles.[14] How was this possible?

These embattled village folks experienced agonizing persecutions in the wake of the Revocation: deprived of the right to worship according to their lights, they were tortured, sent to the galleys, or killed if they would not recant. The king's troops razed their *temples*, compelling many Camisards to take to the forest. There they hid, living for years in caves and worshiping on mountaintops; soldiers hunted them like game. The ones who remained at home in poverty were obliged to quarter troops in their homes and forced to forswear their faith or make pro forma conversions to avoid torture. Their ministers had to flee for protection to Geneva. In their absence, the common folk, among whom but a small number were able to read, write, and memorize written sermons left behind by the pastors or smuggled in from Geneva, gathered to meditate on scripture, sing psalms, and pray.

Like their fellow Huguenots, the Camisards strove to model every detail of their lives on scripture. They replicated important Calvinist practices and beliefs.[15] For example, at home they prayed "in Huguenot style," as they themselves termed it, with the father serving as the "little pastor" of his household, responsible for training his children to read the Bible and to be conversant in the faith.[16] Their public worship was required to be "in conformity with scripture."[17] For instance, in general the Camisard prophets did not themselves go into battle, since the Holy Spirit instructed them, as it had told Moses and Joshua, not to bear arms. And they subscribed to the doctrine of predestination, which had been significantly clarified and solidified in the years after Calvin's death.[18] They shared with Calvin an unshakable belief in divine Providence: "A large army won't save you. No, it's the arm of God the Omnipotent, who can save, who will save you, even with a small number of soldiers, from a larger host, so that to Him all glory and honor will be given."[19]

Like their embattled Huguenot forebears during the Wars of Religion, Camisards claimed the right to worship in the vernacular, that is, in the

Occitan, or southern French, dialect. So strongly did Camisards rely on scripture that contemporaries claimed they spoke "Canaan speech."[20] Camisard children nearly always had biblical names like Isaiah, Elijah, or Abraham, and the Camisard believers thought of themselves collectively as "the people of Israel," as Jews wandering in the desert. Camisard memoirs refer to conditions during the time of trial, both physically and metaphorically, as "le désert."[21] Many Camisards, like those men bathing by the stream when Bâville and his dragoons set upon them, were willing to die for their faith. Theirs was an ardent religiosity of faithful enthusiasts, exemplified by the kneeling man whom Bonbonnoux witnessed seeking spiritual succor and a sign.

Because of the oppression against which they struggled, the Camisards placed great importance on the notion of "the free workings of the conscience," thus reinforcing the Calvinist rationalist and proto-Enlightenment emphasis on this tenet.[22] Calvinist expression of religion was intensified and taken in a more millenarian direction by the Camisards, who were dying by droves in state-sponsored bloodbaths. Camisards preferred more eschatological texts, such as the Gospel of John and the books of Joel, Daniel, and Ezekiel, while Calvinists referred customarily to the synoptic Gospels and the Pauline texts. While Calvinists spoke more of "preaching" and Camisards talked of "prophecy," both practices were intended to edify, exhort, and console.

In many important respects, the Camisards clung to their Reformed roots more tenaciously than Calvinists in Geneva, who might be said to have traded the conviction of the Reformation for the safety of structured ecclesiology.[23] For instance, echoing some of the same arguments as those advanced a century earlier by Calvinist *tyrannomach* theorists such as François Hotman and Philippe Duplessis-Mornay, the Camisard prophets asserted that Louis XIV's agents no longer did God's will, because they persecuted the king's subjects, and that armed resistance to such an abuse of power was allowed by scripture.[24] Gédéon Laporte was one such Camisard prophet, preaching a righteous war against the injustice of the Catholic priests, the king's delegates in enforcing the law.[25]

The Camisard Crisis

The Cévennes mountain region is rugged, rural, and relatively isolated from other European countries and from the rest of France. In this land of country folk, shepherds, and farmers, Huguenot pastors inculcated the fundamental Calvinist principles of reliance on the Bible exclusively as authoritative and the relative equality of laity and clergy. Perhaps because of the region's poverty and widespread illiteracy, the Camisards' reception of scriptural teachings was literal and experientially validated, unlike the more textually sophisticated interpretations made by Huguenots in other parts of France. Because the

Camisards received God's word orally, they distilled its teachings down to pithy truths, formulaic utterances, and memorable images.

After enduring a second century of religious strife, the Camisards were deeply suspicious of Catholicism. They accepted their pastors' scriptural exposition of the Catholic Church as "the whore of Babylon" and the "Antichrist." They believed that clerical intercession and Catholic customs such as the confessional were not found in scripture, and they abhorred the "daily death of Jesus" in the celebration of the Roman Catholic Mass, asserting that Christ had died but once, to atone for all.

The populace in the Cévennes was largely homogenous: there were some Catholics—primarily clergy—but by the late seventeenth century, most lay folk who lived in the area were Protestants. Consequently, Catholic clergy saw the Revocation as an opportunity finally to win back the area for Catholicism. This strategy had been unofficially implemented as early as 1662; Father Meynior, a Jesuit, described in *De l'exécution de l'Edit de Nantes dans le bas Languedoc* a programmatic method "to eat up the adversary."[26]

After the Revocation, Catholic priests and bishops began compelling Camisards to confess, forcing them to go to Mass, and coercing conversions, or at least exterior conformity. The Camisard ministers exhorted their flocks to stand firm, teaching them to "avoid any meeting with the priest, and stay away from the church door."[27] The overt persecution of the Camisards began in 1687 when the abbé du Chayla was given inquisitorial powers in the Cévennes. He mandated the removal of children from Protestant families, and for any Camisards who refused to recant, torture, burning, hanging, imprisonment (for women), and the galleys (for men). Most Camisards refused to cooperate, animated by the strength of their faith; the Abbé Basville marveled at the resolve of this simple folk: "They are mere itinerant preachers, wool-carders, peasants, without any common sense, crazy and flighty folk who continue to face death when there is no need for that."[28]

By 1694, all the Huguenot ministers in the Cévennes either had been killed or had fled. Around that time, an exiled Huguenot pastor, Pierre Jurieu, published a tract in the Low Countries that circulated both in written form and by word of mouth all over the Continent. Addressed to, and sympathizing with, his Camisard brothers, Jurieu's pamphlet identified the pope as the Antichrist and listed harbingers of an imminent apocalypse. Calling God's people to rally to defend the true faith during what he identified as the "end times," Jurieu exhorted the peace-loving Camisards to resist coercion and to rebel. Their leitmotif and rallying cry in battle became to "escape from Babylon." This longing to leave contrasted strongly with the Huguenots' desire, during the Wars of Religion, to "build up the walls of Jerusalem."[29] Huguenots, who were often skilled artisans, expressed their hope for deliverance in the image of a holy city they would help build, while Camisards could only, in their desperate straits, imagine fleeing an unholy captivity.

Stages of Strife: Spiritual Warfare in the Cévennes

Between the Revocation, in 1685, and the massacre at Pont-de-Montvert of the abbé du Chayla on July 24, 1702, the Languedoc, Haute-Guyenne, and Dauphiné regions were periodically troubled. After the Revocation, Louis XIV, on the advice of his Catholic counselors, began a campaign of *dragonnades*, a policy of organized brutality that included the billeting of troops in private homes and the bayoneting and killing of Protestant pastors and faithful. A contemporary memoir penned by the Ursuline sister Demerez stated the choices for residents of the Cévennes: "Either they've got to swallow [Catholicism] whole, or they are deported to America."[30]

The frenzied climate of persecution and resistance was fueled by ecstatic visions. In 1688, a fifteen-year-old illiterate peasant girl, Isabeau Vincent, reportedly began to see visions and to experience a version of speaking in tongues.[31] Although like most peasants in southeastern France, she had been reared to speak only the provençal dialect (Occitan), Isabeau prophesied at length in flawless classical French, a language she may have heard on occasion, but was not conversant with. Although she could not read, Isabeau quoted extensive passages of scripture verbatim and aptly, in well-constructed exhortations. The burden of her "inspirations"—for she identified this phenomenon as a gift of the Holy Spirit—conveyed God's remonstrances to his chosen people, the Camisards: they should repent, abjure Catholicism, recognize the Bible as their sole spiritual authority, and fight to retain their beliefs. Soon after Isabeau's first "prophecy," similar manifestations, voiced by children as young as two or three years old, by adolescents, and by grown men and women, erupted all over southeastern France.[32] Catholics claimed that a veritable "school of prophets," run by a Calvinist minister in hiding, had been set up in the countryside to coach the impressionable in what to say and how to say it.[33]

In her recent study *Huguenot Prophecy and Clandestine Worship in the Eighteenth Century*, Georgia Cosmos provides a typology of the Camisard inspirations:

> Three phases can be identified in witnesses' ordering of the flow of time [in their narration of the circumstances of the prophecies]. The first begins with the Revocation of the Edict and the appearance of child prophets in numerous villages along the river Drôme in Dauphiné, after which the phenomenon of prophecy spread to the Vivarais and Velay. These events were regarded by believers as the fulfilment of Joel's prophecy . . .

The second phase . . . [shows that] in the majority of cases, . . . events [took] place at assemblies for worship in . . . towns in the Cévennes and Languedoc between 1701 and 1705 . . .

The third phase . . . concerns the time to come, during which the deliverance of the afflicted church was to occur as predicted by the inspired children . . .

The apocalyptic imagery expressed in [these] predictions . . . highlights the opposition between the community of the Reformed and its persecutors—evident in the identification of the Roman Church with the false church of the latter days and the Reformed church with the true.[34]

Often, several prophets arose within the same family.[35] Camisards gathered in great numbers to hear the prophecies; greatly consoled and inspired, some in the audience themselves experienced the "gifts." In the absence of clergy, the Camisards viewed these new, experiential manifestations as para-ecclesial ways to continue their conversations with Christ. The prophecies embodied the most literal understanding of the Protestant rejection of the Catholic doctrine of intercession and mediation, and of Calvinist reliance on scripture: these humble folk spoke directly with God through their prophesying, experiencing him face to face. In *Relation sommaire des merveilles que Dieu fait en France* (1694), Claude Brousson describes this belief in immediacy of access to the divinity: "Deprived of the word of God, of evangelism, of a regular worship service, of orderly sermons, of an emotionally appealing but also rational form of religiosity, the Camisards turned toward a belief in 'inspiration.'"[36]

As these prophecies evolved from consolation and instruction to calls for militancy, the Camisards began to select as leaders exclusively men who experienced this gift of tongues and prophecy. If such manifestations ceased, the leader was promptly replaced by another *inspiré*. The Camisards made no moves without receiving directives from on high: before battle, the leader entered into a prophetic trance while the other Camisards sang psalms, recited passages of scripture, and prayed with him.[37] Forming themselves into guerrilla bands under the leadership of such prophets, the ill-clad, poorly armed, and untrained Camisards accomplished miracles in battle against regiment after regiment of elite troops.

The Camisard farmers went into battle singing psalms, certain that God would make them victorious. Fighting with few guns, mostly with stones and sticks, their numbers never, in Misson's reckoning, amounting to more than two thousand, the Camisards fought valiantly, convinced of the Apostle Paul's claim that God uses the weak to confound the strong (1 Corinthians 1:27).[38] They believed that their inspirations had "changed [them], sheep, into lions, and inspired [the Camisards], weakness itself, to face down an army of 20,000 elite troops."[39] Fallen in battle or tortured and martyred for the Camisard cause, these believers were "refined" like gold in a divine furnace: "That is when the Almighty did great things . . . That was the terrible crucible in which the truth and faithfulness of the holy inspired ones was put to the test . . . even as their bones were being broken on the wheel and when the flames were devouring their flesh."[40]

The Camisard resistance from 1685 to 1705 can be divided into six periods: the Revocation of the Edict of Nantes and the banishment of Huguenot ministers from the country; the first outbreaks of "inspiration"; the change from pacifism to armed resistance and the formation of Camisard guerrilla bands; the Camisards' successes in battle, coupled with the redoubling of Catholic measures against them; the reversal of fortune as royal troops, no longer stunned by the Camisards' ferocity and guerrilla tactics, began to prevail against them; and the aftermath, when the few Camisards remaining either fled the country or accepted conversion. Antoine Court, a Camisard scholar who was later ordained a Calvinist pastor in Switzerland, estimated that in 1713, shortly after the uprising had been quelled, more than five hundred thousand Camisards fled France or were killed.[41]

Aggression came slowly to these pacifists. Their first militant feat occurred in July 1702. Some Camisard men, urged on by the *inspirés* and driven to desperation by the *dragonnades* and by the abbé du Chayla's torture of their children, finally decided to act: "Until now, the Protestants had endured persecution patiently, allowing themselves to be killed . . . Now, they could take no more."[42] Led by Esprit Seguier, Pierre Couderc, and Abraham Mazel, a ragtag band of farmers and shepherds armed only with farm implements and slingshots stormed the abbé's château. Stabbing the abbé with pitchforks and knives, the Camisards murdered him in what they viewed as a righteous act of retaliation.[43] The Camisards next armed themselves with guns and other weapons taken from the Château de la Deveze. However, a *dragonnade* troop caught up with them, took Seguier, their leader, prisoner, hastily convened a *chambre de justice* at Florac, and sentenced him to be burned at the stake.

Despite the loss of one of their leaders, the Camisards' resolve was strengthened by the rhetorically gifted nineteen-year-old peasant and visionary Abraham Mazel. He dreamed of black bulls rampaging in a garden, ripping up the ground and vegetation. Mazel, a native of the parish of Falguière in Saint-Jean-du-Gard, had experienced this visionary dream on October 9, 1701, while hiding out in a cave near Toyras. Told by a voice in his dream to chase the beasts away, Mazel awoke convinced that "the garden was the Church, and the big black bulls were the priests who were destroying the Church."[44] God had sent this dream as a sign; clearly, the Camisard cause was just and entailed nothing less than the restoration of Christ's true church.[45]

In Seguier's stead, a new inspired leader, Gédéon Laporte, headed up the rebel band. He and several other Camisard leaders were opposed by Saint-Côme, a Protestant who had converted back to Catholicism for financial gain and social and military advancement. Such recidivists, known as members of *la Croix blanche*, were despised by the Camisards both for their recantation and for torturing their fellow countrymen. After the murder of Laporte at the hands of some Camisards disillusioned by his egotistical style, a regiment was formed under the charismatic leadership of Rolland Cavalier, a twenty-one-year-old former shepherd turned baker. Cavalier directed guerilla operations, setting fire to Catholic churches, executing Catholic priests, killing everyone in the garrison at Servas, and burning down its castle.

Although Cavalier at first did much to raise morale, many Camisards became unhappy with his leadership as its initial mystic tenor yielded to political temporizing.[46] His head may have been turned by the courting he received from some Catholic notables seeking to end the strife: some Camisards felt that "where he was concerned, the man of politics killed the mystic."[47]

After each military operation, the Camisards held an open-air prayer assembly in a clandestine mountain spot. Under cover of night, they sang, prayed, prophesied, and praised God for their victories, asking his guidance for upcoming battles. They referred to their encampment as the Camp de l'Eternel.[48] New Camisard leaders, inspired by the Holy Spirit, came forth to replace those lost in battle. One such leader raised up from the laity was André Castanet, described as having the face, physique, and ferociousness of a bear.[49] Castanet had learned to read and write in his youth, and consequently had great authority among the mostly unlettered Camisard band. He was renowned as a wordsmith and a preacher.

Another military leader, Jean Cavalier, came expressly to the Cévennes from Geneva to bolster the Camisard cause, having received "the direct command from God to go to the aid of his brothers."[50] He arrived in October 1702 and began proclaiming the value of freedom of religion and the imperative of fighting to the death to defend it: "Their birthright religion should be more precious to them than life itself, and they should be willing to risk their lives to ensure freedom of worship."[51] In November 1702, the Camisards chose two new leaders, Nicolas Jouanny and Salomon Couderc, to replace Cavalier and Castanet. Their leadership "stirred the Camisards up even more, and the number of rebels increased."[52]

In the early months of 1703, however, the Catholics began to regroup, retaliate, and win some military engagements. The royal brigadiers Julien and de Parate headed up a new battalion of trained soldiers sent against the Camisards. On January 12, in the battle of the Val-de-Barre, a turning point, Rolland

Cavalier regrouped, slaughtering the Catholic inhabitants of the garrison at Saint-Felix and burning the church at Saint-André, but the Camisards and Jean Cavalier, victorious at the battle of Vagnas (February 10), suffered a crushing defeat the next day.

Some Catholics in the Cévennes formed a guerilla outfit called the Florentins (named after the village of Saint-Florent), turning the Camisards' own hit-and-run tactics against them. The Florentins experienced considerable success, razing several towns that were sheltering Camisard troops, then massacring a group of Camisard noncombatants at a religious assembly in a mill near Nîmes.[53] The Camisards, fearing that they would be annihilated, began to convert in large numbers. Those who did so were disparagingly called the *nouveaux convertis*. Pope Clement XI, adding fuel to the fear and to the Catholics' initiative, proclaimed an internal crusade against the Camisards.[54] One of the few Camisard nobles, the baron de Salgas, a man of considerable reputation and respect, was shortly thereafter arrested and sentenced to life as a galley slave; several local Catholic clergymen came to gloat over his first time at the oars.[55]

The hostilities continued unabated. In June and July 1703, another prayer assembly of Camisards was slaughtered and several more Protestant noblemen were executed. Anyone known to have sold gunpowder or to have provided supplies or munitions to the Camisards was hanged, and villages suspected of having harbored rebels were pillaged or burned to the ground. Large numbers of Camisards were burned at the stake in August. Camisard troops retaliated by burning down churches, but their initiative and morale had weakened, and the superior organization and daunting numbers of the dragoons were beginning to take their toll.

Determined to end the ongoing resistance, the king and his counselors decided to devastate the Cévennes through a scorched-earth policy. The maréchal de Montrevel published an official order decreeing that, if necessary, every Camisard town and village was to be destroyed.

Catholic clergy began to seek conversions by persuading the demoralized, semidefeated Camisards that recanting was their sole hope for survival. Fléchier, the bishop of Nîmes, wrote an open letter to the Cévennols, urging them to repent of their error and encouraging his clergy to use any means to enforce conversions. At the same time, Montrevel published a list of parishes slated for eradication. A special detachment of dragoons, the Cadets de la Croix, was designated to destroy the designated villages and towns. So barbaric were they in executing their project that Montrevel was eventually obliged to send troops against his own men to hinder their depredations.

As news of the persecution of the Camisards spread, England, Holland, Scotland, and the Savoy pledged their support. Men of letters abroad waged a polemic war against intolerance; their campaign was published as *Lettres des*

Protestans Estrangers contre ces ravages. European Protestants and defenders of freedom of conscience elsewhere became increasingly frenzied in their appeals for reconsideration of the policy concerning the Camisards, proclaiming in the title of another polemical tract, *Europe esclave si les Cévenols ne sont promptement secourus.*[56]

A fleet of English ships with reinforcements for the Camisard cause was sighted off the southern coast of France. A detachment of officers and troops sent from Holland to aid the Camisards was arrested by the dragoons. Eugène, prince of Savoy, declared his support for the Camisards. The king's ministers began to take steps to block any foreign aid to the Camisards, sending an ambassador to attempt to dissuade William of Orange from sending troops to help the insurrection.

Throughout this period, the Camisard general Rolland Cavalier continued to experience limited military success, but the king's forces generally reversed those gains in short order. So while the Camisards were victorious at the battle of Roques d'Aubais, demolishing the Catholic fortifications that had been hastily erected there and even causing a Te Deum to be sung for their victory, the troops of the governor of Saint-Hippolyte marched against Cavalier and took back the area at the battle of Tornac.

This oscillation between victory and defeat on both sides continued for several months. In retaliation for any gains on their side, Camisards were executed or deported; many were massacred at Saint-André-de-Valborgne and two neighboring towns. A Camisard nobleman, the baron d'Aygaliers, offered to try to negotiate an end to the troubles. He went to Paris in hopes of gaining the assistance of influential political figures. He succeeded in having Montrevel recalled; it helped that numerous complaints of excessive severity had been lodged against him. The king then sent the maréchal de Villars to Languedoc to confer with Camisard leaders. He visited the Cévennes and reported back on the devastation there.

After several meetings convened by Villars, Camisards were granted the right to hold religious services and preaching was permitted in the town of Calvisson, the first such concessions made during the war. Camisards in Nîmes demanded similar treatment, writing letters to Villars protesting Catholic abuses; forty Camisards who surrendered at Valabrègue made a similar petition. However, Villars published a placard forbidding further concessions. He convoked the chief leaders of all local Camisard communities to offer them terms, but these were rejected as inadequate. In frustration, he resumed the campaign against the Camisards, placing himself at the head of a detachment of dragoons and setting several villages to the torch.

European Protestants, hearing of the breach of the cease-fire and the nefarious actions of Villars, were in an uproar. Camisards, demoralized and in fear for their lives, began to surrender in droves; many met with Villars in Nîmes. D'Aygaliers again traveled to Paris to try to intercede, without success. Villars ordered retaliatory measures against the families and relatives of the rebels; several thousand people were deported or taken from their homes, and more towns were sacked and burned by troops.

Another allied fleet sympathetic to the Camisards appeared off the shores of Languedoc, and one of its ships was captured as a warning to European Protestants not to meddle in France's internal affairs. Several Camisards were caught and executed, along with two captains taken off the ship. D'Aygaliers met with the remnant of the Camisard fighting force, urging them to negotiate, though not to capitulate. His remonstrances having fallen on deaf ears, he was forced into exile. Shortly afterward, most of the Camisard leaders surrendered.

Those who witnessed the surrender were stunned by the poverty, simplicity, and vulnerability of these men who had fought so ferociously. European Protestants were again stirred to attempt to intervene on behalf of the Camisards, although Switzerland sent back to France several Camisard leaders who had sought refuge there. Several Camisard leaders were put to death.

In March 1705, Monsieur de Berwick succeeded Villars as policy maker for the Cévennes—the latter much praised for having ended the rebellion—and proceeded to arrest and kill holdout rebels in Montpellier, Nîmes, and smaller towns.

In Holland, exiled Camisards, encouraged by Cavalier, formed plans to renew the uprising. However, Louis XIV, hearing of this, sent ambassadors to Bern, Zurich, and the Low Countries to discourage support for a new Camisard surge, and the exiled rebels were obliged to flee to Würtemberg. Berwick declared amnesty for any Camisard who would turn himself in; some did, while others escaped into exile. Two leaders who resisted were captured and tortured to death; one, Salomon Couderc, was caught while attempting secretly to reenter France in the hopes of reanimating the Camisard rebellion.

Very few Camisards survived. The Peace of Utrecht was promulgated, and France became, once again, the jewel in the pope's Catholic crown.

Camisards as Calvinists

Once the war-torn countryside regained some measure of normality and it became possible to reintroduce an ecclesiastical structure into the Cévennes, the pastors built on the Genevan synodal model, the cornerstone of Reformed church polity; the first synod of the Camisard Church of the Desert was established at Saint-Hippolyte-du-Fort in 1715. The Camisards called themselves "Calvinistes."[57]

As the Camisards attempted to recuperate during and after the persecutions, although they were not able to worship in *temples*, they held Calvinist services.[58] However, during the time when they were deprived of clergy, the Camisards developed an enthusiastic, ejaculatory prayer style and constantly looked for signs and wonders. This fervent approach to piety eventually influenced the manner of worship of the Pietist conventicle and resembled the Puritan piety they later encountered in the New World. Camisard worship was composed of extensive psalm singing, using the Huguenot Psalter published in 1551 in Geneva; forty-nine of the psalms had been set by Clément Marot, who had been commissioned by Calvin to make vernacular translations. A contemporary Calvinist, Tobie Rocayrol, observed of a Camisard service that it was "exactly the same" as one in Geneva.[59] When the laity felt inspired to proclaim God's word, they spoke in "plain style" biblical exegesis, accompanied by practical exposition applicable to daily life, as Calvin had recommended.[60] Even during the worst times, Camisards kept the Sabbath.

As the Reformed church was slowly reestablished after the persecutions, the Camisards adopted many Calvinist practices and beliefs. They received the Lord's Supper four times a year, as was the custom in Geneva, and "fenced the table" against those deemed morally unworthy or spiritually unready to take Communion. They subscribed to the doctrine, expressed by Luther and continued by Calvin, of the "priesthood of all believers." They recognized two, rather than seven, sacraments and called for an end to clerical orders: "Long live God and the King! Death to the clergy!"[61] Even while on the run from the king's soldiers, Camisard prophets organized a vigilante form of moral surveillance along the lines of Calvin's consistory, punishing lapses such as gambling, obscenity, and blasphemy. Camisards had a concern for social welfare; following the model of Calvin, they emphasized stewardship of and communal access to the few resources they possessed, as well as Christian charity to fellow believers.

Two Camisard Case Studies

Jacques Bonbonnoux, village lad, autodidact, soldier "in the army of God," Camisard pastor, and Reformed minister, began his autobiography with the famous quote from Martin Luther, "Here I stand. I can do no other. God help me."[62] Born in 1673 in the Cévennes, he was reared in the Reformed faith while nominally conforming to Catholicism.[63]

In 1701 he married a fellow Calvinist, but in a Roman Catholic Mass. When his bride died a year later, Bonbonnoux, stricken with guilt, blamed himself for having had the Catholic marriage performed, certain that his wife had been struck down to demonstrate the wrongheadedness of this compromise. One evening after supper three weeks later, Bonbonnoux became a committed Camisard, joining the small troop headed by Laporte, known as Rolland, in 1703.[64] He joined, he stated, "for God's glory and my own salvation," divesting himself first of all his worldly goods, including the tools for his trade as a wool carder, and giving all his money to a relative.[65]

The Camisard guerillas read their Bibles while on the move, carrying them on thick leather straps slung across their backs so as to leave their hands free for their weapons. Although Bonbonnoux could not yet read, he was greatly inspired by the preaching of the prophets who accompanied the troops: "We prayed to God day and night. We sang psalms, we read the Bible, and a young boy . . . of seventeen years, spoke to us every day with prophecies or sermons consisting of passages taken from Holy Scripture, upon which he meditated . . . Our worship was such that I was lost to myself ["ravished"] in wonder."[66] Bonbonnoux's troops lived in the woods and hid in caves or in the cellars or barns of friendly villagers, sometimes going without food for days on end, dodging dragoons, and sleeping on the ground, often with no covering. Their precarious existence did not prevent regular worship: "Prayer services were customary with us. We had [scripture] readers . . . and especially preachers . . . People came from all over to hear them. Often we heard two exhortations and two sermons each day. We were constantly on the run; rarely did we stay more than two days in the same place. Those of the Reformed faith would come from all around to where we were camping, bringing us food."[67] His *Mémoires* include reports of torture of villagers by Catholics, accounts of battles, descriptions of impassioned open-air prayer services, and many nights spent in hiding.

Their custom was to use prayer and prophecy to whip the Camisard soldiers into a frenzy before battle: "Before we went into battle, a young preacher named Daire, about thirty years old, would exhort us with great zeal to fight even to the death . . . [When we sang] Psalm Fifty-one, the words shouted out by a sixty-year-old shoemaker named Adam, my enthusiasm was . . . great."[68]

Bonbonnoux also recorded several "miraculous" happenings. He called an event a "miracle" in his *Mémoires*, then observed, "perhaps it might not seem like a miracle to everyone, but it sure seemed one to us, and we counted it among those things for which we gave God thanks."[69] Another time, when dragoons searching for him and a fellow soldier passed right by them unawares, he commented, "God blind[ed] them."[70] On yet another occasion, having not eaten for days, discouraged, and thinking of giving up, he and his troops suddenly came upon the house of a Camisard, who fed them well; Bonbonnoux considered this aid "miraculous": "God brought us right to them that very evening . . . it was a dream, an extraordinary thing."[71] Bonbonnoux also described hiding from dragoons in an attic: "It was a miracle, how I was able to hide."[72] Every once in a while, the Camisard soldiers were able to worship in one of the few *temples* still standing: "After supper, we went to the local church, one of the few that had not been burned . . . where we prayed, sang Psalms and heard preaching."[73] Since the Reformed ministers had been chased out of France by the dragoons, Bonbonnoux and a soldier friend, Claris, took matters into their own hands: " 'All our preachers are either dead or have surrendered,' Claris, very moved, said. 'What then shall we do?' 'God will provide,' I replied . . . After I had answered him thus, Claris pulled a child's alphabet out of his pocket and said, 'Friends, let's start studying. We shall yet become ministers.' What a challenge for men who did not know how to read! . . . I can tell you, nonetheless, that three of our company learned to preach the Gospel, by God's grace, and me among them."[74]

Bonbonnoux was an astute and discerning man. He constructed a typology of Camisard belief through which he was able to distinguish between those whom he assessed to be genuinely concerned with preserving the Reformed faith and those who, prey to bloodlust, manifested "the fanaticism of the visionary Reformed believer."[75] The definition of a good Camisard, for him, was "one who has not surrendered and has protected the faith."[76] Demonstrating an Enlightenment sensibility surprising for one of his background, Bonbonnoux also exercised his critical capacity on the pronouncements of the Camisard prophets; they had to meet certain criteria for him to accept them as legitimate, and in at least one case, he judged a prophet to be in error: "Unfortunately, this prophet's inspiration was mistaken."[77]

In 1714, the renowned Camisard pastor and Reformed minister Antoine Court called together the remnants of the Camisard preachers, among them Pierre Carrière, known as Corteiz (whose account we shall examine next), Durant, Rouvière, Vesson, Huc, Arnaud, and Bonbonnoux himself. Bonbonnoux came out of his self-imposed exile in Switzerland to participate in this meeting in the Cévennes. He remained in France, and on November 21, 1718, he participated in the provincial synod of the Reformed Church of Bas-Languedoc as a "proposant" (a postulant studying for the ministry). On April 24, 1721, he wrote to his second wife (his "sister in Christ"), who had remained in Geneva, that he was "not ashamed to claim the Gospel of Jesus Christ as the power of God"[78] and described for her his itinerant life and material deprivation: "Therefore Christ's minister walks where God leads him and considers all earthly things as nothing. He disregards material wealth and puts his confidence in God, saying humbly, but with confidence, 'God is my firm foundation!' "[79] Bonbonnoux's life as a Reformed minister was marked by almost as many hardships as he experienced while a Camisard soldier. On many occasions his life was threatened. He took numerous risks for his faith, carrying contraband Bibles back into France: "The Lord inspired me with courage; that is how I was able to come into town carrying my Bibles. Sometimes I'd pull them out of my little bag, and hide them in my pockets and in my breast; sometimes I'd wrap them up in my kerchief, or cover them with leaves and carry them in my hands like a head of lettuce . . . I came and went with my Bibles; I was even arrested while in possession of them, but they were never discovered, and never caused me any problems."[80]

Finally, after twenty-seven years of fighting, preaching, and church building, Bonbonnoux returned to Geneva, old and sick, where he helped found the Reformed Seminary at Zurich, along with his closest friends, Antoine Court and Pierre Carrière.[81] Bonbonnoux died in 1755 at the age of eighty-two, and his body was taken back to Languedoc to be buried in the Cévennes mountains. In homage to his friend and fellow believer, Antoine Court edited and published the first edition of Bonbonnoux's *Mémoires*.

Bonbonnoux epitomized the active life of a Camisard who was integrated into Reformed ecclesiology. The life of Pierre Carrière, known as Corteiz, offers a model of a Camisard who worked to reestablish the Reformed Church in France.[82] Corteiz, born in 1680, was one of the first Camisard pastors ("pasteurs du désert"), a self-termed "Réformé" preaching "fire and the sword"[83] and calling the faithful to "abandon all [for God]."[84] He was first inclined to the Reformed faith when, as a youth in 1697, he began to read works by the Calvinist pastor Pierre Du Moulin, sermons as well as books like *Le Bouclier de la Foi* and *Du combat chrétien*.[85] He then went to great lengths to obtain a Bible so that he could read for himself the scripture passages that had been cited in his readings. Coached by his parents, devout French Protestants, Corteiz began to feel "repugnance"[86] for Catholicism. His father took him to secret nocturnal *assemblées*, where he was urged to articulate his faith publicly. It was at this point that Corteiz became an *inspiré*; experiencing a visitation of the Holy Spirit, he preached and prophesied: "And suddenly I was filled with courage, and I spoke with confidence about God's word. Ever after that, our village folk eagerly petitioned me to preach."[87] Soon, the nearby town of Nogaret sent for him to preach there.

Throughout his preaching career, and somewhat uncharacteristically for a Camisard, Corteiz, like Elie Neau, counseled passive resistance to Catholic oppression.[88] He distinguished between a just war (self-defense) and the actions of those *inspirés* who slaughtered aggressively rather than simply to protect themselves. Corteiz believed that such actions would be met with the withdrawal of God's favor: "God removed the column of his protection."[89] He distinguished, like Bonbonnoux, between fanatics[90] ("false, or self-anointed, prophets": the phrase is striking, since he himself had experienced the gifts of the spirit!) and believers ("les Réformés").[91] For instance, when the Camisard captain Abraham Mazel arrived in Languedoc and began to raise an army, Corteiz was concerned: "I did everything possible to change his mind, but [he] told me that the Holy Spirit does not lie, and that the Holy Spirit had told [him] that [he] had been chosen to deliver Israel from her oppressors, and that victory was assured."[92] Six months later when Mazel was killed in battle, Corteiz wrote, "The news saddened me, but I regarded this event, as all others, to be directed by Providence."[93] Further, he criticized Nicolas Tony, the leader of a militant Camisard troop: "I took the liberty of telling them that killing priests, burning churches, such behavior is not found in scripture, nor did the early Christians do such things."[94] In 1703, dragoons came and burned down Corteiz's village. Practicing what he had preached ("to obey Jesus, who told us, 'When someone persecutes you, leave that place and go to another'"),[95] Corteiz, along with the few Camisards who survived, were compelled to seek shelter in the maquis.[96]

In 1704, he fled France, finding refuge in Lausanne; however, a community of exiled believers there begged him to return to France to encourage the persecuted faithful. Corteiz left for Geneva, but was not able to get back into France until 1709. Martyrs were in the making in the Cévennes: scores of Corteiz's family and friends were hanged, burned, or shot down at evening worship. Corteiz, always on the run and in hiding, fell deathly ill. In 1712, friends were able to spirit him back out to Lausanne, where he convalesced and then married.

Unable to forget the plight of the Camisards, Corteiz felt called to return, alone, to the Cévennes, where he started to associate with other preachers, among them the Camisard preacher Jean Huc de Genouillac, and to form gatherings for preaching and prayer. In Marseille, the young preacher Antoine Court heard of Corteiz, and later met with him in Nîmes. Corteiz pleaded with Court to come help in the Cévennes, and Court complied.

Thus commenced the revival of the Camisards and the gradual reinstatement of the Reformed Church. Court and Corteiz cobbled together some twenty *assemblées* (congregations) in the Vivarais, and "the Cévennes, its fervor having been suffocated into indifference, began to awake and to revive, spurred by the preaching of the Gospel."[97] In 1716, Corteiz met with Bonbonnoux, and in the Dauphiné, they and others established "order in [re]born churches,"[98] drafting "appropriate rules . . . for this new church polity."[99] Among these rules were the requirement that the synods convene at least twice a year and that they establish a school for pastors for young men aged fourteen to twenty-five. Provisions were also made for fines for swearing and immoral behavior, the endorsement of the Confession of Faith of the French Reformed Church, specified days for prayer and fasting, a welfare chest for indigents, and mandatory public confession before being allowed to take Holy Communion.[100] They established a synod in Languedoc and formed ten churches in the dioceses of Nîmes, Montpellier, Alais, and Mende.

It was decided that at least one pastor from each diocese would be sent to Geneva for ordination so that the Lord's Supper could be properly celebrated, and in 1718, Corteiz was nominated by his synod. Although Corteiz, like most Camisards, did not feel that ordination was necessary, he agreed to the official procedure in order to be integrated into the church hierarchy.[101] He was ordained a Reformed minister by the laying-on of hands in the Église française in Zurich on August 15, 1718. Upon his return to the Cévennes in October, Corteiz ordained Antoine Court, then convened the Synode Réformé. Corteiz, leader of the remnant of the Reformed Church in France, exercised his ministry in the county of Foix in the Ariège and, especially, in the hills around Montpellier, where there had been no Protestant preaching for several years. After preaching to, encouraging, and catechizing the youth of the area, he soon reaped the harvest he had sown: "Then Truth began to triumph over error; then did the zeal of the faithful awaken, and religion awoke, and faith was strong, and all was well. In a very short time, the number of preachers swelled."[102]

Calling the reestablishment of the Reformed Church "a marvelous act of God,"[103] Corteiz recorded inspirational occurrences such as the celebration of the Lord's Supper with more than one hundred Camisards clustered into a cave at night. Corteiz jubilated: "In this way, our churches became strong in our mountains, and the Catholic priests were denied any hope that the Reformed could be [coerced back] into the Roman Church."[104] A few months later, however, Louis XIV condemned Corteiz to death. Corteiz escaped to the Bas-Languedoc, where he preached until 1752. Pursued by dragoons, he fled to Würtemberg, where he joined a community of French refugees.[105] He died in exile.

The lives and textual witness of Bonbonnoux and Corteiz represent Calvinist theology in a "spiritist" Camisard form. Together, these voices articulate a morphology of Camisard piety. That of Jacques Bonbonnoux is the firsthand account of an illiterate village boy, reared a Calvinist, who took up arms against the Catholics to protect his village, and who learned to read in order to be able to read scripture and preach, and who encouraged others in the absence of ordained ministers in the Cévennes. His account, riddled with grammatical and lexical errors, epitomizes the grassroots religious, as well as political, understanding of the Camisard Everyman. The narrative of Pierre Carrière (Corteiz) provides a refined, theologically astute portrait of a Camisard pastor who ultimately took refuge in Geneva, reflected on his experience, then returned to the Cévennes to play an extremely influential role in the reestablishment of the Reformed church there. He became a man of international reputation, and the sophistication of his reasoning as well as the conviction of his account command attention.

Preachers, prophets, and pastors, those Camisards who survived the persecutions committed their stories to paper; or, if illiterate, they recounted them to a transcriber. The Camisards realized the need to encourage fellow believers who were still in straits because of their faith, offering their personal experiences as templates for the revelation of God's will even in the midst of suffering. Their stories are fascinating and fully embodied; they recount the testimonies of men whose temperaments had been shaped by trial and who were willing to annihilate "self" for their understanding of God and of freedom.[106]

CHAPTER TWO

Survival Strategies

Prophets, Preachers, and Paradigms

The Camisards gathered in their fervent, covert nightly assemblies to hear the prophetic and apocalyptic pronouncements issuing from the mouths of wool carders, shepherds, chestnut gatherers, and day laborers, calling for an end to the Antichrist and Babylon (Rome), foreseeing the Day of the Lord, claiming the right to worship as they pleased, and inspiring scores with the desire to defend their faith.[1] "After 1700 prophesying was widely experienced among dispersed Protestant communities in the Cévennes. It was a force which sustained the inhabitants of these communities during a time of violent religious persecution . . . The principal characteristic of the [prophecies] is their immediacy: the voices . . . reach us directly . . . reveal[ing] the various manifestations of prophesying and how this phenomenon was experienced by people in the contexts in which it had occurred."[2]

Camisard prophecy, occurring in a "pressured" or peripheral social context, conforms to the typology developed by Robert Wilson in his study *Prophecy and Society in Ancient Israel*. Wilson's typology may serve as a lens through which to view the distinctive characteristics of the Camisards' experiences and perspectives. The Camisards fit Wilson's category of "peripheral": they were on the margins of Reformed society by virtue of their straitened socioeconomic situation, and they rejected the normative Roman Catholic theology espoused by the French theocracy.[3] However, a subgroup of Camisards, those who became prophets, became central to the Camisard community. These prophets filled the preeminent function of developing a "working theology"—even a militant one—in very specific circumstances of strife and persecution. For one thing, the fact that illiterate Camisards made their prophecies in "the King's French" shifted them, at least in their own minds, in from the periphery—by either a miracle or a strategically subversive use of the idiom of the very state that was attempting to deny them existence—to a more central position.[4] The prophecies, taken as divinely inspired, allowed the Camisards to reposition themselves in a theologically legitimate place: they believed that they constituted the true church.

Thus, the Camisards derived their strength of purpose, unity, and conviction of legitimacy from their prophets. The prophesyings were usually public performances during assemblies at which lay preachers shared the vast amount of scripture they had memorized. Only a very few Camisards, generally taught by their pastors, could read, but they all were familiar with Reformed doctrine, which stated that any individual believer could interpret the Bible for himself. The primary source for the vocabulary and content of their pronouncements was the Bible. Their utterances were not symbolic, but rather were meant to be taken literally. Scripture created the "horizon of expectation" in the listeners or "social support group," to use Wilson's term, of the Camisard prophets.[5]

Drawing on Old Testament models of prophecy, such as the book of Joel, and influenced by New Testament paradigms of inspiration, such as the gifts of the Holy Spirit received at Pentecost in the book of Acts, and especially from apocalyptic literature like the book of Revelation, the Camisards began to articulate a theological stance that arose directly out of the social crisis in which they found themselves, yet that also situated them in reference to the early Christian church—whose oppression by imperial Rome served a prototype for the persecutions that the Camisards were currently enduring. On the whole, Old Testament models of prophecy motivated the function and role of Camisard prophecy, while New Testament apocalyptic writing provided most of its content.

In these models of prophecy, the Camisards discerned a process by which individuals might speak both for God and for the community, as well as the means to authenticate prophecy; further, the energies and abilities of the prophets could be channeled into structures essential to the preservation of the Camisard subculture. While a potent charisma attached to prophets, making them seem powerful in themselves, the Camisard community actually used the prophets to perpetuate itself.

The "Support Group" and Its Significance

Robert Wilson's model of prophecy contributes to an understanding of the Camisard experience through his emphasis on social context and community. No prophet arises in isolation, he observes, and once one does appear, the "social support group" provides important functions of recognizing, validating, enabling, and sustaining the prophet.[6] Camisard prophets received messages that offered reassurance to the subculture, stating what the community wanted and needed to hear. This aspect is typical of prophecy acting within, and having an effect on, a social context.

One of the more intriguing puzzles concerning the strength, cohesiveness, and remarkable resilience of the Camisards may be explained by the composition and nature of the support group they provided. The social legitimation accorded to prophecy as a means of communal self-perpetuation created a paradox: the prophecy, a creative riposte to the experience of persecution (that is, an anti-institutional response), was itself, already, protoinstitutionalized, since the support group appropriated prophecy as a formal mechanism for ensuring military leadership, social cohesion, and theological validation.

There were several kinds of support communities for the Camisard prophets. The first was that of the Camisards' Huguenot brethren, but their support was, on the whole, rather lukewarm. Many Huguenots were scandalized by some of the enthusiastic "excesses" of the "French Spiritists," or Camisards.[7] For instance, when the three Camisards known as the "French Prophets" arrived in England, they united with Huguenot coreligionists at the French Church of London, but some days later were barred from worshiping there because of their urgent millenarian prophecies. The Huguenots had too much invested in perpetuating their own institution to take a risk by supporting the ecstatic Camisards.

Nonetheless, there was some explicit and official support for the French Prophets and other, less well-known Camisard immigrants. François Misson, son of an émigré Huguenot pastor in Niort and himself a former jurist under Louis XIV, became persuaded by the French Prophets' firsthand accounts of the Camisard sufferings. He arranged for witnesses to the prophesying in the Cévennes to testify before a judge and to give sworn testimony over a period of several days in a London court. Misson then collected this testimony, added a preface, and published the collection in French under the title *Le Théâtre sacré des Cévennes* (1707) and in an English translation as *A Crie from the Desart*; the collection was reprinted all over Europe.

Protestants in Geneva might have constituted a support group, but Calvinist Protestantism had become so thoroughly institutionalized there that its original spark was tamped down, intellectualized, whereas the Camisards brought with them a vibrant, lived experience of contact with the Holy Spirit, and of being led by its wisdom, that recalled the sort of back-to-the-source conviction that had first animated Calvin. In many respects, the Camisards, perhaps uncomfortably, recalled the Calvinists to their origins. In the Cévennes, the Camisard Protestants had maintained close ties with Geneva and practiced a Protestant piety consistent with Calvin's prescriptions. By 1702, when Camisard refugees began to arrive in Geneva, however, warm-hearted piety and preaching on the gifts of the Holy Spirit had been subsumed to a latter-day need for political and social stability.

The second support group was much less ambivalent about, and consequently more helpful to, the Camisard cause. This group consisted of the Walloon churches and the community of Reformed resistance to Catholicism in the Netherlands. The Walloon churches poured money into the Cévennes to try to ease the Camisards' plight, supported individual Camisards who managed to escape, and welcomed the Camisards into their churches. In the Netherlands, Pierre Jurieu, a Huguenot minister and philosophe of international prestige and impressive theological credentials within the European Reformed community, was one of the most significant sources of support for the Camisards. He provided a theoretical apparatus that legitimized the prophetic pronouncements of the movement. His publications provided step-by-step descriptions of the upcoming Apocalypse, of which he identified the Camisards as a prefiguring sign; he also programmatically refuted the Catholic abuses against which the Camisards were reacting. Jurieu wrote book after book and transcribed portions of written testimony attesting to the power of Camisard prophecy.[8] He was widely read throughout Europe and in the North American colonies.

A third support group arose within the community of Camisards themselves. This group is somewhat more elusive to define, since not much documentation exists. The enthusiasm shared among the Camisards, their belief in divine inspiration and visitations by the Holy Spirit on their entire community but especially on the prophets, sustained them in their time of trouble. They were reputed to blow into each other's mouths to confer the gift of the spirit;[9] they experienced ecstatic manifestations of the spirit; and, while in the spirit, they prophesied and prayed to God to lead them in a holy war against their persecutors. Prophecy lifted up the plight of the poor, enjoining support, protection, and continued steadfastness within the Camisard community.

The support group was a small persecuted minority including all Camisards except the "Croix blanches." These were Camisards recruited by Catholics during the "active" phase of prophecy to serve as informants against other Camisards and even, at times, to fight against them. The *nouveaux convertis* were Camisards who had converted back to Catholicism under pressure or fear of reprisal.[10] Because they tended to be somewhat wealthier villagers, they were less likely to join in behavior that might be perceived as threatening the social order. However, many of the younger *nouveaux convertis* underwent counterabjuration, thereby rejoining the support group and often playing an active and positive role in it.

The *nouveaux convertis* seem to have been especially important to the prophetic phenomenon. Perhaps the prophets recognized that these *convertis* felt great guilt over having abjured their faith and now more eagerly than ever wanted to defend their Reformed stance. Characterized by great fervency, the reconverted *convertis*, once again having rejected Catholicism, seem to have formed, in large part, the social set from which Camisard military leaders were drawn. Robin Briggs notes that "the attempt to eradicate Protestantism . . . left an unfortunate legacy of the 'nouveaux convertis' whom the church never managed to assimilate."[11]

The Camisards selected military leaders from the ranks of those who prophesied. Toward the end of the uprising, when the Camisards began to lose battles, their leaders became discredited in the eyes of their closest support group. Once its members doubted the integrity or inspiration of its leaders, the Camisard cause began to falter.

A Paradigm for Prophecy

According to autobiographical accounts and the testimonies of witnesses, the Holy Spirit persuaded the Camisards of the veracity of prophetic phenomena. The sources detailing Camisard prophecy are both varied and problematic. The first consideration is what might be called the absent presence of prophecy, since it was uttered primarily by illiterate peasants of whom we have no record or only fragmentary recollections. Nonetheless, there are a number of paraphrased transcriptions of their statements, either by someone who witnessed the prophecy or by a secondhand writer. For example, the pastor Pierre Jurieu recorded them in his letters: "A lay preacher, an uneducated man . . . believed he had a vision, hearing a voice telling him, 'Go, comfort my people.'"[12]

A few of the Camisard prophets who survived the persecutions went on to become ordained ministers in the Reformed Church, and later wrote their memoirs as retrospective testimonies to the effect, nature, and content of their own prophecies (Antoine Court) and those of others (Jacques Bonbonnoux). Furthermore, a few hardy pastors hid among their flock before fleeing. They compiled accounts attesting to signs and marvels, such as hearing voices in the air near where *temples* once stood, or seeing unusual stars guide the Camisard troops out of danger by night, and they authenticated their accounts by appending their signatures. This was during a "latent phase" of Camisard prophesying, early in the persecutions, when the Camisards did not actively resist.

The Camisard *inspirés* provided the spark to activate scripture. Since Camisard culture was primarily oral, those few who had literary or verbal memory were expected to be able to quote biblical texts extensively and apply them to current circumstances. Since Catholic priests and the king's soldiers were confiscating Bibles, the function of recalling, repeating, and interpreting remembered scripture became very important. Only a privileged subset of the subculture was able to perform this function. Prophets had to be able to enter into a trance and be possessed of the spirit, command an audience and get a hearing, compose a message drawn from scriptural knowledge, and tailor a message to current circumstances.

The Camisard support group would then become galvanized by the *inspiré*'s dynamic enactment of scripture. The group fulfilled certain criteria: it recognized the accuracy of the scriptural passage being quoted and validated such verses by applying them to daily life, either for comfort, encouragement, and direction, or for revolutionary and militaristic guidance. The message served to confirm the elect status of the support group and the *inspiré* status of the prophet.

The message thus stabilized the threatened and persecuted Camisard social structure, defending it from the hostile Catholic majority by pronouncing a biblical verdict of impending judgment in which majority and minority status would be reversed.[13]

Pierre Jurieu and the Theory of the End-Times

Pierre Jurieu, born in 1637 to pastor Daniel Jurieu in Mer, France, went on to study in Calvinist academies in Saumur, Sedan, Holland, and England, and in 1674 was appointed professor of theology and Hebrew in Sedan, France. This chair was suppressed by the order of Louis XIV in 1681, and Jurieu went into exile around the time of the first wave of forced conversions in the Cévennes. The author of numerous anti-Catholic polemical tracts, among them the *Preservatif contre le changement de religion* (1681) and *Politique du clergé* (1681), Jurieu also ministered to the Walloon church in Rotterdam, continued to attack the pope as the Antichrist, and criticized Louis XIV for his policy of *dragonnades*, denouncing the dragoons as "missionaries booted for battle."[14]

Probably Jurieu's most important work on apocalypticism, the *Accomplissement des prophéties*, was first published in 1687 and then expanded until his death, in 1713; in it, Jurieu maintained that God would deliver his people shortly after the Revocation.[15] In his *Lettres pastorales*, Jurieu defended the Camisards as embodying a religious orthodoxy harking back to the early Christian church.[16] He contrasted Camisard prophecy with the abuses and distortions that he perceived in Catholicism, claiming—as many other Protestants did—that Rome, in many respects, did not conform to scripture. The original title of the *Lettres pastorales*, "To our brothers groaning under Babylon's yoke,"[17] conveys Jurieu's partisan perspective. It also shows his pastoral desire both to encourage his "frères," the Camisards, and to urge the Huguenots to affirm solidarity with them: "*our* brothers."

Although Jurieu himself, by background, education, and even theological training, was on the whole very different from the Camisards whose cause he espoused, he wrote about them in a style accessible to all,[18] describing his work as "meant to be read and understood by simple folk . . . with as much profit as others will derive."[19] Jurieu had a significant influence on the *nouveaux convertis*, causing many to reconsider their decision to go over to Rome. The Catholic bishop Fénélon, trying to minister to the *nouveaux convertis* in Saintonge, hated Jurieu for this reason, and Bossuet wrote against Jurieu in *Avertissements aux Protestants, sur les lettres du ministre Jurieu* (1689–1690).

Jurieu headed up an international support group for the Camisard prophets in two ways. First, his writings on the apocalypse provided proof texts for a theory of the end-times as presaged by the Camisard rebellion.[20] "This persecution must be the final one," Jurieu wrote to the Camisards; it was "the same message as the one penned by the author of Revelation."[21] Second, by soliciting, compiling, and publishing letters from Camisard refugees in London, Castres, Metz, Valence, Dublin, Geneva, and Berlin, Jurieu compiled an evidentiary corpus of the Camisard experience. The epigraph to the *Lettres pastorales* reflects this program: "As we intend to include with the letters the most important acts of our Confessors and Martyrs, anyone who has any sure knowledge of them should trouble to let us know about it."[22] Thus, Jurieu was the apologist of the Camisard cause as well as the interpreter of their version of popular, pietistic Reformed theology.

Like many Enlightenment Europeans, Jurieu was appalled by the figures summarizing the persecution: by 1686, more than 40,000 Camisards were in prison, more than 2,000 were serving as galley slaves, and more than 200,000 had clandestinely fled the country.[23] Jurieu was persuaded by the intensity both of the Camisard experience—their sufferings, their steadfastness in the face of persecution, and their spiritual conviction—and of the authenticity of what he called their "sentiment intérieur" (what the Camisards called the inspiration of the Holy Spirit). As a Huguenot, Jurieu believed that grace enlightened the individual interpretation of scripture; this enabled him to affirm that the Camisard interpretation of scripture—however controversial it might be—was accurate and trustworthy. Jurieu sought to expand support for the Camisard cause by persuading other Huguenots of their kinship with "their brethren in Languedoc."[24] Further, he showed the Camisards their solidarity with the Huguenots: "God shall save His people . . . this will remind Huguenots of flagging faith of their individual and collective election, their minority identity apart from the rest of the world, as both a privileged and a persecuted people."[25]

Jurieu's eighth pastoral letter, written on September 23, 1686, is especially significant for the Camisard cause. In it, Jurieu described, as he titled the letter, "Songs and voices heard in the air in various places."[26] He affectionately called the Camisards "les petits prophètes" and argued that their prophecy was an expression of divine will. Jurieu determined that the onset of the phenomenon conformed to the paradigm established in the apocalyptic book of Joel.[27] Jurieu noted that in the earliest forms of their prophecy, the Camisards attempted to perpetuate a communal worship predicated on scripture and psalm singing: "We left their Assemblies in the dead of winter. And we saw that, despite the harshness of the season, the precipices bordering the paths, and the thick evening shadows, the faithful continued to gather in such places for the purpose of praying to God together."[28]

By the beginning of 1689, the *inspirés* had come to the forefront as leaders of these gatherings. The pastors having fled, the support group gave a layperson the power to preach or to administer the sacraments. Jurieu defended this decision: "You should not assume that they are guilty of irregularity in this. For it is ever so that true vocation is determined by the people and by the choice made in assemblies."[29] Jurieu went on boldly to assert that "the ordination of a pastor is really only a formality, which can be dispensed with in cases of emergency,"[30] showing how the Camisard message demonstrated the characteristics of direct inspiration, egalitarian dualism, and the world upside down (a topos reflecting the anticipated reversal of social structures in the end-times), as well as markedly accommodating the role of women in prophesying. The Camisards' idiom reflected a well-developed persecution mentality.

Jurieu characterized the Camisards' testimony as factual. He explicitly contrasted their accounts of signs and wonders, which he accepted as true, with what he called the "evil tales"[31] of Catholicism, characterizing the latter as staged deceptions at saints' tombs, the misguided adoration of holy images, a mistaken belief in the intercession of saints, and "a thousand" other "superstitions."[32] To these "false signs" of Rome, Jurieu opposed the truthful testimony of the Camisards.[33] He based his argument for the validity of Camisard miracles on God's ability to reveal himself when, where, and how he so chose: "Nothing happens without God willing it. Could it be possible that God would entirely hide himself behind his creatures, under the veil of secondary causes, and never pull the curtain even the slightest bit aside to reveal himself?"[34] He also based his thesis on the prototype provided by Old Testament prophets—"at the time the authors of Holy Scripture were writing, that sort of thing occurred"[35]—and cited examples of such divine interruptions of the natural order: "God granted Gideon a sign in nature"[36] and "Ezekiel received a sign in the heavens."[37] Jurieu argued against Enlightenment rationalism's skepticism concerning what he deemed to be miraculous occurrences: "This is a miracle that deserves our attention. We would indeed be ungrateful to God, were we to overlook such a stunning testimony of His approval."[38]

In short, God was on the Camisards' side, and would soon intervene on behalf of his persecuted people, Jurieu argued, by bringing about the end of the world. Jurieu identified several unusual occurrences as signs prefiguring the end-times. Numerous witnesses heard psalms being sung "in the air" near lo-cations where Camisard *temples* had been destroyed at Louis XIV's command. This was first attested to in Béarn, the first province to which dragoons had been sent. For instance, Jurieu quoted one eyewitness as saying, "I attest that the younger Monsieur Bazin, living in the town of Orthez in Béarn, told me that, while walking with one of his friends one afternoon near the town of Orthez, he heard voices singing psalms . . . This happened some months after our church had been placed off-limits to us."[39]

The narration of the phenomenon conformed to a pattern. Jurieu used legal language to relate the incident and relied on testimony collected by pastors before their flight. The pastors conveyed the information "par certificat" and signed and dated the testimony they had transcribed ("written in Amsterdam on November 23, 1686, signed by Magendie, former Minister"),[40] and the tes-timony was given by witnesses who used the formula "je déclare que" to attest to their truthfulness. The eyewitnesses provided precise time and place infor-mation as well as autobiographical material about themselves to enhance their reliability.[41] They also added affective material to dramatize and make more credible the emotional quality of their experience: "Even now as I write, I can still hear their cries."[42]

The witnesses or the support group then speculated on possible motivations for, and interpretations of, the sign. Some readings of the signs included state-ments such as the following: "I told him, Sir, if men fall silent, the very stones will cry out";[43] "We can not doubt for a moment that these are bands of angels whom God sends to us to console us and to assure us that God has not com-pletely abandoned us, and that our deliverance is at hand."[44]

Next, the event recounted was examined for its effect on the support group; for example, it might "fill this poor persecuted people with an extraordinary joy and consolation."[45] The support group might feel comforted or consoled, con-firmed in its course of action, or, occasionally, corrected for being off course, as in the case of one pastor who interpreted the phenomenon as God trying to reach hardened hearts: "God has made mouths to speak in the middle of the air . . . He is causing a great change in your lives, to make you worthy to receive Him . . . the time of your deliverance is near, but he will not come until the time of your repentance has come . . . and the spirit of piety and devotion make a home in your heart."[46] The support group's assessment of the event's authentic-ity and the reliability of the witnesses was recorded: "Some will say that she is only a woman, but she is a woman who is reporting on something that occurred in public and for which she had as witnesses several hundred people";[47] "Made-moiselle de Vebron has always belonged to the Reformed faith, and God has saved her from falling away as others have."[48]

Finally, the support group—and Jurieu—gave thanks to God for the inspiration and direction that he had provided: "We gave thanks to God for the grace that he has shown us in reminding us of our duty to him through the means of heavenly voices which melodiously sang sacred songs."[49] Similar phenomena were viewed as linked and reinforcing: "the very same thing happened in the Cévennes";[50] the sites of the testimonials shifting geographically and chronologically from the Dauphiné to small towns in the Cévennes mountains.

Jurieu used the Camisard miracles and prophecies as a paradigm. He urged all those of the Reformed faith to emulate the model that the Camisards established for those apocalyptic times: "You must gather together as often as you are able; read scripture together . . . Console each other with good prayers and sermons . . . Finally, *you must imitate the zeal of our brothers in Languedoc.*"[51]

Ultimately, Jurieu's aim in writing the *Lettres pastorales* was not only to provide an apology for the Camisard cause, but also to reinforce his earlier anti-Catholic writing. He used the case of the Camisards as a touchstone for true faith: those who persevered, however persecuted, were the true Christians; those who kept themselves pure from Catholic abuses were exemplary martyrs to be emulated: "I have told you this story about the strength of faith of our brothers in Languedoc and how they have persisted in gathering together, risking martyrdom and death in so doing, in the hopes of persuading you of what I have just shown you in this letter: that you must not go [back] to the Roman church."[52] Jurieu's own support group—his readership—had multiple constituencies, and the support that he provided to the Camisard cause implicitly exhorted other Protestants to strengthen their resolve against Rome.

Pierre Jurieu became a formal apologist for the Camisard cause, offering a coherent scheme of apocalyptic interpretation as a lens through which to explicate the prophetic pronouncements. Contemporary Camisard depositions testified to the overwhelming influence of Jurieu's writing even upon this predominantly illiterate folk: his publications circulated widely, and many could quote him as well as they could quote scripture, having memorized and passed on extensive passages of both after hearing them read aloud. Jurieu's writings assured the Camisards of the support of the spirit and the biblical warrant for their faith, empowering them to persevere in a time of trial.

CHAPTER THREE

The Testimonials

The French Prophets and the Inspirés

of the Holy Spirit

There would be no end of all the Wonders reported to have come to
pass in the Cévennes.
—Madame M. R. De Montpellier, 1707, quoted in Misson, *Le Théâtre
sacré des Cévennes*

One evening early in 1701, a cluster of friends gathered clandestinely by candlelight in the town of Vernon, where a thirteen-month-old baby,
still in swaddling clothes, convulsed and then prophesied. Despite having no
knowledge of "the King's French," nor even, yet, of his native Provençal, the
Camisard infant reportedly spoke his first words as prophecy in perfect French.
He audibly and intelligibly exhorted the Camisard folk to persevere in the face
of tribulation. According to Camisard observers, "The child, aged between 13
to 14 months, was wrapped up in his cradle. He had never before spoken or
walked. The child spoke clearly in French. His body shook at the beginning."[1]

Doubters and detractors called such phenomena impostures; the "little
prophets" were prey to illusion, possession, and "maladies," and a purported
"school for prophets" had been established in the Cévennes to dupe the credu-
lous and deceive the king's subjects.[2] In the case of some of the younger prophets, great efforts were apparently made to give the lie to their claims. Pierre
Jurieu reported, for instance, that Isabeau Vincent was suspected of being
possessed and that Catholic clergy attempted to exorcize the demon with holy
water. Although some skeptics regarded her "comme si elle eû été possédée,"
Jurieu, like most Camisards, was confident that her prophecies were attribut-
able to miraculous intervention.[3]

This is the stuff of which the Camisard legend was made. As one recent
scholar puts it: "Can we in fact speak of 'legend'? It's very likely . . . that isolated
cases, reported by word of mouth or by letters recopied with a greater or lesser
degree of accuracy . . . became the rule rather than the exception."[4]

How much of it was true? While absolute veracity is nearly impossible to ascertain, the effect of the prophetic phenomenon on the Camisard support group was undeniable. Without the encouragement of the ecstatic utterances, the ragtag band of Camisard peasants could never have accomplished their military successes: "It was by inspiration that we forsook our parents and relations, and whatever was dearest to us in world, to follow Jesus Christ . . . This was what gave to the inspired a zeal for God and undefiled religion, a hatred of idolatry . . . It was only by the inspirations . . . that we began the war for the enjoyment of our Holy Religion; a small number of simple young people, without education, and without experience, how could they have done so many great things, without help from above? We had neither power nor counsel, but the inspirations were all, our refuge and support."[5]

Several years later, as the Camisards were being slaughtered by the hundreds in the Cévennes, the tide of war having turned against them and, perhaps, their "little prophets" no longer sufficing to uphold the survivors in the face of such devastation, Elie Marion, Durand Fage, and Jean Cavalier de Sauve fled to England. This Camisard remnant, which would come to be known as the French Prophets, arrived in London battered, but determined to preach the gospel and plead their cause.

The prophecies did not cease with the end of the war and the surrender of the last of the rebels; rather, prophecy continued across the Channel, communicated by Marion, Fage, and Cavalier, who made converts not only among French Protestant refugees in London, but also among the English.[6] While they initially received a welcome, succor, and a hearing from the primarily Huguenot French colony in exile (the Consistoire de Savoie), their more conservative Calvinist coreligionists quickly became alarmed by the French Prophets' apocalyptic urgency. Concerned about maintaining peaceful relations with its Anglican hosts, the established French Church in London viewed the three accomplished public speakers, who were both millenarist and militant, as being beyond the pale.[7] Determined to safeguard the measure of tolerance and religious freedom it had won, the Huguenot *temple* adamantly dissociated itself from what it saw as Camisard extremism.

In August 1706, the twenty-five-year-old prodigy prophet Durand Fage reached England and began preparations for the arrival of Elie Marion, who began his apocalyptic preaching in London on September 16, hoping to resuscitate support for the Camisards.[8] Fage, Marion, and Jean Cavalier met at the home of a sympathetic Presbyterian minister, Thomas Cotton, where all three uttered warnings of the approaching end-times.[9] Cotton had witnessed the persecution of Huguenots in Poitiers and Saumur and had been greatly affected, returning to England to lobby on their behalf.[10]

In England, where millenarian sentiment had been inflamed by the hopes raised during the Glorious Revolution, thinkers such as Bishop William Lloyd sympathized with Camisard apocalyptic beliefs, declaring that the Cévennol Protestants were one of the two witnesses cited in the book of Revelation as attesting to the imminence of the end-times.[11] Other English clergymen as well believed that the persecution in the Cévennes prefigured the Apocalypse. The Reverend Thomas Burnet wrote that "the resurrection of the Witnesses goes on very well in Savoy and Dauphiné."[12] As a result, many in London accepted the preaching of the French Prophets, including their claims that the dead would soon rise, as authoritative pronouncements from God.[13]

A group of English men and women, mostly Anglicans, influenced by the apocalyptic preaching of John Mason, the rector of Water Stafford, near Buckingham, had begun as early as 1689 to anticipate the Second Coming of Christ. Calling themselves Philadelphians, they sought to reform the church through personal piety, belief in direct inspiration, and theosophical principles. They welcomed the refugee French Prophets with great enthusiasm as heralds of the impending Apocalypse.[14]

However, the Huguenots already established in *temples* on Threadneedle Street and in the chapel of the former Savoy palace were strict and staid Calvinists. The established French clergy and their flocks were nearly a generation older than the French Prophets, and had originated in the southwest of France.[15] The Threadneedle Church had taken action to prevent its dissolution in 1660, seeking royal protection as a conformist church, and so had a conservative interest in avoiding potential controversy or divisiveness.[16] Further, the Huguenots, nearly riven by a disagreement over predestination at two points in their early history, were concerned to present an appearance of orthodoxy and acceptability.[17] The younger Camisards, fresh from persecution and martyrdom in southeastern France, looked askance at their carefully respectable and conformist confrères.

At first, the French Prophets got quite a hearing. Some, hoping to be convinced by miracles, became disenchanted, however, when the prophecies were slow to be realized.[18] Further, since the Camisard prophets stressed personal inspiration and spiritual gifts as signs of true Christianity, they entered into direct conflict with many in the Threadneedle French Church who denied the validity of such phenomena.[19] On January 5, 1707, the Savoy consistory published a statement called the "Acte noir," announcing from the pulpit that "the Agitations of these pretended Prophets are only the Effect of a voluntary Habit, of which they are entirely Masters, though in their Fits they seem to be agitated by a Superior Cause."[20]

The French Prophets responded with metaphors derived from their experience of exile, persecution, and estrangement, their rhetoric prefiguring the eventual Huguenot and Camisard diaspora to the New World. Marion cried: "Faith and Truth are dead upon the Earth . . . I have no place of Abode. I have no Habitation upon the earth; I am driven away from all Places: I am wandering, I tell thee, like the things of nought."[21] On March 30, 1707, the Savoy consistory took further action, refusing to give Communion to the French Prophets. However, during the next week, seven members of the French Church began to prophesy. London now had the evidence of the Holy Spirit for which it had been looking. Ten days later, a mob in Soho set upon the French Prophets, accusing them of wanting to destroy the French Church and to supplant orthodoxy with a "new" gospel. Riots continued throughout April.

Marion and Fage were brought to trial in the Queen's Bench Court, accused by the Savoy consistory of blasphemy and sedition. As the trial dragged on, the Philadelphians merged with the French Prophets, adding many English converts to the ranks of the few French followers. In July, the French Prophets were found guilty by the court, but yet more followers flocked to their side. Many experienced glossolalia, often speaking in Greek, and saw signs in the heavens, as had the original Camisards in the *désert*.

On the fourth of September, Marion declared that London had become the New Jerusalem. Millennial expectations rose to a fever pitch. As penalty for the guilty verdict, the French Prophets were condemned to stand on a public scaffold wearing placards decrying them as false prophets; they exulted in being persecuted for Christ's sake. English followers continued to hope for miracles, the resurrection of the dead, and the end of the world. At this point, the French Prophets were not in control of the movement; rather, it was using their renown to make its own claims, among them John Lacy's assertion that an English prophet, Thomas Emes, who had recently died, would be raised from the dead. Female prophets sprang up, providing further fuel for the Anglican fire, since prophecy by women was not condoned in scripture, Anglican clergy argued.

Marion took steps to reestablish some order. He merged the French and English groups into what he called the Sign of the Reunion of the Two Alliances, published a French and English New Testament, and assigned followers to one of the twelve tribes of Israel as a sort of para-ecclesial structure for the bourgeoning body of followers. Agape feasts took place. On Christmas Day 1708, more than two hundred participants in the new alliance celebrated the Eucharist.

In a controversial step toward institutionalizing the movement, Marion and others decided that only the *inspirés* and their secretaries were to meet together in formal assembly. Many were angered at this hierarchy of inspiration, among them Jean Cavalier, and split off into separate groups. In 1712, some of these prophets left England to begin prophesying in Scotland; on the Continent, Pierre Jurieu welcomed others. In general, Huguenots opposed their prophesyings throughout Europe.[22] But one influential figure, François Misson, deemed them "witnesses."[23] He can be thought of as seeding a Camisard support group in England, as Georgia Cosmos notes: "Misson was the Camisard *inspirés'* first vital link to the French refugee community in London. He remained an influential supporter."[24]

Misson's Case for the Camisards

The affaire of the French Prophets became a cause célèbre; their message galvanized London, with French and English believers quickly taking sides and arguing the merits of each case. The French Prophets called into question political, social, and intellectual partis pris, with the Cévennes featuring as a sort of laboratory for theological veracity.[25]

One of the most prominent and articulate of the few public figures to rally to the Camisard cause was François Misson. Misson was a London neighbor of the French Prophets, two of whom (Marion and Fage) had been given shelter in a home near his.[26] At first keeping a skeptical distance, but eventually fascinated by their experiences, Misson engaged them in dialogue during the seven or eight months they lived nearby.[27]

Misson defended Marion, Cavalier, and Fage against the London ill wishers who, on April 32, 1706, burned to the ground the house in which the Camisards had been staying. When the clergy of the established French Church preached against the French Prophets in the Savoy consistory on the following Sunday, calling them "impostors and public blasphemers who can provide no proof [for their representations],"[28] Misson was outraged; his sense of fair play and his own convictions now called into question, he decided to provide precisely the proof that was alleged to be lacking.

Determined to make a thorough exposition of the Camisard claims, he formed the project of having eyewitnesses,[29] among them the three French Prophets, provide sworn depositions[30] before a London judge.[31] These statements would provide the documentation needed for the case to be judged on its own merits and would, Misson believed, determine exactly what had transpired in the Cévennes. He worked to put the proceedings on a legally defensible footing: "Witnesses who came forward between November 1706 and March 1707 to give testimony were cautioned against making false or inaccurate statements; they were to report 'la vérité pure et simple,' speaking only of events they could distinctly remember."[32]

Misson himself was present at the time of the collection of the depositions; he had them transcribed, translated into English, and published at his own expense.[33] The collection of twenty-six lengthy and detailed testimonials, along

with excerpts from contemporary publications concerning the Camisard uprising, was circulated all over the Continent in both French and English versions;
copies reached the New World.

Entitled *Le Théâtre sacré des Cévennes ou, récit de diverses merveilles nou-
vellement opérées dans cette partie de la Province de Languedoc*, the collection
demonstrated the application of Enlightenment historical methods to a situation possessing a confessional slant. The English title, *A Crie from the Desert*,
recalled the wanderings of the ancient Hebrews in the desert as well as the
persecution of sixteenth-century French Calvinists, figured as latter-day Israel-
ites under siege.[34] Misson aimed at shaping a sympathetic audience among the
Huguenots in London for their Camisard confrères, reminding the former of
the common experience of persecution. The witnesses themselves also made
this association at times in their testimonials. Sarah Dalgone, for instance, referred explicitly to the war-torn France of a scarce century past, saying, "I was
frequently at the assemblies, which our poor persecuted Protestants held in
secret, for the worship of God according to the ancient manner of our churches
in France."[35]

The compilation began with verses from the book of Acts and other New
Testament writings, implying that the French Prophets' testimonials were similar to the testimonies of the apostles—seemingly equally incredible—and the
founders of the early Christian church. For instance, Matthew 5:11 and 12 was
cited as justification for the Camisard positions: "Blessed are you when you
have been persecuted and reviled, and when they speak against you. Rejoice
and be glad, for your reward will be great in heaven. For this is how they persecuted the Prophets who were before you."[36]

The French Prophets were represented as "three brave Christian soldiers,"
similar to the martyrs of the early Christian church. Their utterances, despite
Misson's claim to neutrality, assumed the aura of undeniably truthful statements. Misson himself noted that what he had collected was not ammunition
for a polemical battle—although the *Théâtre sacré* did indeed galvanize a war of
reason versus faith waged on the printed page—but was rather proof of truth:
"These are simple truths, simply told and legally deposed. Read, and consider
them all, and draw your own conclusions."[37]

Applying the Enlightenment to Revelation

Misson's method of assessing evidence took on an Enlightenment quality when
he provided the reader the opportunity to be the judge: after studying the testimonials, the reader would be qualified to weigh the evidence and arbitrate the
case. This method illustrated the Enlightenment belief, as well as the Christian

conviction, that through the accumulation and presentation of documentation, truth would prevail: "When a truth is established on a firm foundation, nothing can unsettle it."[38] The documents were construed as representative stand-ins for the witnesses, almost corporeal substitutes.[39] In addition, the fair and thorough collaboration of other potential witnesses was solicited: Misson stated, "If any-one has any serious and reasonable objection or light to cast on the subject, I will be glad to receive from them the signed, concise statement of their objec-tion."[40]

Orderly, rational, and meticulous in his method of collection, Misson estab-lished a typology for the testimonials in the *Théâtre sacré*. He stipulated that the accounts of only selected people—those who, because of their integrity, were deemed worthy of having perceived or heard—would be included: these would be "special witnesses, persons whose faith and faithfulness [had] been especially proved."[41] The confessional composition of the collection would thus be mixed, including not only Camisard but also Catholic contributors, "pious Catholics, such as the author of the Marquis de Guiscard's *Mémoires*, as well as the public figure and writer Mr. David de Brueys."[42]

Misson enumerated the sorts of evidence that he deemed admissible: "ex-cerpts from books"; "letters handwritten by their authors," such as those penned by a Dutch pastor, a noted galley slave, and two Camisard noblemen named Caladon and Puysieulx; and "depositions tendered in London . . . by twenty-six reliable witnesses who saw and heard the things they were reporting."[43] Misson repeated that the representations rendered in writing were credible precisely because they had been duly attested to in the presence of witnesses, among them himself and his translator, "who was present at the time that most of the statements were made":[44] "My consistent method was to make very clear to those testifying how very important it was that they speak only the truth and make no statements of which they were not entirely sure, concerning only mat-ters to which they were prepared to swear solemnly."[45]

To ensure reliability of translation, as well as to secure the broadest possible audience, Misson appointed a bilingual secretary: "an English gentleman, who understands our language well, worked together with me on his translation."[46] This translation went into two English editions. However, for some readers, Misson somewhat undermined his purportedly neutral methods when he pos-ited the conclusion to be drawn from the assessment of the evidence before its display: "The various matters taken up in this book collectively form *a very sub-stantial justification* of those people against whom one has been waging such a horrid, tyrannical war."[47]

Misson went further, revealing his religious beliefs, which he deemed not incompatible with Enlightenment objectivity, despite his case for earthly events that attested to a supernatural order.[48] Misson affirmed a belief in divine inspiration and in present-day miracles: "I am one of those who believes that God's hand has not been shortened: that just as he performed miracles in the past, he continues to be able to do so in the present."[49] God's Providence was not curtailed: God could, and would, do as he purposed, and what human could dare to contest that ability, Misson argued. Indeed, Misson observed scientifically, "closely and, as it were, with a microscope,"[50] and reached a theological conclusion that apparently did not conflict with his Cartesian philosophy: "Divine wisdom governs the world that it created . . . This adorable Providence seems to play a large role in surprising occurrences [miracles]."[51] If the French Prophets claimed to be inspired by God, and if events seemed to bear them out, why not believe them, Misson argued.

The more Misson heard of the Camisards' story, the more compelled he was by their cause. This proponent of Cartesian logic, heir of Montaignian skepticism, defender of Enlightenment reason, offered as a paradoxical explanation for his conviction the rationale that the Camisards' case was so extraordinary that it would be unreasonable to dismiss them as crazy men: "Their case was characterized by such miraculous happenings that he could imagine nothing more unreasonable than to dismiss them as ill, or as fanatics."[52] So swayed was he by their accounts that this educated member of the well-to-do, professional *haute bourgeoisie* staked his reputation on the veracity of the lowly Camisard prophets' claims:[53] "I have no shame in testifying . . . I myself know, I who write this . . . I am sure that they are innocent."[54] In fact, in an unexpected reversal of the solid front that a moneyed class customarily opposes to that of a less enfranchised or educated group, Misson exalted the itinerant French Prophets above the established Londoners, labeling the latter "the unenlightened and misinformed mob": "The basic aim of the *Théâtre sacré* is to help you to see, as opposed to the false ideas of the noisy, crazed, and unenlightened mob, that it is really true that, for about six years now, in the Cévennes there has been a large number of people, of every age and of both sexes, who have been and continue to be in similar circumstances [of oppression] to those in which we see Marion, Cavalier, and Fage."[55]

Rebutting the Testimonies

Misson's project looked both backward, with the Camisard prophets featuring as models drawn from the New Testament, and forward, with the French Prophets construed as living emblems of the devastation wreaked by Louis XIV's *dragonnades*.[56] Most importantly, though, the *Théâtre sacré* revealed a theater of destruction that threatened any thinking person anywhere in the world, for it portrayed the systematic undermining of a primary Enlightenment credo: that of freedom of conscience. The occasionally outrageous pronouncements of the French Prophets and of other Camisard enthusiasts were thus enrolled in Misson's project as proof cases for truthful speech and freedom of expression. What some might view as religious fanaticism was now presented as an argument for the dispassionate exercise of reason and analysis. Little wonder the *Théâtre sacré* provoked such strong reactions.

Reaction from contemporary readers across the Continent was not always favorable. More than 147 works on the subject of the French Prophets and Camisards, of which 38 were in French, 101 in English, and 8 in bilingual editions, were disseminated throughout Europe, generating a highly polemical discussion. While the *Théâtre sacré* undeniably helped raise public consciousness concerning the Camisards' plight, other voices sought to use the testimonials against the Camisard cause. They did so in two ways: either they denigrated the value of the witnesses' statements, or they tried to discredit Misson's method. Three groups manifested this negative response: the Huguenot Church in London, Catholics decrying Camisard error, and some Enlightenment readers exercising their critical capacity.

The first negative reaction came from the consistory of the French Church of London on February 25, 1707, and again on March 7, 1707, when it promulgated two "Actes" explicitly taking aim at the testimonials. Misson's open-mindedness extended to appending the texts of these *actes* near the end of his volume. By including both points of view, prosecution and defense, he intended to allow readers to determine for themselves where truth resided. The *actes* published several purported retractions by some of the witnesses. It is not inconceivable that pressure from the tightly knit émigré community, or from church authorities, had been applied.

For instance, it was asserted that "Jean Cabanel from Anduze declared to those assembled that he never really believed that those who claimed to be divinely inspired were true prophets."[57] The Huguenot church authorities declared several narratives to be "purported testimonies, which were in fact willfully falsified by impostors in order to try to encourage this sham of pretended prophecy."[58] They also attempted to discredit the prophets by claiming that they had been given privileged information before prophesying, and so were culpable of manipulation, not gifted with clairvoyance: "For that reason they said anything they wanted and called it an inspiration, passing it off as a revelation from the Holy Spirit."[59] Finally, the documents asserted that some of the witnesses either did not exist or had assumed an alias, as in the case of Sarra d'Algone: "We were only able to find one woman by that name, and she stated that the declaration was pure invention."[60]

It appears that Misson had anticipated the criticisms of the second group, Catholic clerics. In his preparatory remarks to the *Théâtre sacré*, he provided a detailed statement of the Christian orthodoxy of Camisard beliefs: "The enemies of these innocent folk try to make them responsible for abominable acts in order to defame them. They accuse them of not being Christian and of hating the ministers of the Gospel, but the Camisards protest even more strongly that they believe in the Father, Son, and Holy Ghost, and that their hope of salvation is founded solely on Jesus Christ's redemptive act of salvation, [that] they love and revere God's ministers. They also state that they are poor, having trampled underfoot earthly riches in order to take up Jesus' cross."[61] Some of those who testified also incorporated such criticisms as though to anticipate and defuse them. David Flotard, from Vigan in the Haute-Cévennes, testified on March 6, 1707, and observed that he was convinced of the authenticity of the spiritual manifestations that he had witnessed, despite the fact that some priests would question them as "impostures . . . fanaticism . . . Satan's wiles . . . [and] drunkenness."[62]

The third group, Enlightenment rationalists, found fault with Misson's evidence and exposition, asserting that the information lacked "credibility."[63] Others reacted out of a class bias, exhibiting the social snobbery that Camisards eschewed. While not denying that some of what the Camisards reported might be true, these critics cast a cloud over their witnesses' credibility because of their low social standing: "This is the sort of hysteria [one can expect from] low-class people."[64] Other detractors averred that there were errors in transcription;[65] one critic maintained that only twelve of the twenty-six eyewitnesses "have sworn to their statements."[66] These critics claimed that since not all the statements had been made under oath, numerous depositions had been fabricated, and might even have been penned by the same hand: "Let me say here something that holds true for the entire *Théâtre sacré*: it seems that the author is more concerned to write good French than to tell the truth. All the statements appear to be written by the same person . . . Most [purported witnesses] are people who hardly know how to speak, yet one makes it sound as if they were very eloquent, an eloquence of which they are entirely incapable."[67]

The phrase "more concerned to write good French than to tell the truth" was meant not only to undermine Camisard prophecy, but also to tar Misson as a fabricator: the transcribed testimonies of these patois-speaking prophets were written, impossibly, in flawless French—the French, it was argued, of an educated man like Misson, who wrote their stories for them; therefore, their use of French was not miraculous but rather a strategy to perpetuate lies. Misson was judged to have fostered the scheme and to have provided the elegant idiom in which it was expressed. However, this appears most unlikely, since the transcriptions were taken down verbatim from oral statements and in the presence of witnesses. That is why Misson went to such elaborate lengths to receive the statements in a legal setting: so that their veracity could not be challenged.

Misson was not without his champions. In a compendious addendum to the *Théâtre*, titled *Meslange de littérature historique et critique sur tout ce qui regarde l'état extraordinaire des Cévenols, appellez Camisards*, numerous contemporary figures contributed their supportive comments as well as testimonials to Misson's character and credentials.[68] Misson's publisher declared that "the author of this collection, believe me dear reader, is a man of the world entirely without prejudice. He is the self-declared enemy of the false ideas held by the mob."[69] Misson's bookseller defended the integrity and the neutrality of his client's method and stance, "his theory being that the way best to apply one's reason in the search for truth is to begin by firmly and clearly establishing all the facts, before denying or affirming anything."[70] Finally, Misson's apologists turned the tables on the critics who had excoriated him for allying with the uneducated masses, asserting that those who did not listen to reason and conclude that the Camisards' cause was just were, themselves, the ignorant horde: "What the wise man has to say is not meant to serve as a dam against the unbridled torrent of erroneous opinion. Rather, it is meant for those worthy to receive it."[71] The reader of merit would recognize the validity of the Camisard cause.

On the other side of the Atlantic, theology and Enlightenment rationalism made strange bedfellows: the Puritan Cotton Mather was moved by the tales of Camisard suffering and persuaded by Misson's documentation. Mather went on to write on behalf of the Huguenots in Boston; he also wrote what is arguably the first history of what had happened to their Camisard cousins.

The Text as Theater and the Theater as Text

The Camisard witness Mathieu Boissier coined the phrase "le théâtre sacré des Cévennes," which Misson adapted as the title of his collection of testimonials: "It is notorious to all, or may be, that the wonders God has shown, from the commencement of this century, upon *the sacred scene of the Cévennes*, and upon the borders of the Rouergue, are the same in all their circumstances with those that have made so much noise, ever since the year 1688, in our country of Dauphiné, as well as in the Vivarais and Velay, districts commonly taken to be part of the Cévennes."[72]

The geographical region was designated as a supernatural terrain: it was construed as the arena, or "theater," in which God had chosen to display his miracles and acts of Providence. The Camisards thus became, in a rhetorical reversal of fortune, the privileged ones, for it was within the confines of their territory and experience, and exclusively within those frontiers, that God was working out his purpose.

This topographical and theological theater offered high drama: the visual—indeed, synesthetic, because also aural, tactile, and even olfactory—experience was compellingly conveyed. "The landscape of the Cévennes was dramatically transformed as sites in isolated parts of the countryside were converted into places of worship in Reformed congregations. It was on these sites that a forbidden religion flourished despite violent persecution . . . In their representation of the *désert* experience during the Camisard war, the witnesses of the *Théâtre sacré* described a spiritual reality which gave rise to the conviction that they were acting out a history which had been willed by God."[73] The phenomenon of being conduits for God's inspiration, recipients of the indwelling of the Holy Spirit, and vehicles for divine pronouncement was dramatized in the collection. This experience was referred to in several ways throughout the *Théâtre*: it was termed "to be caught up by the spirit," "to receive the gift," "receive inspiration," or simply by the noun "ecstasy."[74] The first three locutions fittingly emphasized the passivity of the recipient. These were simple folk, without means or method to aid themselves; only through a form of divine possession could they find the ability or the conviction to oppose secular and ecclesiastical authorities.

The prophetic ecstasy also was linguistically distinctive. Despite the fact that the Camisards communicated with their peers habitually in dialect, "all those whom I [Castanet] viewed in an ecstatic state spoke French better than they ever could do if not in a trance."[75] They seemed transported beyond themselves: as one man claimed, " 'Twas not himself who spoke, but the spirit of God by his mouth."[76] Often, they professed to be unaware of their competence while in this state: "I heard several of those who had just spoken while in an ecstatic state say that they would not be able to repeat the things that they had [just] said."[77] It was as though they sought to prove that their utterances were not their own by a sort of dispossession of self—and of regional identity and marginal status vis-à-vis the absolutist nation-state: "He appropriately cited passages from scripture, as if he knew the Bible by heart. I am certain he could not read."[78] This appropriation of classic French was tantamount to a symbolic and semiotic subversion of the backwoods status to which the Camisards had been relegated.[79] The democratization of inspiration reinforced this perception—not only young men, but also many young women, prophesied.[80]

The various witnesses—both to the empirical, historical persecution of the Camisards and to the phenomenon of prophecy—responded to the two manifestations in the *Théâtre* in different ways. Some simply recounted what they had seen. Others stated where they were from, what they had seen, and what experiencing prophecy was like, providing only the rudiments of a personal history. Others recounted a nearly complete autobiography. Among the witnesses who described a "conversion experience" was Cavalier. He initially doubted the claims of his Camisard countrymen: "My little reasoning thereupon went no further than to suspect that these people might be some sort of conjurers, as I had heard say . . . I hoped to escape . . . and wished myself twenty miles off."[81]

However, his skepticism was ineluctably overcome by both the strangeness of the manifestations and the sincerity of their reception: the young man he had at first suspected of being a fraud, Cavalier eventually called "the inspired lad."[82] Cavalier's account was one of the most interesting, not only because he was one of the three French Prophets in London, but also because he offered a complete psychological itinerary of a spiritual reawakening.

The testimonial texts included in the *Théâtre* offered, then, a theatrical performance: the documents presented the Camisards' tribulations and their enactments of the assurance of salvation. However, critics continued to contest the efficacy and authenticity of this dramatic representation: "After examining these people, we were convinced that they were not whom they claimed to be. Twenty 'sacred theaters' couldn't make angels of light out of them."[83]

Mathieu Boissier was among the first to give his deposition. He described how a group of friends invited him to worship with them at Loriol, in the province of Dauphiné, his birthplace. A large band had gathered to hear a young girl prophesy. She spoke with authority and conviction: "There was a girl [who] preached with an eloquence and fluency, to me most admirable . . . after the spirit of God."[84] Suddenly, she fell on her knees, begging God to give her the gift of tongues so that she could proclaim his will.[85] Boissier was so moved by her eloquence that he believed he had heard the voice of an angel or a supernatural being.[86] Inspired by her example, Boissier determined to travel to Holland, where Jean Cavalier was prophesying. In his later travels, Boissier met many other "prophets" and heard of occurrences that he could only term "miracles."[87]

The next witness to take the stand, on January 14, 1707, was Jean Vernet of Bois-Châtel in the Vivarais. He gave this testimony: in 1702, he had left Montpellier, where he had been working, and returned home to find his house transformed into a site of collective prophecy. His mother, brother, two sisters, and a cousin were all "in an inspired state."[88] Shortly after, his mother was put in prison for prophesying. What Vernet found most striking about the phenomenon of prophesying transmitted from one family member to the next was that it was in classic French rather than the provençal dialect ("She spoke at the time of inspiration only French, which surprised me exceedingly, because she never before attempted to speak a word in that language, nor has since to my knowledge").[89] Further, his mother's prophesying was characterized by great heavings of the chest and stomach.[90]

Another witness, Jacques Bresson, added the detail of incessant movements of the head: "They had every one agitation of the head, breast, stomach, arm, or otherwise, which attended their prophetic discourse . . . and [they] always spoke French."[91] Jeanne Castanette recounted a collective scene of prophecy in her deposition of January 14, 1707. She seemed to be aware of the Pauline scripture (1 Corinthians 14:31–33) mandating that glossolalia occur to one person at a time so that each message might be heard clearly and interpreted for the edification of the community, and a lawless babble prevented: "At another of those meetings, several falling into the inspiration began to speak at once; whereupon one of them said to the next, 'In the name of God, be silent.' Then the others held their peace, but afterward they spoke one after the other."[92] Another witness, Jean Cabanel d'Anduze, noted that people chosen to prophesy had not always lived exemplary lives. After receiving the gift, however, they "ceased their libertine conduct, and some who had been debauched now became well behaved and pious."[93]

Some of the depositions spoke of miraculous sightings, of lights appearing in the sky to guide the Camisards through the dark of night past Catholic troops, and other supernatural phenomena. Claude Arnassan from Montel recounted that he had spent three years in Marseille as a galley slave, the penalty for having fought in Rolland Cavalier's troop. While soldiering, he had witnessed lights like torches in the sky, which appeared fortuitously on occasion: "He was no sooner on his knees, than there appeared in the air a light, like a large star, which advanced, pointing to the place where the assembly was met."[94] As he was leaving, a young *inspiré* told Arnassan of a vision he had experienced, in which he saw that Arnassan would be imprisoned unless he immediately put himself back under Cavalier's leadership. Shortly after, he was jailed in Nîmes until 1704. Jacques Du Bois, who made his way from Montpellier to Geneva and then to London, witnessed "balls of fire fall from heaven to dazzle the eyes of their enemies"[95] on several occasions. Similarly, Guillaume Bruguier, who had been captured at Usez, incarcerated for three months, then impressed into the king's service in Spain before deserting near Portugal, was guided in his flight by "le Ciel": "I saw, as it were, stars directing toward the place, where it was, which I always looked upon as a guide, and never failed to find it true."[96]

Testimonies of the French Prophets

While nearly all the testimonies contained compelling details and an accent of personal conviction, one of the most extensive and personalized narratives was that of Jean Cavalier. He made his deposition in January 1707 and opened by describing an "assemblée" that he had somewhat reluctantly attended near Sauve. A young prophet of about fifteen was speaking, and Cavalier's first assessment was that this was some sort of "Devin," or mind reader. Immediately, the adolescent began to articulate out loud, practically verbatim, Cavalier's own internal ambivalence. Cavalier considered leaving, but someone was blocking the door. Gradually, Cavalier began to consider the possibility that this young man and two others preaching with him might truly be inspired: "I began then to conceive a quite different opinion of those people there."[97] The reasoning he gave was that because these prophets all spoke of, and gave glory to, God, they must be legitimate, since Satan "could never glorify God's name."[98]

The prophet was preaching on a particular text, Isaiah 55:2, a piece of prophetic literature that invites all those who "thirst" for God to "come to the waters." This invitation seemed to be extended to Cavalier in particular, since one prophet had this message for him: "His good pleasure was to put his word also into my mouth."[99] Cavalier was touched, and comforted, by this assurance.

His recounting of the event was not unlike a conversion experience. He described his initial doubt and subsequent conviction, including a detailed account of the violent bodily agitations he endured for a period of nine months and that culminated in his own "ecstase" in his father's house: "One Lord's Day, being at home in prayer, I fell into an extraordinary ecstasy, and God opened my mouth. I remained then for forty-eight hours under the operation of the spirit."[100] Cavalier described hearing God's voice within him, an illumination of the Holy Spirit that took time to work out its purpose: "The hand of God often striking me, before my tongue was loosed; 'tis true that on the other side, I experienced consolations, for I readily yielded to the inward motions of the spirit unto prayer, I immediately forsook my plays and usual diversions, and above all I found a perfect abhorrence of the train of public worship among the papists."[101]

Cavalier not only experienced his own inspired trances; he was emotionally shaken by the experience: "Rivers of waters ran down my eyes . . . I wept in secret continually."[102] The preaching had an immediate physical effect on him, a feeling almost of oppression, as though the word of God were weighing heavily on him: "When the sermon ended, there seemed a beating as of a hammer in my breast, which kindled a flame that took me and dispersed all over my veins and put me into a sort of leaping, which flung me down; I rose again without any harm, and as my heart was lifted up to God with unutterable fervor, I was struck again, and my flame increased; my prayers grew also more ardent, speaking and breathing with mighty groans . . . [and] sudden violent agitations of the head and body."[103] He also testified to marvelous workings of the Holy Spirit in other Camisards. For example, he related the story of the Camisard

Clary emerging untouched from the heart of a blazing fire that he had caused to be built in order to test his resolution for the cause of Christ; Cavalier also recounted how the Camisard Compan, "in a state of ecstasy," was thrown like a ball against the gates of heaven.[104] Cavalier's testimony transmits strongly the theatrical, performative, and symbolic element of the Camisard experience.

A theme of Cavalier's testimony illustrated the apocalyptic reversal of world hierarchies that Christ's reign would bring about, a reversal particularly likely to resonate with the poor and powerless Camisard peasantry: "When he said the least of children and the meanest among men were yet of great price with God, I was overjoyed."[105] Other witnesses echoed this leitmotif, a more militant version of the Beatitudes' teaching about the meek inheriting the earth. Those who experienced the gift were joined together in a new, familial arrangement: they called each other "brother" ("frère") and the Holy Spirit deemed them "my children" ("mes Enfants").[106] "God uses the simple, and, in our weakness, he is strong," claimed Monsieur de Caladon. An illiterate peasant girl who prophesied compellingly reminded him of Balaam's ass ("une Asnesse de Balaam"), which had dumbly refused to go forward when a celestial host barred his path, and was beaten by Balaam for his pains (Numbers 22:21–34): "There was a certain poor woman, not very intelligent . . . When they told me she was going to preach . . . I couldn't believe she would be able to . . . But she did wonderfully well. This 'Balaam's she-ass' had a golden mouth: divine intelligence helped her speak . . . She was a flood of eloquence; she was a marvel . . . She became an entirely different person, being transformed into a great preacher . . . This was nothing short of miraculous."[107]

Both the meticulous detail with which Cavalier rendered the account of his own visitation by the spirit, and the care with which he recorded others' similar experiences and reactions, are significant for several reasons. First, Cavalier's narrative offered a step-by-step "born again," or conversion, account. He specified that he endured "almost nine months of sobs and agitations"[108] before receiving the gift of prophecy, a laborious birthing of spiritual speech, described in unusually complete spiritual, psychological, and physiological detail.[109] Second, since Cavalier was destined to become one of the three French Prophets, his account attests to the compelling, charismatic force of his personality, which led him to wield such influence. This persuasive personality may have been genetic charisma; Cavalier's cousin, Rolland, had been one of the most renowned guerilla captains of the Camisard cause. Cavalier was a good spokesman for the Camisards; his ability to use rational, logical discourse while also occasionally breaking into highly emotional rhetoric appealed to Enlightenment rationalists such as Misson as well as to the man in the street.[110] Cavalier was also definite on the issue of divine inspiration: "I here declare solemnly, without any equivocation whatsoever, by this public act, upon the oath I make of it before God, that

I am in no wise the framer of the bodily agitations I suffer in my ecstasies; I do not move my own self, but am moved by a power independent that overrules me."[111] Cavalier had no doubt—and hoped to leave his reader with none either— that the words he spoke while prophesying had been given to him by God: "I was very happy to be found in the company of those whom God had called to be replenished with his grace, which was freely communicated to them, . . . and to put his words also in my mouth."[112] This inner certainty was essential if the otherwise dispossessed Camisards were to stand firm against the overwhelming might of trained, uniformed, professional troops.

Jean Cavalier was incarcerated at Perpignan by the king's troops because of his inspirations. His father eventually was able to secure his release, and Cavalier went into exile in Italy. The Holy Spirit then ordered him to leave Italy, where he was serving as a mercenary in the army, and to go to Geneva to enroll in his cousin Rolland Cavalier's militia regiment.[113] However, Cavalier became very ill during the sea voyage and was put off the boat in Ostende. He made his way to Amsterdam, and then to London.

Cavalier met up with Elie Marion, the second of the French Prophets, in London. Marion was born in Barre, in the Hautes-Cévennes. He gave his testimony for the *Théâtre* in January 1707. His statement, like that of Cavalier, was significantly lengthier, more detailed, and more "autobiographical" than those of most other witnesses. Marion decided to leave his birthplace because he was repelled by rampant "Idolatrie" in the Catholic Church.[114] He was tired of being coerced into a religiosity that he found repugnant, "[having been] from my infancy forced by some to go to Mass."[115] At about age twenty, Marion determined that the Catholic Church was "superstitious . . . And the more I mused and reflected upon it, the more shocked I became; I had not then so much as ever read the holy scriptures, but it was my own natural reason . . . that put such thoughts in my heart."[116] While at Barre, he witnessed the raptures of more than forty prophets, and then himself experienced the phenomenon: "Afterward, when I had been at several assemblies, wherein several of the inspired spoke with more strength of argument and persuasion . . . I was struck to the heart by the powerful energy of the divine language."[117] Not unlike Cavalier, Marion felt spiritual confirmation ("a secret joy—an inner feeling of God's grace") as well as physical discomfort: "A certain fire filled my chest and caused such a feeling of heaviness that I sighed heavily. My body was thrown back, and I remained for a good fifteen minutes in this state."[118]

Like Cavalier, Marion underwent trials before he prophesied, reinforcing the scrutiny of self that characterizes both their narratives, making them seem more like micro-autobiographies than narrowly focused depositions. Marion's first experience of prophesying had also occurred in his father's house: "The first day of 1703, as we were going to bed, our whole family and some relatives, after having spend the day praying, . . . I suddenly felt a great heat around my heart and spreading throughout my body . . . A force that I could not resist took hold of me . . . God struck me and encouraged me simultaneously . . . My God made me a new heart . . . and it pleased him to loosen my tongue and to put his word into my mouth."[119] And like Cavalier, Marion responded to the phenomenon of prophesy by soon taking up military service: "This same spirit of wisdom and grace told me that I needed to take up arms . . . for God's cause . . . and so I joined up with a band of Christian soldiers."[120] While fighting, Marion continued to prophesy, to have visions, and to weep tears of blood. He claimed, while "part of the Camisard band,"[121] to have witnessed other miraculous occurrences, such as bullets turned away in midair from their targets by divine intervention.[122]

He eventually fled to England so that he could testify from a place of safety and the trials of the Camisards would thereby not go unheard or unheeded: "I am a French Protestant, escaped out of the great tribulation . . . to seek refuge in a foreign country."[123] As one of the French Prophets, Marion continued to proclaim to the Continent the justice of the Camisard cause. Like Misson, he concluded that so many extraordinary proofs of God's Providence surrounded the Camisards that it was impossible not to accept the veracity of their claims.

For instance, Marion ended his testimony by recounting yet another miraculous intervention. This was the story of how Abraham Mazel, one of the most respected Camisard prophets, who, while incarcerated for life ("prison perpétuelle") in the notorious Tour de Constance, from which escape was said to be impossible, dug through its thick walls under cover of night, used ropes to lower himself and other prisoners down from the tower, fled past sentries and through marshes, going days without food or water, and escaped to Geneva. Marion reiterated what Mazel had told him—to trust in God—and he survived.[124]

One of the few women to testify for the *Théâtre sacré*, Marie Chauvain, was a widow from Provence. On March 15, 1707, she also claimed that after witnessing another person prophesy, almost as though through a process of contagion or imitation she herself began to speak in tongues. A young girl of fifteen lodging at Marie's house began to pray out loud. Marie's husband, a Catholic, left the room, and Marie then cautioned the girl to beware, "since we lived among Papists, and might suffer for what she did."[125] The young girl responded that she had no choice but to pray, and she was required not only to prophesy, but also to confer that gift on others with whom she had contact.[126] The young girl disclaimed any responsibility or authority for her actions, dismissing herself as a simple shepherdess.[127] Marie Chauvain interpreted this prophet's presence as a divine sign: she had been sent by God to convince Marie's husband to forswear Catholicism and become a Camisard ("as he did afterward").[128]

Another female witness, Isabeau Charras, from Ruches in the Grandes Cévennes, stated on March 5, 1707, that she had witnessed several prophets between 1689 and 1696, when she left France. In describing one of the prophetic experiences she had seen, Charras stated that the accompanying physical movements were not extreme or disruptive[129] and that the overriding characteristic was "great joy."[130] She discerned the guiding principle of these "inspirations" to be an "inner voice": "She abandoned herself to the spirit, which guided her so well . . . [through] an inner voice."[131] Charras also mentioned having heard, on numerous occasions, "singing in the spirit": "Psalm singing which [we] heard in many places, as if coming from high in the air . . . This divine melody [was heard] in broad daylight . . . in places far from houses, where there was no wood, no hollowed rock, and where, in short, it would be impossible for anyone to have hidden."[132]

Like Elie Marion, she felt that it was "another undoubted proof of the holiness of the inspirations . . . which is, that the events have always answered the predictions."[133] And like other witnesses relating miracles, Isabeau seemed both awed and matter-of-fact. The miracles did not come as a surprise to the Camisards, but simply provided proof of God's presence among them.[134] Like a member of the early Christian church privileged to behold miracles, Monsieur de Caladon averred that the Camisards were being transfigured: "It seemed to us that these were the wonderful fruits of holy inspiration."[135]

Inspiration, scripture, and the French language were closely intertwined, as Georgia Cosmos has pointed out:

> What exactly did the witnesses mean when they stated that an inspired person spoke "en bon françois"? The clue to understanding what they meant in this cultural context—where, as noted by LeRoy Ladurie, to speak French was to speak in "a holy tongue"—is their observation that the inspirés, most of whom could not read, appeared to know the Bible by heart . . . It would seem reasonable to infer a connection between prolonged familiarity with pious texts and the prophesyings . . . however, this is not how this phenomenon was understood by those who witnessed these events.
>
> . . . When infants and youths were heard to prophesy in French, this was perceived as a "gift" from God . . . the words . . . were thought to have come directly from the Holy Spirit.[136]

Durand Fage, the third French Prophet, also gave testimony. He spoke before the judge in London in January 1707. His account was more marked by enthusiasm and fervor than those of the others. Unlike Cavalier and Marion, he did not provide many autobiographical details, but rather felt compelled to bear witness to miraculous acts. He recounted an occasion when a Camisard band, lost in a foggy night, prayed for guidance, only to see "a Light fall from Heaven, [illuminating the way forward] like a Rocket flare;"[137] he proudly called the Camisards "children of God" ("Enfans de Dieu"); he related witnessing numerous children prophesy ("The spirit poured out on several young children . . . It pleased God to cause the mouths of innocents to speak of his wonders");[138] and like Cavalier, Fage told the tale of "Frère Clary," who willingly entered the fire "en Ecstase" to prove his faith, and emerged unharmed. Fage's identity seemed entirely absorbed into his understanding of acting as God's agent: "God would give us the victory."[139] Like the Camisard troops, he did nothing without first praying, and unfailingly received an answer, inspiration, or sign: "Should we attack the enemy? Were we being followed? Would night fall while we were still en route? Did we fear an ambush? Would an accident happen? Should we mark out the location for an assembly? We first prayed . . . [then] immediately the spirit would answer us, and his inspiration guided us in all things."[140] So precious to the prophets were the visions and trances granted to them, Fage recounted, that even when parents of young *inspirés* threatened them or beat them to make them stop, the children persisted in their pronouncements.[141] Fage might have been identifying with such treatment from his own experience—if not as a youth, then certainly as one of the French Prophets reviled in London by the Huguenots.

Most of the witnesses stated that they had thought logically about the prophetic phenomena, yet had come away persuaded, despite the surprising youth or apparent unsuitability of many of those who spoke in inspirations. This was the case with the majority of readers as well. Richard Holford, one who read the testimonies, swore an affidavit on April 1, 1707, to this effect.[142]

The *Théâtre sacré* concluded with a brief appendix consisting of letters and other relevant documents, many purporting to contain "miraculous stories."[143] Finally, Misson ended as he had begun, asserting that only his absolute conviction of the truth of the Camisard claims could have induced him to risk his reputation with this publication: "I will tell you first what caused me to love the Camisards, and what compelled me to sacrifice my good name and my material wealth for them: it was the zeal and the piety that they manifested. You would have to be completely blind to not see that it is the hand of God that upholds them."[144]

Misson acted like a judge, summing up the case before sending the jury out for deliberations. Tellingly, he gave the last word to the French Prophets. Elie

Marion, Jean Cavalier, and Durand Fage, in the face of yet more persecution, confidently asserted on April 24, 1707: "God is our sheltering place and the rock of our salvation."[145]

The influence of the French Prophets, a remnant of the Camisards, would be felt for years to come on the Continent and in the American colonies, particularly in social, political, and religious movements. Camisard concepts of personal empowerment resulting from unmediated communication with God resonated with similar views held by Puritans and others. Foremost was the issue of freedom of conscience, held dear by Enlightenment thinkers as a condition for discovering the truth, and cherished by the Camisards because of their experience of horrific persecution.

CHAPTER FOUR

"From a Farr Countrie"

An Introduction to the French Protestant

Experience in New England

French Protestants arrived in the North American colonies from the Bas-Languedoc, the Cévennes and Vivarais regions, and the Dauphiné.[1] Some joined British colonists on plantations in North and South Carolina and Virginia; others headed for New York or Boston.[2] But wherever they came from and wherever they landed, they had to make their way alone, without much aid from the new community in which they found themselves. After arriving in Boston, a native of the Languedoc wrote to friends in France: "You must disabuse yourself of the Impression that Advantages are here offered to Refugees . . . Whoever brings Nothing, finds Nothing."[3] The French Protestants had to find a way to survive in the New World.

Strangers in a Strange Land: Survival Strategies

Several models have been proposed to explain what happened to French Protestants when they arrived in the British colonies. Perhaps the most influential model for the past two decades has been that proposed by Jon Butler in *The Huguenots in America*. Butler maintained that French Protestants assimilated completely within two generations of being in the New World. He did not find their religious adherence to have been a major obstacle to such assimilation, which he attributed to intermarriage and a desire to conform. Much recent scholarship rejects this thesis: "The one-dimensional linear framework employed by many historians of the American Huguenot experience virtually 'predetermines' the rapid decline, 'assimilation,' and 'disappearance' of Huguenot culture in New York. Although this monolithic approach documents simple superficial evidence of their absorption into the dominant English culture, it is too shallow to confront change as process."[4]

Butler estimated that more than 160,000 French Protestants fled Europe between 1680 and 1690.[5] Several thousand came to the New World, making this the largest immigration of a homogeneous ethnic population since that of the

Mayflower and the Puritans, and the first major continental European refugee group to come to America. Butler noted that most seemed to have disappeared from the record.[6]

He argued that they quickly shed their linguistic, ethnic, and religious identity by assimilating, intermarrying, and converting.[7] Butler adduced a socioeconomic motive for them having done so, since English was the lingua franca of the colonies and the English-speaking merchants were the most successful and prominent. Butler found no more than fifteen hundred French immigrants identifiable as Huguenot in the colonies by 1700. He argued that there was often near-total assimilation. However, such assimilation was often arguably only skin deep; it constituted an adaptation for socioeconomic survival.

Janine Garrison concurs that most French Protestant émigrés in Europe integrated quickly and relatively easily. Mixed marriages and language proficiency by the second generation made the difference, she claims. Those who went to England triply assimilated, since they were rapidly incorporated into the Anglican Church.[8] However, conditions were different across the ocean: there were no nearby support communities, no preexisting exile routes (as was the case in Geneva, where Huguenots had sought refuge for years), and not much of a multilingual cultural climate.

Thus, a second model developed during a period roughly contemporary with Butler's work. This model was proposed by scholars of American religious history such as A. G. Roebber, Ned Landsman, Randall Balmer, and Richard Archer. In this model, a complex pattern of ethnic regionalisms characterized the New World, a rugged coexistence of diverse confessions striving for cultural prominence in certain areas, such as New Amsterdam.[9]

A third thesis has recently been proposed by Neil Kamil. In *Fortress of the Soul: Violence, Metaphysics, and Material Life in the Huguenots' New World, 1517–1751*, he argues, in part, that once French Protestants came to the New World, the majority of them Huguenot craftsmen, they "creolized" or hybridized material culture by applying their artisanal techniques to existing, predominantly English and Anglican, goods.[10] Kamil also asserts that, consistent with a long-standing French Protestant response to persecution, what John Calvin called "Nicodemism" was in play: Huguenots "hi[d] in plain sight."[11] Kamil asserts that for self-protection French Protestant piety in the New World took, of necessity, a more private than public turn.[12]

The model that Kamil offers goes a long way toward accounting for French Protestant responses to the New World.[13] However, he does not deal with the Camisard factor, that is, the contribution of the Camisards to yet another model of French Protestant adaptation to the New World.[14]

Finally, it should be recalled that Huguenots and Camisards did not immigrate exclusively to New England, the primary focus of the present study. In

Pennsylvania, William Penn advertised the availability of land and religious toleration to the Huguenots, for instance, and, as Bertrand Van Ruymbeke has documented, a preponderance of Huguenots settled in South Carolina.[15] In particular, the Dutartre Insurrection of several Huguenot families there (involving the murder of an entire family so as to liberate it from the Last Judgment), sparked by reports of Camisard enthusiasm, demonstrates a clear Continental influence.[16] On the whole, Van Ruymbeke's pattern is akin to Butler's model of assimilation in which "integrating rather than remaining separate was the norm."[17]

What remains to be examined is the variety of ways in which French Protestants, influenced by Camisard piety and experiences, lived out their faith in the New World.[18] The Camisards' identity as French was not ever something that they chose deliberately to renounce but rather was much less significant than their identity as believing Christians. For a similar reason, the Naturalization Act passed by Great Britain in 1697 was important to the Huguenots, since it legally ensured liberties in the New World that had not been explicitly protected, ones that had been taken from them during the Wars of Religion despite their status as subjects of the king. The act solidified social and financial opportunities as well.[19]

Confessional perspective was bedrock for these émigrés—not something they chose to alter at will. In every other domain there is evidence of flexibility on their part, but not in that of religion. In *A Perfect Babel of Confusion*, Randall Balmer wondered why it would be surprising that French Protestants in America would renounce their identity as French, given that their homeland had so badly persecuted them.[20] His is a reasonable query. National identity seems not to have held central importance for them.

Religion was another matter altogether. After all, the Camisards and Huguenots fled in order to retain their religious beliefs.[21] Their writings and political stances do not indicate any hesitancy about professing their belief publicly.[22] However, as far as living out that faith and creating institutions within which to do so, Huguenots pursued a strategy of protective coloration designed to prevent a repeat of the Camisard experience. Thus, French Protestant religiosity became more private than public, pietistic rather than institutionally maintained and formally expressed, during this period.[23]

The Camisards and the Huguenots did not abandon their faith; they reaffiliated for social, political, and financial gain while retaining their religiosity, their Bible studies, and their reputation for biblical literacy and personal probity.[24] When the colonies began to pass laws banning conventicles, or small, private assemblies, primarily to control Quaker enthusiasm, French Protestants in the colonies sympathized with the Society of Friends, remembering the *dragonnades*, the forced conversions, and the prying of Catholic clergy into Protestant creeds. When George Whitefield's Methodist revival swept across New England, it seemed not to elicit any Huguenot response, perhaps because, at least for the Camisards, personal piety and belief in a God concerned with the everyday affairs of each person were already firmly in place. From this perspective, the Camisards were the earliest revivalists in the colonies, antedating Whitefield by several decades.

French Protestants preserved their religious distinctiveness by adopting an inward-turning devotional attitude and pietistic expression. Camisard enthusiastic piety contributed to an international strain of pietism that influenced the thinking of, for instance, German Pietists and the practice of warm-hearted piety.[25] And both Cotton Mather and Increase Mather maintained correspondence with the German Pietists, especially those at Halle. This was the earliest link in Mather's "French connection."

The Camisard experience was fresh in the collective memory of French Protestants and relevant to their changed circumstances. While German pietism was certainly part of the cultural bath in which a variety of faiths was dipped during the colonial period, the Camisards offered a more immediate and compelling model to Huguenots in the New World.

Old World to New World: Models

Eventually (and rather paradoxically), the Cévennes and other Camisard areas were brought back and normalized in nonenthusiastic orthodoxy by a handful of Camisard pastors who went to Geneva to be ordained, including Pierre Durand. A document housed in the Montpellier archives, the journal of a Durand family member, is illustrative of this phenomenon.[26] Imprisoned for thirty years in the Bastille because of her participation in Camisard *assemblées* and because of belonging to the Reformed faith, Marie Durand recounted her own story as well as those of her father, Étienne Durand, and her brother, Pierre Durand. In her diary, Marie Durand related how her father held a prayer meeting in his house in defiance of the authorities. Dragoons imprisoned Pierre, whom they suspected of having led the meeting. Pierre escaped and fled to Switzerland. During her long incarceration, Marie corresponded with the Camisard pastor Paul Rabaut.

The story of Pierre Durand provides an instructive illustration of the shifts from Reformed practice to Camisard, then back to Reformed. Durand was born (circa 1700) in Le Bouchet, a tiny hamlet in the commune of Pranles, near Privas. His father, the town clerk, taught him how to read. Durand became Antoine Court's successor as pastor in Languedoc after escaping to Geneva, where he was ordained.[27] After being urged by another refugee Camisard pastor there to return to France and "embrasser le Désert," he did indeed go to the Vivarais.[28] He remained there at great risk to himself: on May 14, 1724, an edict had been promulgated sentencing any pastors found in the area to life labor as galley slaves.

Changed historical circumstances shape theology. For example, Pierre Durand was very proud of having "restored order" to the church in the *désert*, which involved stripping away its Camisard characteristics and restoring its former, basic Reformed nature: "He had the joy of eradicating prophecy from his province . . . [He determined that] even more than persecution, prophecy, by its excesses, posed the greatest danger to the Reformation."[29] Despite Camisards' enthusiasm during the worst of the persecutions, Pierre, like many surviving Camisard pastors, came to believe that the structure of a *temple*, the order of a church service, and the guidance of an ordained clergy were needed to control some of the excesses and abuses that enthusiasm had produced. These pastors sought to reclaim and perpetuate Reformed theology (which, at least for Pierre and his flock, followed the Genevan model), seeing the Camisard variant as a distortion born of trauma.

The lives of Pierre and Marie Durand exemplify how Camisards were finally brought back to a more recognizably Reformed orthodoxy in the years from around 1720 to 1730. Ironically, this was when Huguenots in the New World were developing a more personal and pietistic slant—implementing the Camisard strategy—to protect their own spirituality. During this time in the colonies, "Calvinists in this region [the Vivarais] engaged in diverse and wide-ranging varieties of Protestant practices. A number were internationalistic, heterodox, and often pietistic . . . Formal confessional connections seem to have been far less important than the quest for intensity and variety of spiritual experience."[30]

French Protestant émigrés in the colonies became characterized by an interiority that fostered conviction rather than by outward attempts to resist or undermine the primarily English—Anglican and Puritan—structures that they found there: this accounts for the generally positive reception they eventually received and for their ability to adapt as well as they did.[31] The inward turn was in part responsible for safeguarding Huguenot identity, and that turn derived from Camisard pietism. Camisards were acknowledged by Quakers, Shakers, Pietists, John Wesley, Madame Guyon and the quietist movement, and, later, the Oxford Movement, as having had an influence on their piety or of having actually been their progenitors.[32] The Huguenot inward turn found parallels and a sympathetic reception among like-minded Puritans of the day.

This reception was in part due to the Camisards' decision, upon arriving in the New World, to tamp down their religious enthusiasm. They emulated their Huguenot confrères in conforming—though not fully assimilating—to prevailing norms in the colonies for a more measured, intellectualized piety. Consequently, when the revivalism of the Great Awakening broke out in the 1740s, Huguenots and Camisards seem not to have participated. Just as the Huguenot churches in England forty years earlier had shunned the French Prophets, the Huguenots and Camisards in America went to some pains to dissociate themselves from a similarly sensationalistic phenomenon; people like the radical preacher Daniel Rogers (Exeter, New Hampshire, 1740s) and the gospel minister James Davenport (New London, 1740s) apparently left them cold.[33] These preachers were suspected of "cessationalism . . . [and] bogus miracles that smacked of Catholic piety."[34] The French *immigrés* wanted at all costs to avoid being associated with Roman Catholicism.

Case Studies for This Model

Two ways for trying to tease out the experiences, motivations, and influences of these hidden Huguenots and elusive Camisards in the colonies diverge from customary techniques of traditional historiography, borrowing from the realms of theological inquiry and literary explication. One method is to sift through primary sources as a way not only to tell their stories, but also to reconstitute their individual voices and thereby assess their particular personal piety.[35] The testimonials of representative individuals and eyewitnesses, like those in Misson's compendium, fleshed out the records of the Camisards' Old World experience. It is now time to add information about their lives in the New World.

The second approach is to establish a lexicon for these tale-tellers, to examine the rhetoric they employed when talking about their faith, justifying changes in their practice of piety, acknowledging an awareness of any such changes, or describing how their piety harmonized or clashed with the surrounding culture. How the stories were told shaped both the storytellers and the audiences, revealing belief systems.

Both methods can be fruitfully applied to the experiences of Gabriel Bernon, Elie Neau, and Ezéchiel Carré. Bernon went first to Boston when he left England, as did Neau and Carré, Bernon's cousin and the first pastor of the Reformed Church in Boston. Bernon appears to have encouraged Neau's conversion to Anglicanism in 1701. Neau, a Huguenot sentenced to the galleys, fraternized with and was influenced by Camisards. While in prison, he wrote emotional, highly personal songs, poems, and prayers resembling Camisard expressions of piety. After his release, Neau eventually converted to Anglicanism in America. He cooperated with other Protestant denominations as part of his fund-raising activities for ecumenical outreach and early abolitionist protest. Neau's early work with African Americans antedated, and most likely influenced, the explicit abolitionist endeavors of Benjamin Colman and Joseph Bean.[36] In *Souls Flying to Jesus Christ* (1740), Colman's rhetoric is remarkably similar to Neau's: "You that are Servants, and the meanest of our Household Servants, even our poor Negroes chuse you the Service of Christ; He will make you His Freemen."[37]

Neau minimized the significance of his ethnic identity as a Frenchman, but never forswore his identity as a Christian. He saw himself as a citizen of what scripture calls "the far country" (Luke 19:12), the Kingdom of Heaven.[38] Because his identity resided primarily in his piety, Neau was concerned to safeguard his freedom to worship as he chose. Neau's influence led Bernon to emancipate his slaves in 1728, some ten years before his death—an unusual decision at the time and one animated by Neau's model of advocacy for slaves, their children, and former slaves through his schools. His schools were the first ever established to teach literacy to African Americans.

There are many parallels between the lives and careers of the three men examined in the chapters to follow: all were members of the French Reformed Church; Bernon arrived in Boston less than ten years before Neau; Neau was from Saintonge in Poitou, while Bernon was from La Rochelle, in the same province; both were merchant privateers in the West Indies; both eventually converted to Anglicanism. As for Ezéchiel Carré, "the name Carré is found in the Bernon genealogy . . . it is very probable that [the] Reverend Ezéchiel Carré was a relative of Gabriel Bernon."[39] Bernon may have originally gone to Boston to join his cousin, and this may also explain why Neau went there.

Cotton Mather, an important supporter of French Protestants in the New World, provides another link. He wrote the preface to Carré's *The Charitable Samaritan* and translated and published Neau's prison poetry as *From a Farr Countrie* (1698), which appeared in print two years before the publication in Rotterdam of the original French-language version. "Mather's understanding of the outworking of piety in the practical [spreading of Christianity through endeavors such as Neau's] is an epitome of Puritan theory on the subject; but it was enriched by his eager adoption of new strategies of mission from London and the Continent," all of which had been influenced by reports of the persecution of the Camisards, the Huguenot diaspora, and the revival of Protestant piety in the Old World due to both.[40]

Although Mather's *Magnalia Christi Americani* (1702) makes no mention of Carré, Neau, or Bernon, his interaction with at least the first two is a matter of historical record. Mather, ever responsive to the needs of individuals and the causes of the day, played a significant part in plaiting together the strands of the Huguenot and Camisard tapestry of experience. Through his translations, prefaces, and publishing contacts, he facilitated the transcontinental conversation of French Protestants, triangulating among groups located in France, Switzerland, and the Netherlands; in London; and in the New World. In Boston, Newport, Providence, and New York City, Mather enabled such conversations to continue among French-speaking Protestants and other groups of the Reformed faith, some not Francophone.

Bernon was a prominent citizen in all walks of life during Mather's tenure in Boston. Also, Bernon helped establish the Society for the Propagation of the Gospel in Foreign Parts (1701) and urged Neau to convert to Anglicanism (1704) so that he could obtain funds from the society to endow his school for slaves.[41] Bernon was instrumental in establishing Anglican churches in Rhode Island, and he founded a French-speaking town in Massachusetts. His piety and practice were intertwined; both thrived in a network of like-minded French Protestants.

Camisard experience and expression influenced Neau's role in the revival of Protestant piety in early eighteenth-century New York City, his involvement with the Society for the Propagation of the Gospel and the Society for the Propagation on Christian Knowledge, and his school for slaves. Further, the French connection sheds new light on Cotton Mather. After learning of experiences such as Neau's, Mather became "the most active spokesman of his generation in New England on behalf of the ministry to American blacks and native Americans."[42]

The paradigm of rapid, near-total assimilation of French Protestants may have been the case on the surface; however, it is undeniable that a unified core of ideologies and modes of operating in the world, a French Protestant *mentalité* derived from Huguenot and Camisard experience, persisted. Carré, Bernon, Neau, and others of whom they are in some measure representative retained their faith, finding ways to make it work in the New World. Their lives, writings, and accomplishments offer case studies of how Huguenots, influenced by Calvinist and Camisard experiences and forms of piety, forged a faith adapted for their New World circumstances. Examples of this strategy of accommodating without relinquishing one's theological identity include Bernon's extensive program of church founding, church building, and construction of "refuge towns" like New Oxford; Neau's schooling of slaves; and Carré's social witness in texts such as *The Charitable Samaritan*. Rather than assimilate, they retained their theological distinctiveness but channeled it into a private piety coupled with corresponding public action.

CHAPTER FIVE

Protestant and Profiteer

Gabriel Bernon in the New World

When he arrived in the New World, Gabriel de Bernon (1644–1736) jettisoned the particle in his name, the "de" that designates nobility, and graphically revised the venerable family shield of the Bernon family, descended from a fourteenth-century count of Burgundy. Rather than retain the symbolic representation of his Old World lineage, Gabriel reinvented himself in a New World idiom. He did so through a cunning play on words, not in French but, significantly, in English, and even with an American accent. Gabriel Bernon's new, self-designed shield featured a bear and a circle, or "naught": *Bar-none*: Bernon. Bernon thus represented a way of being in the New World that epitomized self-fashioning in the best American frontier tradition. He knew how to assess his situation and use what he could to his advantage. He was a consummate code shifter, adroit at manipulating the vernacular of two cultures. His profiteering combined with his piety in resourceful and often unexpected ways throughout his New World experience. Because Bernon was so prominent and pervasive a presence in the American colonies, more is known about him than about virtually any other French Protestant refugee.

"Everyone That Hath Forsaken Houses"

Bernon, several of whose ancestors had been mayors of the great port city of La Rochelle, became a wealthy and influential merchant.[1] Throughout his time in the colonies, he exemplified certain coping strategies implemented by French Protestants when they came to the New World. He adapted successfully, attaining commercial and civic prominence. He appears to have been a communicant in good standing in the Anglican Church, but retained his Reformed beliefs. Because of the force of his character, will, and diplomacy, he was on familiar terms with most of the famous men of his day in the colonies and in England, and parlayed these relationships into personal power, though he never neglected to lobby for the needs and best interests of his coreligionists.

Bernon contributed significantly to the socioeconomic and political development of the towns in which he settled. Even as he pursued personal advancement, Bernon clearly also felt a responsibility for fellow believers and for those in need and showed a concern for the poor that may have derived from some contact with, and sympathy for, the persecuted and impoverished Camisards back in France.[2] Bernon was frequently in London on business when the French Prophets were active, so he, like Wesley, Whitefield, and their contemporaries, would have heard their message and been influenced by aspects of it. Especially appealing would have been the Camisard emphasis on a personal and inner experience of the Holy Spirit. Similar to the Camisards, Bernon consistently upheld the importance of laypersons—such as himself—in maintaining theological orthodoxy.

Also like the Camisards and other pietist groups of his day, Bernon frequently referred to God's Providence. Uncharacteristically for a Calvinist, Bernon manifested a belief in the "openness" of revelation: believing like the Camisards that miracles could and did still occur, he asserted that God continued to provide signs to lead and succor his people.[3] Further, Bernon was a staunch defender of freedom of conscience; reiterating this Camisard catchphrase, he stated that "Roger Williams and all those, that have settled in our Providence town, have been persecuted, bruised and banished out of Massachusetts government, for not submitting themselves to the arbitrary power of the Presbytery and we fear nothing more than this arbitrary power of the clergy. Power before Popery did ruin the world, and, since Popery, the arbitrary power of the clergy hath ruined Europe."[4] Notions of freedom of conscience and freedom of thought (*libre pensée*) became part and parcel of French Protestant thought, and Camisards and Huguenots alike continued to advocate for these concepts in various ways in the New World.

A Profile in Adaptation

The de Bernon family "had been one of the first in La Rochelle to adopt the Reformed religion, and it was in the Bernon mansion that many of the earliest Protestant services were held."[5] After the Revocation of the Edict of Nantes, Gabriel, having become, like his father, a merchant sea trader, refused to convert to Catholicism.

He fled France in 1682 for Quebec, where he hoped not only to escape religious and political persecution, but also to profit from the lucrative fur trade in which his family had already been involved. However, hostilities ran high between Huguenots and Jesuits, and in that same year, Jesuit priests influenced Québecois authorities to remand Bernon back to France, where he was imprisoned for his faith in the Lantern Tower at La Rochelle.[6] The records indicate some reluctance on the part of political authorities to eject him from Quebec, because of Bernon's entrepreneurial success and influence. Governor Denonville of Quebec called Bernon the principal merchant there, adding, "It is a pity that he cannot be converted . . . as he is a Huguenot, the bishop wants me to order him home this autumn, which I have done, though he carries on a large business and *a great deal of money remains due to him here*."[7] This event was to have a great influence on Bernon when he later returned to North America; never again would he allow himself to forget that even when one was an upstanding and moneymaking contributor to the social order, politics and theology could cause one to be ousted. Strategies of adaptation were clearly in order.

Back in France, his brothers, less scrupulous than Bernon, had converted under pressure. They now used their influence to try to obtain his release from prison.[8] Their efforts unavailing, in 1686, with Gabriel near death from deprivation of food and water, they arranged for him to be smuggled out of prison in a wine cask and delivered to safety in Amsterdam. He briefly remained in Amsterdam, then went to London in 1687.

There Bernon became a naturalized British citizen, already demonstrating the reasoned, practical, and chosen conformity—so long as it did not compromise his faith—that he was to practice for the rest of his life. Naturalization was a route that many Huguenots chose; as the anonymous writer of the *Report of a French Protestant Refugee in Boston* (1687) counseled, "Those who desire to come into this Country should get themselves naturalized in London in order to be able to carry on Business in any Sort of Merchandise, and to trade with the English Islands, without which they cannot do so."[9]

Shortly thereafter, Bernon set sail for the New World, bearing letters of recommendation that quickly launched him into a successful career in commerce. He was listed as a "leading citizen" of Boston in 1688.[10] There Bernon was reunited with his wife, Suzanne, and their three young children. His wife had feigned conversion in order to escape from France.[11]

In Boston, he began to manufacture rosin and salt for sale to naval outfitters. In 1693, Bernon obtained a patent from the Royal Navy to manufacture and supply naval stores to His Majesty's fleet. In 1698, Bernon moved to Newport, after a brief visit to England to attract additional commercial investors. Developing an extensive and lucrative trade with Nova Scotia, Cape Breton, and the West Indies, Bernon became one of Boston's luminaries. "He did not put business first, however, but was always scrupulous to discharge his obligations as a Christian and a member of the state," one early biographer enthused.[12]

An early type of venture capitalist, Bernon began an initiative in faith-based "real estate development" after going to London to obtain proprietary rights to develop a tract of 2,672 acres in New Oxford, Massachusetts. Remembering his own travails and the persecution of his fellow French Protestants, Bernon intended to establish a French colony in New England, a site to be modeled specifically on the biblical paradigm of "cities of refuge," where future Huguenot refugees from Old World persecution might shelter.[13]

In 1687, Bernon, in commercial association with another French refugee, Isaac Bertrand du Tuffeau, and accompanied by the Reverend Daniel Bondet, a French Reformed pastor, went with fifteen families to establish a plantation seventy-five miles west of Boston. Bernon obtained a captain's commission from Massachusetts governor Joseph Dudley so that he could protect himself and defend his fledgling settlement. Bernon quickly caused a Huguenot *temple* to be built there.[14] He also built a fort, palisades, and a gristmill.

The short-lived settlement experienced troubles, including economic difficulties and what some deemed shady business ethics: Oxford farmers cultivated wine grapes and also milled grain, but in 1691 Bondet, working for the Society for the Propagation of the Gospel (SPG), complained to the Massachusetts authorities that the settlement was selling alcohol to the Indians, thereby undermining his attempts to Christianize them.[15] The Oxford settlement was further shaken when a band of Indians, believed to have been incited by Jesuits, massacred several settlers in 1694. Two years later, the husband and children of the Sigourney family were also murdered. Suzanne Sigourney, sole survivor of this Huguenot family, which had fled La Rochelle in 1681, returned to Boston with Bernon and the remaining settlers, all of whom were originally from Saintonge, with the exception of Paiz Cassaneau, a Camisard from Languedoc.[16]

In 1699, Bernon attempted to reestablish the settlement at New Oxford. He returned to the site, accompanied by a Huguenot minister recently arrived from London, Jacques Laborie, and the surviving original settlers, some eight to ten refugee families. However, the new leather business Bernon started had little success, and there was virtually no population growth. Consequently, and subsequent to the killing of settlers at Deerfield by Indians in 1704, Bernon abandoned the project, and the remnant of settlers dispersed to Hartford and New Milford, Connecticut. Bernon determined in 1704 to move his business venture to Rhode Island, selling the land in New Oxford to English settlers in 1713. The ruins of the settlement, one piece of masonry called the "old French fort," can still be seen today.

Bernon's Piety and Practicality: Negotiating Loyalties in the New World

Bernon's commercial prominence, coupled with the contemporary recognition he received as an important figure in the French Protestant community, is attested to in the extensive correspondence he maintained with the Providence church, the established and thriving French Church in the New York colony, and prominent merchants and government figures such as the Huguenot Benjamin Faneuil.[17]

Bernon's correspondence with the Providence church had to do with such matters as the appointment of ministers and the soliciting of funds for church-building projects, significant issues for the French Protestant community of believers.[18] His involvement attests to the respect that his coreligionists felt for Bernon and to his high standing in both church and commercial circles. Bernon's correspondence also documents the extensive network of relations that French Protestants maintained with one another, and their ongoing dialogue about doctrinal, ecclesiastical, and quotidian issues in the colonies; some of these letters were sent to South Carolina and some to transatlantic destinations. One such issue, for example, concerned the receipt of remittances. Bernon regularly received sums sent on behalf of emigrated Protestants by their relatives in France who had converted to Catholicism. They "looked after the interests of relatives who had fled . . . and transmitted to them with scrupulous fidelity the revenues from funds left in their keeping, or the portion that fell to them upon a division of inherited property."[19]

Bernon's first documented letter to the New York church community is dated March 25, 1699.[20] Bernon's name turns up in the registers of the Church of Saint-Esprit in New York as early as May 22, 1699.[21] Because he was well regarded and socially prominent, Bernon was involved in many governmental negotiations that strengthened the influence of the New York and Boston Huguenots at a time when the French were held in suspicion by other colonists.[22] The Church of Saint-Esprit in New York City was a wealthy and powerful community, numbering in its ranks many illustrious financiers and traders. Its clergy was predominantly French, though there were some Dutch ministers; regular Sunday services were held in French. The church was officially founded in 1628, although the French community had been gathering to worship since 1624. The community was substantial: by 1697, 15 percent of the 4,000 inhabitants of New York City were Huguenots.[23]

At roughly the same time that Bernon was breaking ground for his refugee town at New Oxford, a change of command occurred in the colonial government, concomitant with power shifts and other alterations across the Atlantic. In 1698, Richard Coote, the first Earl of Bellomont, was appointed colonial governor of New York, Massachusetts, and New Hampshire by William III (the former William of Orange) and Mary II. This appointment was potentially incendiary because of its resonance with what became known as Leisler's Rebellion. In 1689, a minor merchant named Leisler and his son-in-law Milborne led a popular uprising against the wealthy in the Middle Colonies.[24] Leisler and Milborne, supporters of William of Orange, who had been reared in the Dutch

Reformed faith and remained militantly Protestant, were nostalgic for what the Dutch Reformed Church had been—as they believed—before it had been co-opted by Anglicanism and exploited for crass commercial motives. It had clearly become advantageous to convert to, or at least coexist with, Anglicanism, since the British were now really the socioeconomic masters of the colony. Many New Light Dutch Reformed believers, increasingly pietistic, were disgusted by what they saw as political and religious collusion for economic gain.[25]

The rebellion, at length, was suppressed, and Leisler was ultimately hanged for his rabble-rousing. But his legacy of discontent persisted, attesting to an ever-deeper cleavage between the moneyed class—primarily merchants and clergy—and the poorer, artisanal class. For the latter, most avenues for social advancement had been closed off by English domination of the colony and their inability to master the English language. The struggle also attested to deep doctrinal splits among different religious confessions.

Ten years after Leisler's Rebellion, those in power still shuddered at how the world might have been turned upside down, and were at great pains to prevent any recurrence. In 1698, it was the Huguenots who enjoyed significant social prominence, as they had not done a decade earlier. Circumstances had changed favorably for them, not only in Boston, as with Bernon, but also in New York.

> The French community held the balance of power in New York. They seem to have been opposed to the administration of Lord Bellomont . . . [who] did not hesitate to slander them . . . In a report to the Board of Trade on August 21, 1698 he writes: "I must acquaint your Lordships that the French here are very factious, and their numbers considerable . . . At the last election, they ran in with the Jacobite party." It seems that the Earl of Bellomont had found himself maneuvered into the party of the old Leislerians, and so aroused the hostility of the New York merchants and therefore of the leading people coming from La Rochelle . . . The Governor invited M. Gabriel Bernon who was a native of La Rochelle and personally acquainted with a great number of the French in New York, to come from the Huguenot settlement of New Oxford, Massachusetts to [intervene], but without success.[26]

It seems odd at first to find a titled English colonial governor, a man of power and wealth, linked with Jacob Leisler. However, Bellomont had actually supported Leisler, and had been responsible for the episode in which Leisler's and his son-in-law's bones had been disinterred by his supporters and paraded through the streets of New York.[27] Leisler had been opposed to the wealthy merchant class, and most of the constituents of the Church of Saint-Esprit were, after considerable effort, members of the social elite—a position they wished to safeguard. Although he had on occasion advocated aid to French refugees in Boston, Bellomont did not want the French to exercise what he believed was undue influence in the commercial life of New York.

There was another connection that worried the Huguenot community. The larger issue for Leisler had been that of money and influence. But this concern went hand-in-hand with a rabid anti-Catholicism.[28] In 1698, when fears ran rampant in New York that the Jesuits were trying to suborn consciences and when conspiracy theories hatched daily, it was claimed that the French fleet was about to invade New York and take it over.[29] Consequently, most French were stereotyped as Catholic.[30] Bellomont himself articulated this conflation; when he said that the "French . . . at the last election . . . ran in with the Jacobite party," he meant that the French were Catholic sympathizers, perhaps even Catholic themselves, like James II and the Jacobites.[31]

Much as Bellomont and others did not appear to want to acknowledge the fact, however, the Huguenot community was, of course, Protestant. In this particular case, the Huguenots feared being included in anti-Catholic sentiment. And since they construed Governor Bellomont's attitude toward the French community as unsympathetic at best, they believed they had cause to be concerned. Further, they were furious. They told Bernon that they would prefer to "go to the Mississippi rather than submit to Lord Bellomont."[32]

Remembering their experiences of persecution in the Old World after the Revocation, the Huguenots were adamant on the matter of freedom of conscience and their right to worship as a church separate from governmental interference. Many of their forebears had been affiliated with the Separatists in Leyden, who sailed on the *Mayflower*.[33] They took any interference in their affairs—even if apparently secular—as an unwelcome and unwarranted intrusion and an attempt to usurp those basic rights for which they had already suffered so much.

Bellomont hoped that Bernon would use his prestige and influence to persuade his confrères to cease their opposition to the government. Bernon complied, adhering to Calvin's principle regarding duly constituted governments: they were to be supported and obeyed, except in the most extreme cases of abusive behavior. But Bellomont also relied on Bernon because, as a perspicacious pragmatist, he had begun to attend an Anglican church, mainly to strengthen his social and economic position in the colonies.[34]

Perhaps the most interesting of all reasons for Bellomont's selection of Bernon—and for Bernon's acquiescence in Bellomont's request—is theological. The Huguenot community in New York was then undergoing a form of revival influenced by Camisard mysticism. The Huguenot poet and erstwhile galley slave Elie Neau had, upon his liberation, come to the colonies, where he became an influential member of the French Church in New York and an elder of the church after 1704.

Neau was noted for his mystical piety, which flowered in the songs, canticles, and poems he had composed while in prison.[35] Further, Neau organized the first school for African slave children in New York; he identified with their plight because of the trials that he had endured. Neau was known as "heroic and saintly, [living] in the realm of the Spirit."[36] He knew Bernon, and the two corresponded.[37] In addition, Pierre Peiret (or Peyret) had arrived in 1687 to become the new pastor of the Church of Saint-Esprit. A native of Languedoc, he likely had participated in the ecstatic worship, prophecy, and glossolalia that marked this area of Camisard piety. Like Neau, Peiret penned poetry of a mystical tenor. His *Tresor des consolations* was published anonymously in 1696.

Camisards like Peiret were more "enthusiastic" in their worship and less institutional in their piety than their Huguenot coreligionists. Consequently, the same sort of schism that drove Leisler, the New Lights, and the revivalist, pietistic Labadists away from the practical-minded, more socially ensconced members of the Dutch Reformed church—including its ministers, who drew their salaries from the government, not from the congregation—may have been occurring here: "a cleavage between charismatic and traditional religious authority."[38]

Bernon, the pragmatist, was therefore invited to New York to lecture his Camisard-influenced Huguenot confrères about the need to temporize and compromise, to "live and let live" with established governmental authority.[39] The New York Huguenots, who had implemented a characteristic pietistic response to persecution, had to be brought back, through reason and diplomacy, to considerations of social, political, and institutional stability. Bernon recalled his fellow Huguenots to an awareness of their primary, that is, theological, identity, and as a good Calvinist, he reminded them that scripture enjoined them to submit to secular authority.[40]

Unfortunately, the Huguenots in New York refused to heed his request, whereupon Bernon reproached them in a letter dated March 25, 1697, indicting them for disloyalty to the governor. In so doing, he criticized those of his own religious and ethnic identity and background, aligning himself with the authorities: a calculated stance of political expediency galvanized probably primarily by socioeconomic considerations. His rhetoric was not unlike that of the Dutch ministers in New York who wrote to Amsterdam in 1680: "It would be a great folly in us, and an unchristian act of discourtesy, should we either misuse or neglect the privileges granted us by treaty by the English . . . We are in a foreign country, and also governed by the English nation . . . We must exercise much prudence in order to preserve the liberties granted us."[41]

Worried about the charge of disloyalty, Pastor Peiret and the leaders of the Church of Saint-Esprit petitioned the governor for an audience in order to rebut this direct accusation coming from one of their own. Ultimately, they exonerated themselves. Nonetheless, the Crown did not disburse its customary supplemental funds to Peiret—at least not that year.[42]

That Bellomont eventually pardoned the Huguenot community suggests that his concerns had most likely arisen from what he felt to be its excessive domination of trade in New York. The Huguenot community, for whom theological, not mercantile, concerns were uppermost, had in a somewhat alarmist fashion misconstrued his reaction as anti-Catholic sentiment erroneously ascribed to them.

Trouble in Providence

Bernon was a man of many accomplishments, not least the founding of three churches. And though he was skilled in the arts of compromise and cooperation, not all his interactions ended as positively as the Bellomont incident. In November 1716, the General Assembly of Providence Plantation met to censure Bernon for "contemptuous and disorderly" conduct:

> Gabriel Bernon, having exhibited a petition before this Assembly, wherein were divers foul charges against Capt. John Eldredge, an assistant of this colony; and the matter being duly debated, the said Capt. John Eldredge was deemed innocent of the slanders . . .
>
> The Assembly do order the said Gabriel Bernon to sign two acknowledgements; the one, for his causelessly charging Capt. Eldredge, and the other for contemptuously and disorderly behaving himself before the said Assembly.

Bernon, realizing that his petition was unavailing, and ever with an eye toward self-interest and profit, expressed regret: "I, Gabriel Bernon, do hereby acknowledge myself to have causelessly charged Capt. John Eldredge . . . I am heartily sorry for the same, and desire him to forgive my fault in so doing."[43] Interestingly, no record of the second acknowledgment exists. Perhaps Bernon refused to make it a matter of record that he had behaved in a "contemptuous and disorderly" manner—very likely, for a truth-telling Protestant, if he truly felt himself innocent of that charge. Whatever the case, this documentation further supports the portrait of Bernon as someone adept at code shifting, deft at maneuvering socially once he had ascertained the lay of the land. Finding himself outnumbered, Bernon adroitly stepped aside, again demonstrating a strategy of adaptation and accommodation.

As his personal papers, held in the Rhode Island Historical Society, attest, Bernon became the ancestor of many of Rhode Island's earliest—and soon to become most prominent—families. Many artifacts formerly owned by Bernon are extant; all are costly. Several carved chairs, a gold rattle, his psalm book, and an ancestral sword dated 1414 remain in the possession of his descendants, the Carpenters and the Allens of Rhode Island. Bernon's effects include correspondence, family documents, autograph memoranda, contracts, the papers of some of his descendants, and a sketched map of the settlement at New Oxford.

A Huguenot in the New World

Bernon became involved with other Huguenot businessmen in trade: he traded in Virginia and Pennsylvania along with the Faneuil family of Boston, and he exported to England and the West Indies in partnership with Daniel Ayrault after Bernon's only son died on a trading ship off the West Indies in 1712. In addition, he invested in shipbuilding, manufactured nails, and set up a salt works, an enterprise in which the Rochelois had been involved along the Atlantic seaboard for generations. In 1710, Bernon moved to Providence, where he experienced great commercial success and local fame.[44] While living in Boston, Bernon had been a "devoted" member of the French Reformed Church (the pastor was Ezéchiel Carré, his cousin), but "on coming to Rhode Island, where there were not enough of his countrymen to support such an organization, he immediately allied himself with the Anglican communion."[45] In Rhode Island, Bernon was a prime mover in establishing at least three Anglican parishes: Trinity Church in Newport, St. Paul's in Kingston, and St. John's in Providence. Although Bernon attended the Anglican church—and was listed as a vestryman in 1718—he may never officially have converted.[46] He is buried beneath the foundation of a later addition to St. John's Church.

In 1712, Bernon, at age sixty-eight, married a second and much younger wife, Mary Harris, and moved with her to Wickford, Rhode Island. They returned to Providence in 1719, where Bernon died in 1736, having spent his later years in semiretirement, writing correspondence "mostly of a primarily religious character."[47] Four years before he died, Bernon wrote a will manumitting all his slaves and their children.

A Calvinist to the last, Bernon could not abide anything that smacked of Catholicism and clericalism. In a letter to the vestry of Trinity Church, Newport, Bernon denounced a pamphlet on church order that seemed more "high church" or Romish to him, stating, "I am a born layman of France, naturalized English, which I hold a greater honour than all the riches of France, because the English laity are not, like the laity of France, slaves of the clergy and hackneys of the Pope; wherefore rather than submit to this I abandoned my country, my fortune, and my friends, in order to become a citizen under the English government."[48] First and foremost, Bernon upheld his religious convictions, adapting to new circumstances but refusing to assimilate seamlessly.

Significantly, in the Bernon archives can be found some correspondence that Gabriel Bernon maintained with George Berkeley, bishop of Cloyne in the

County of Cork, where he led a more Reformed version of the Anglican Church in Ireland.[49] Because the Anglican Church on the Continent was, during this time, so much influenced by the Reformed ideas coming from Scotland in particular, and Ireland and Wales as well, it is not difficult to envision a French Calvinist sympathizing with or converting to Anglicanism.[50] The Reformed influence on Anglicanism included recourse to the Calvinist Geneva Bible, stronger insistence on good preaching, and an emphasis more on personal piety and justification by faith: "The one thing that mattered now was faith and the responsibility of each individual to put his or her whole trust in the mercy and forgiveness of God."[51] This sounds much like the pietistic Camisard strategy that some Huguenots adopted in the New World.

Like Cotton Mather, Carré, and Neau, Bernon set great store by the role of the laity in calling ministers to accountability and in ensuring that ecclesiology conformed to scriptural standards. Thus, his attendance at an Anglican rather than a French Reformed church was in no way an assimilation process that diluted his faith, but rather a reasoned selection of a benign alternative that enabled him to maintain intact his essential core beliefs.

Further, it was a choice that reflected his admiration for the Enlightenment principles of English society and government, principles that had been woefully lacking when Louis XIV abrogated the freedom of conscience of his Huguenot and Camisard subjects. These beliefs and principles continued to inform Bernon's life: on his tombstone, it is written that Bernon was "a Huguenot [who] *died in the Faith*."[52] Despite adversity, and having surmounted all challenges by his use of creative adaptability, Bernon seemed to have fulfilled the trajectory announced in the scriptural passage engraved on his headstone: "Everyone that hath forsaken houses, or brethren, or sisters, or father, or mother, or wife, or children, or lands, for My name's sake, shall receive an hundredfold, and shall inherit eternal life."[53] In his own words, Bernon's "most fervent desire" was "to sustain [my]self in the fear of God."[54]

Bernon's obituary, published in Boston in 1736 with an accompanying encomiastic commentary, summarized Bernon's life and influence: "He behav[ed] himself as a zealous professor of the Protestant religion and dying in the faith and hope of a Redeemer, and with the inward assurance of salvation; leaving a good name among all his acquaintances, and by his upright life giving evidence of the power of Christianity in sustaining him through his great sufferings in leaving his country and a great estate *that he might worship God according to his conscience*."[55]

Bernon was one of the key players in a network of social, political, and theological influences concatenated around the Boston area and centering in unexpected ways on the person of Cotton Mather.

CHAPTER SIX

Cotton Mather, Ezéchiel Carré, and the French Connection

> Do what thou wilt with mee; kill mee; for thy Grace hath made mee
> willing to dy; Only, only, only, Help mee to Delight in thee, and to
> glorify thy dearest Name.
> —Cotton Mather, recorded in his diary, 1681

In his biography *The Life and Times of Cotton Mather*, Kenneth Silverman strove to revise the austere picture that had come to be taken as representative of Mather, positing that "many different features of his life and time drew Mather, popularly imagined as the quintessential Puritan bigot, into the vanguard of religious toleration."[1]

Cotton Mather's machinery of piety derived from his dedication to the channels of grace, methods of cultivating growth in the Christian experience. His piety was creative, capacious, and elastic. The sort of spiritual ecstasy that Mather appeared at times to experience does not at first fit with the popular profile of Puritan religiosity, nor with the customary portrait of a severe and reserved divine.[2]

In many respects, Camisard piety was not dissimilar from Cotton Mather's piety. And, indeed, Mather imported elements from other religious backgrounds, demonstrating, for instance, a penchant for reading devotional manuals so as to "take piety to the masses," a concern other Puritans shared with him. Mather's piety was channeled by meditation and prayer. His journals and diaries amply attest to his prayer life being erratic and volatile, alternately exalted and despondent. Speaking of himself in the third-person singular, a rhetorical strategy that can convey trauma and disorientation, Mather often recorded periods of abject silence, as if God had stopped up his mouth: "On the 13th of March, 'in the Assurances, the glorious and Ravishing Assurances of the Divine Love, my joyes were almost insupportable.' On the 19th, he was depressed; on the 3rd of April, he was again ecstatic; on the 8th, he suffered from a 'silence of God' in prayer-time—punishment for an 'Idle Fraud of Soul.'"[3] His speech returned to him, it seemed to Mather, only with the enabling power of the Holy Spirit.[4]

The similarities between Mather's private experiences of piety and those of the Camisards are undeniable. He "had for years been a religious enthusiast whose constant ecstasies brought him into . . . direct communication with Heaven."[5] Perhaps for this reason, Cotton Mather became a sort of "support system" for French Protestants in his day, often taking up his pen in their defense, forming friendships with them, and advocating on their behalf in church.

Mather's Unexplored French Connection

Most scholarly histories of Cotton Mather refer briefly to his—and many other British colonists'—distrust of French Catholics and Jesuits.[6] They generally do not mention his friendship with some French Protestants in New England.[7] Nor do they discuss his occasional espousal of their cause.[8] This "French connection" warrants exploration. It was important not only in providing aid to the French Protestants themselves, but also in influencing the political and theological direction the colonies would take toward freedom of conscience and freedom of worship.

While colonists worried about the possibility of imminent invasion by the French or waxed furious at Jesuit proselytizing in French Canada and the Jesuit incitement of Indian massacres of British settlers, they tended to be blind to the fact that one could be Protestant as well as French.[9] They habitually conflated the categories of French ethnicity and Catholic religiosity.[10]

However, Cotton Mather knew Frenchmen who were devout Protestants. Indeed, one factor enabling him to support Huguenot churchmen was their ineradicable distrust—perhaps even more vehement than his—of French Catholics. The Huguenot refugee and minister Ezéchiel Carré, Mather's friend and coauthor, lamented the religious persecutions launched by Louis XIV, which Carré had experienced firsthand in the Old World. Even without a personal experience of persecution, Mather excoriated Louis XIV as a tyrant and a despot, labeling him "the French Moloch" and "the Greatest Adversary of Christianity, that ever was in the World!"[11]

Mather's interaction with, and support of, French Protestants opens a new, vital chapter in his early career and in the life of the colonies. It coincides with a crucial period for Huguenots and Camisards in the New World. Mather had close friendships, almost a relationship of protector to protégé, with the refugee French community in Massachusetts. Mather seems, despite cultural opposition in the contemporary climate, deliberately to have decided to promote the cause of the French in New England. In a diary entry in September 1686, he wrote of several resolutions, one of which was "to be kind to the French refugees."[12]

In times of trouble, Huguenot refugees in the colonies,[13] influenced by the tribulations and ecstatic professions of faith of their more radical and enthusiastic Camisard confrères, felt the Holy Spirit constantly and personally intervening in their lives, and did not hesitate to attribute their recent tribulations to divine Providence, God working out his purpose in history over the long term.[14] For them, new scientific perspectives could only be manifestations of a larger divine order; scientific theories were always handmaidens subordinate to divine perspective.[15] Mather, too, "longed for evidence of the Spirit."[16]

However, since some Puritans were skeptical about such "enthusiasm," he also sought to corset much experiential phenomena within prescribed ecclesiastical and scriptural confines. The battle between reason and faith often led him to "doubt the reality of the Spirit himself."[17] The apparent dissimilarities between Mather's avowed yearning for spiritual manifestations, and his inclination to conform to the Protestant community (which, in general, cautioned excessive reliance on such "stirrings") can be explained by examining evidence from Mather's French connection.[18] No surprise, then, that in some respects Mather should have felt such an affinity with French Protestants: "Mather's theology is ... essentially Reformed Orthodoxy stripped back to biblical essentials."[19]

Mather had connections with German Pietists such as Philipp Jakob Spener. Mather's biographer asserts that their influence on his thought was significant: "The immediate German Pietist influence on Mather's own ecumenism *was likely* Philip Jakob Spener, who reduced the whole of Christianity simply to a confession of sin and a profession of faith in Christ."[20] However, such affiliation derived first from the French Protestant model, since the German Pietists were themselves influenced by, and involved with, Camisards and Huguenots. Mather encountered German Pietism "sometime in the early 1700s through his connection with the Anglican Society for the Propagation of Christian Knowledge in Boston."[21] French Protestant *immigrés* such as Bernon and Neau were key figures with whom Mather interacted in the SPCK.

Mather met and interacted with Huguenots in the French Church of Boston, as evidenced by his correspondence and copublication with Ezéchiel Carré, while no evidence is available for direct conversation with Auguste Francke or Spener. Further, just as the Shakers claimed affiliation with the Camisards, so did the Pietists, and so did John Wesley, who participated in prayer meetings led by German Pietists but who also responded favorably to the message of Camisards who preached in London.[22] The French connection is therefore even more significant.

Early in his ministerial career, Mather was drawn to emotional and spiritual manifestations of the workings of the spirit, a tendency he shared with Camisards and the Huguenots influenced by them.[23] Mather's beliefs and temperament predisposed him to be favorably drawn to French Protestant refugees. Shortly after his ordination on May 15, 1685, "his private devotions . . . were more prolonged and more ecstatic than ever; his emotional condition throughout the year was more and more overwrought"; "he recovered [from these states] in a somewhat disturbed spiritual condition; he had an excessive ecstasy."[24]

The fact that Mather himself deemed these spiritual "movements" "excessive" showed an awareness that he did not always experience what the Puritan community expected. Mather also documented others' responses to some of his "enthusiasms," not all of them favorable.[25] A heightened awareness of spiritual forces at work in daily life was also a perspective Mather shared with his father. Increase Mather had long prayed for what he called "special providences" and angelic guidance.[26] In the 1680s and 1690s, Cotton Mather's journals show that he began to pray for direct communication from angelic beings. Kenneth Silverman observes that "Mather's prayers for communication with angels were highly unusual for a Puritan . . . While Mather's views on good angels were entirely traditional, *his hope for close communion with them was not*."[27] On the whole, the Reformed community believed that revelation was "closed": no miracles or overt spiritual manifestations, such as speaking in tongues (which the Camisards practiced), were to occur after the special dispensation that had been given to the early Christian church.[28] The contrasting attitudes toward gifts like inspiration affected even the interpretation of scripture: "To the enthusiast, the Bible is infallible when interpreted by an inspired person. To the Reformers, it possessed an inherent infallibility, and needed only clarification, which was a matter for the learned."[29]

Mather, however, at least at an early stage, appears to have attempted to live his life in accordance with spiritual "messages"—direct, specific words of inspiration akin to "personal prophecies." "Cotton Mather had for years been a religious enthusiast whose constant ecstasies brought him into direct communication with heaven."[30] This was a pattern akin to the reverence in which the Camisards held the prophetic word delivered to the individual believer.[31] In matters affecting public polity, Puritans, like Huguenots but unlike Camisards, tended to subject matters of faith to the scrutiny of reason. They did not deny personal faith, but they did expect its manifestations to be orderly. Mather expressed similar concerns that piety comport well with Puritan mores, cautioning against "such . . . excesses" in his 1705 preface to a tract by the enthusiast minister John Danforth.[32] In his private prayers as well as in some public sermons, Mather seems to have conceived of his spiritual life as being somewhat different from the Puritan norm, bringing him closer, at least unofficially and in the sense of personal interactions, to the more expressive Camisard minority than to the more orderly and staid Huguenots. It is true that he was not unlike his father in this respect, for Increase seems to have battled with mania or extreme and unaccustomed forms of ecstatic experience.

However, with Cotton the phenomena seem to have occurred primarily during his youth, although some returned after the death of his second wife.[33] These states seem to have been fairly sustained, and Mather's diary indicates that they were deliberately induced or prayed for. Further, "this Pietist strain [did] remain within Puritanism, . . . and Cotton Mather cultivated personal and intellectual connections between English Puritanism and Continental Pietism."[34] Cotton Mather "considered the missionary, charitable and evangelistic work" of the Pietists to be "among the brightest signs of revival around the globe in the early 1700s."[35]

Some of the entries in his diaries sound like descriptions of the ecstasies experienced by Camisards.[36] For instance, Mather described becoming so spiritually transported that he detained his congregation for more than two hours while he prayed aloud and rapturously, perceiving his own soul "soaring and flaming toward Heaven."[37] He referred to what he called his "Particular Faiths"[38] and spoke of "the rapturous Touches and Prospects"[39] and ecstasies beyond description. Camisard enthusiasts' descriptions of their ecstatic states sounded much like Mather's account of labile emotional states and spiritual oscillations: "The beginning of this month . . . brought with it . . . multiplied Experiences of Strange Dejections and sad Buffetings upon my mind . . . and then a more than Assistance and Enlargement in the service."[40] While the almost physical quality of the spiritual struggle described may not seem much dissimilar from typical Puritan journal accounts of the period concerning spiritual wrestling,[41] the vocabulary is not similar to theirs,[42] but rather is more akin to the highly sensory, personal, and inspired quality of Camisard pronouncements.[43] In addition, Mather's emphasis on the Holy Spirit is like that of the Camisards' on spirit-filled prophecy. Mather advised one man, "See what a vast difference there is between the Spirit of your language, and the language of the Spirit."[44]

Huguenots, like Puritans, were more likely to speak of the first person of the Trinity and of God's Providence, and to adhere to the *stylus rudus*, or plain style, of scripture; they distrusted "fictional" innovations and were wary of subjectivity as a guarantor of spiritual validity.[45] However, Mather used a more enthusiastic tone when describing a wave of church memberships, presumably conversions, to his North Church during a revival in September 1694; he claimed to have witnessed "a strange descent of Shining Spirits, that had upon them great marks of their being such Angels as they declared themselves to be," and he gave reports of having heard angelic music in the heavens,[46] phenomena frequently reported in Camisard testimonials.[47] In journals from his early twenties, Mather recounted how he was visited in his study by an angelic being who auspiciously foresaw the transcontinental influence that Mather's writings would eventually wield: "And in particular this Angel spoke of the influence . . . of the books this youth [Mather] should write and publish, not only in America, but in Europe. And he added certain special prophecies of the great works this youth should do for the Church of Christ . . . Lord Jesus! What is the meaning of this marvel?"[48]

Also like the Camisards, the young Mather professed to distrust rote or formulaic prayer. Huguenots, on the other hand, customarily included set prayer in their services.[49] Mather was aware of his pietistic divergence from other Puritans, as the parenthetical inclusion of the rhetorical interrogation in the following passage suggests: "this Day as I was (*may I not say?*) in the Spirit."[50] The need to include the question attests to some acknowledgment that he was making a departure from the normative, sanctioned style of writing about spiritual matters.

Mather's early piety thus appears to have fostered a predisposition for sympathy with French Protestant refugees. Certainly there was dialogue and mutual influence after their actual coming into contact. Though the causal link is not clear, the relationship and influence cannot be questioned. Mather wrote prefaces to numerous Huguenot publications in which he acknowledged friendship beyond public support for these individuals—as he did for other causes and confessions.[51] In his diary for September 1686, Mather penned his first mention of French refugees.[52]

Further, many of his Huguenot associates had been influenced in their thought and piety by the recent persecutions visited on their Camisard confrères. Mather actively espoused their cause—not always a popular thing to do.[53] For instance, "in October [1683] he was active in forwarding a plan, objected to by some as superstitious, that devout people should devote a given hour every Monday to pray for [French] persecuted churches abroad."[54] Mather's preaching politicized the matter, bringing the persecution of Protestants on the Continent home to the colonists: "[Mather's] weekly prayers for threatened Protestants in . . . France seemed to make New England Puritans participate in the struggle against Louis XIV . . . and [against] an aggressively reactionary Catholicism."[55] Catholicism, as here contrasted with Protestantism, was "firmly identified in the [contemporary British] mind with absolutism."[56]

Perhaps one factor accounting for Mather's involvement in French matters both abroad and locally, as well as for the friendship and empathy he evinced toward the French refugees, was his avowed transcontinental ambitions.[57] Fluent in numerous languages, Mather published tracts in French and Spanish and made translations into various Indian tongues; he was a member of the Royal Academy of Sciences in England and held an honorary degree from the

University of Glasgow. Although he never left his native land, Mather worked to develop and sustain a polished reputation abroad. Along with such courting of recognition from the intellectual elite of the day, Mather also espoused the notion of freedom of conscience, which was prevalent among Continental intellectuals of the time. But he did so only up to a point. Mather's politics were quite liberal, although his theology was essentially conservative. For him, freedom of conscience meant that Protestants should not be coerced by a Catholic king into forswearing their faith and converting.

Another factor contributing to his taking up the French Protestant cause may have been the ecumenical notion of pan-Protestantism, which he professed at times in the early stages of his career. He envisioned such an approach as a concerted riposte to Catholicism. Mather's *Bonifacius*, for instance, reminded readers that "for the advance of the larger Reformation . . . [the church] needs to look outside New England . . . , reposing its hopes for the future of Protestantism not in a Puritan City on a Hill which might be its vanguard, nor even in an alliance of English Protestants, but in a worldwide Pietistic evangelical movement."[58] Mather espoused this position, too, only up to a certain point. For instance, he briefly cooperated with the Society for the Propagation of the Gospel in Foreign Parts, an Anglican body, but essentially he distrusted Anglicanism, and furthered the cause of the society only in hopes that it would obstruct the work of Jesuit missionaries.[59] This was such a pressing matter for Mather that he, along with Robert Thompson, a London member of the New England Company, suggested in 1692 that the New England commissioners should contact Huguenot ministers to "instruct some ingenious converted Indians in ye French tongue" so that these Indians would not be likely to succumb to the blandishments of French Jesuits.[60]

Mather established several important relationships with French Protestant refugees. At some point in the late 1680s, Mather became the close friend of Ezéchiel Carré: Huguenot refugee, fellow polemicist against the Jesuits, former pastor at La Rochelle, and the first Protestant pastor of the French Church in Boston.

Ezéchiel Carré: Pastor to a Remnant and Mather's Protégé

Ezéchiel Carré was born around 1646 on the Ile de Ré, off the coast of the town of La Rochelle, an important Huguenot stronghold. Carré studied philosophy and theology at the academy in Geneva founded by Calvin. He ministered to congregations in the Saintonge and Guyenne regions of France for twenty years before the Camisard uprisings began in the Cévennes; he fled France during the wave of persecutions initiated at the behest of Louis XIV. Approximately forty-five French families fled France in the fall of 1681.

They settled in the area of Narragansett, Rhode Island. Carré was the pastor of this group.[61] They received aid, encouragement, and instruction on the naturalization process from the French Church in London. Along with the Huguenots Daniel Ayrault and Pierre Berton, Carré petitioned the proprietors of Narragansett, Rhode Island Colony, for permission to establish a place to be called Newberry Plantation (October 1686).[62] However, finding the area too remote from the sea to be suitable, three weeks later they requested permission to settle in Kingstown—today East Greenwich, Rhode Island, commonly known as "Frenchtown."[63] The anonymous publication titled *Report of a French Protestant Refugee in Boston* (1687) noted that "there are at Noraganzet [*sic*] about one hundred Persons [of the faith]; M. Carré is their Minister."[64]

Each family received a parcel of 100 acres and a meadow. The band of refugees planted vineyards, planted mulberry trees to support sericulture (the raising of silkworms was a traditional Huguenot trade), and anticipated being joined by some five hundred refugees still in France or England.[65] As minister, Carré was entitled to 150 acres at no charge. Some 100 acres were also set aside as glebe land to support the church, and provision was made for a school. The colonists were pleased to find what they believed to be a place where they could in safety "enjoy our worship to God" and where they "had the government's protection in our improvements, no person disturbing us."[66] They eventually made excellent wine, which was much admired by Governor Bellomont.[67]

However, English colonists from East Greenwich and Kingstown soon began to dispute the French claims to land, occupying their fields and carrying off their hay. Carré, as pastor, was delegated by the French community to protest this usurpation to Governor Andros, who upheld the French titles on the condition that the refugees swear an oath to the English crown in 1693.[68] Nonetheless, by 1691, Kingstown had been broken up by a band of colonial rabble, and most of the French settlers relocated to New York. For instance, Louis Carré from Poitou, a relative of Ezéchiel's, later turned up on the registers of the Church of Saint-Esprit in New York, where he was listed as an elder.[69]

The Kingstown settlers lamented, "We were in a dismal state . . . what little we had preserved by flying from France, we had laid out under the then improvements [here]. It looked so hard upon us, to see [ourselves] . . . ruined. And when we complained to the Government, we could have no relief . . . They soon pulled down and demolished our church."[70] It was the Huguenot and Camisard persecutions from the Old World revisited on the New.

Carré, however, went with some of the Huguenot refugees to Boston, where he had frequently been summoned to preach to the French congregation, which at that time had no permanent minister. The refugees noted that "the town [of Boston] is built on the slope of a little hill, and is as large as La Rochelle."[71] They sought to establish formally a French Church there.

In Boston, Carré became the first minister of the French refugee church. This had been started the year before, when a small band of refugees linked up with a few French acquaintances who were already scattered throughout Boston and who had been gathered for worship by Pastor Pierre Daillé shortly after his arrival in 1682.[72] Daillé's friendship with Increase Mather prefigured the tie that was to develop between Ezéchiel Carré and Cotton Mather. A structure for the French Protestant Church in Boston was designated in 1687 (it was the Latin schoolhouse), and along with Daniel Bondet, another Huguenot pastor, Carré preached often in Boston.[73] A French Protestant *temple* for this congregation was finally erected in 1715 on a plot of land purchased ten years earlier.

The inhospitable conditions suffered by French Protestants made it a struggle to maintain the church early on: "Here in Boston there are not more than twenty French families, and they are every Day diminishing, on Account of departing for the Country to buy or hire Land and to strive to make some settlements," the *Report of a French Protestant Refugee* lamented.[74] This account, found in Antoine Court's papers and not published until February 1868, is one of the few Camisard accounts extant (the writer was a native of Languedoc).[75] A second part, chronicling the anonymous author's journey to Rhode Island, has never been found. Intended to quell French Protestant fears about the New World, the *Report of a French Protestant Refugee* reassured Camisards and Huguenots alike that there were few Catholics in the country: "As for Papists, I have discovered since being here 8 or 10, 3 of whom are French and come to our Church, and the others are Irish."[76]

The author was charged with investigating whether propitious conditions might be found to encourage French Protestant immigration to the New World: "He was commissioned to collect on the spot such Advices as might serve to guide his comrades in the Faith, and facilitate their establishment in the Land of Exile . . . [The account is] the simple, honest narration of [one] who . . . notes everything in his Passage . . . in short, the Statistics, both material and moral, of a dawning Community."[77] The document is written as a series of questions and answers. Presumably, other Camisards, and Huguenots, drafted their questions, and the author then tried to find the answers. His text attests to the difficult conditions in which Carré labored to establish a French Protestant Church in New England.

The first French Church in Boston lasted until 1748.[78] Carré was supported financially by members of his Huguenot church, among them Jean Latourette.[79] Latourette may have accompanied Pastor Pierre Peiret to London and later to New York, where a tightly knit community of a few hundred French refugee families were pastored by Peiret throughout the 1690s. Latourette likely first landed in what is now Rhode Island, and left after the failure to thrive of the first Huguenot colony there in 1686 (as did most of the original settlers by 1690). He died in 1708 in New Rochelle; his family continued active in the French Church of Saint-Esprit in New York.

Carré was a seminal figure in the colonies, as the road named after him in East Greenwich, Rhode Island, attests. He was also a friend of another influential Huguenot who settled in the Northeast, James Bowdoin.[80] Bowdoin offered financial support to the Huguenot community and aided in the construction of the church.

Cotton Mather sponsored Carré's new church, publicly advocating relief aid for refugee Huguenots. His support for Carré should come as no surprise, since the Reformed piety practiced by the refugees was in large measure recognizable to the Puritan community. Carré was even claimed as a "Presbyterian minister" in some contemporary accounts.[81] Mather spoke highly of the Camisard French Prophets, word of whose prophesying and plight had reached him from London. Mather averred that he had reason to expect the imminent resurrection of the Camisard martyrs, as called for by the controversial French Prophets: "*We have cause* to think, that *the Resurrection of the slain Witnesses in France, is now very near*; and if any of us have been Compassionate Samaritans towards their afflicted people, we shall rejoice with them, in the *Redemption which draweth nigh*."[82] Mather made this statement despite contemporary reticence over taking such overt and firm positions on matters of the spirit, and despite the controversial nature of the French Prophets' claims.[83] Mather's statement and his actions on behalf of French Protestants in Boston constitute a strong gesture of solidarity.

A Parable for the Times

Carré's two surviving texts, *The Charitable Samaritan*, a sermon preached in Boston in 1689, and the *Echantillon: De la doctrine des Jesuites*, published in 1690, played an important role in alleviating the suspicion that many New England colonists felt toward the French refugees at a time when hostilities with Catholics were at a peak: French and Indians from Canada had committed many depredations, and a renewed outbreak of hostilities threatened. The colonists assumed anyone French was likely to be Catholic and therefore an enemy.[84] The fact that the Huguenot refugees experienced persecution at the hands of the Jesuit-incited bands of Indians helped allay the colonists' fears of French Protestant treachery, especially after the massacre at Deerfield, Massachusetts, in February 1704, when the Huguenot refugee town founded by Gabriel Bernon was raided and razed.

But Carré's theological convictions, shown to conform to Puritan doctrine—and interpreted for a broader audience by Cotton Mather—were the primary factor in easing these tensions. In *The Charitable Samaritan*, he wrote, "Our little Colony will chiefly have obligation to you, for hereby you will in some sort justify them against those Calumnies, whereby some would render our Retirement into this New World suspected."[85] Carré then stated his intention to dispel the confusion of the colonists over French theological stances. Addressing an influential French merchant, John Pastre, another refugee in Boston, he observed that "persons may easily perceive, that those who maintain such Doctrine, and have exposed themselves to so many dangers and miseries on the account of it, cannot reasonably pass for Papists, and that it is uncharitable and uncompassionate to accuse them as such."[86]

Mather endorsed Carré's arguments. Not only did Mather fraternize with Carré, he also wrote the preface to at least two of Carré's publications. In fact, it is likely—and the preface bears this out—that Carré's work would not have been published without Mather's intercession.

The Charitable Samaritan was written in English because of the difficulty of having it published in French: "Moreover, if it appear in English, it is not because we have a mind to trespas on the Rights of others, but 'tis because it was impossible here to print it in its natural tongue."[87] The Reverend Nehemiah Walker was the translator, his involvement also attesting to the degree of collaboration encouraged by Mather between Puritan and French churches. Carré's tract is the only surviving printed text of a pulpit oration penned by a Huguenot refugee preacher of the period.[88]

Popular suspicions of the French ran rife in the colonies in the late seventeenth century. In October 1692, the General Court of Massachusetts passed a resolution that expressed the concerns of British colonists regarding the French presence: "Considering that amongst the many French Gentlemen and others that reside among us who pretend to be Protestants, there may be sundry of them that are Papist and enemies to their Majesties and the weal of this province . . . if they [do not] give a satisfactory account of themselves, [they are to be] seize[d] and br[ought] away to Boston, there to be proceeded against."[89]

However, despite this fraught climate, Mather attempted to appeal to a sympathetic audience—even crafting such an audience rhetorically—drawing Huguenots and Camisards into the fold by calling them fellow Protestants: "The New-English reader is here entertained with a Sermon pronounced in the French Congregation at Boston, by a Reverent Minister of that Nation, at this time a Refugee among us; and the Doctrine therein delivered sufficiently discovers the Worthy Author to be a Christian, and a Protestant, that may challenge a Room in our best affections."[90] Mather thus took pains to break the mistaken presumed equivalence between being French and being Catholic.

In addition, Mather hoped to bolster the fledgling French Protestant Church and enable it to settle in New England, also a goal of Carré's. The sermon motifs of the traveler and the exiled wanderer must have been particularly poignant to Huguenots.[91] Carré's homilies take up this refrain: "Jesus Christ left his Countrey which was Heaven; [and] he appeared here below as a Traveller."[92] The figure of the traveler embodied some aspects of the Huguenots' and Camisards' sufferings and tribulations—the church wandering in the "Desert"—and translated into emotional terms the sense of displacement they felt, the tension between Old World and New World experiences. For instance, Elie Neau wrote a collection of mystical songs that was published first in English rather than French—a linguistic displacement that mimed the actual, physical sense of alienation experienced by Neau. The title, *A Present from a Farr Countrie*, alludes to the leitmotif of the traveler.

By taking as his text the parable of the Good Samaritan, Carré accomplished many purposes. He could call his fellow refugees to support one another; he could gently admonish Puritan colonists not to judge his confrères falsely or harshly. This was a timely injunction, since the French in Narragansett had recently been judged by the provincial government of Massachusetts to be "good Protestants . . . well approved of," despite the recent controversies and alarms.[93] Carré, anglicized with the moniker "Monsieur Corey" in *The Charitable Samaritan*, was thus reminding his auditors that the English government had, in fact, confirmed the probity of the French Protestants in the region.

Carré wove a theological theme of repentance, sin, and salvation into his sermon; and perhaps most surprising for a relatively orthodox Huguenot, he identified implicitly with the experience of his more radical and glossolalic Camisard cousins who had been recently martyred for their faith in France. He equated the current circumstances of his Huguenot flock in Boston with the plight of the humble and humiliated Camisards by using the biblical figure of the beaten man as emblematic of French Protestant straits: "What doth not this Samaritan do for this wounded person, he alights from his Horse and helpt him on his Beast. Christ was abased to advance us, he made himself poor to make us rich, he came down from the highest degree of glory to raise us up; he was King of the World . . . and yet took on him the form of a servant, for to make us Kings."[94] Carré told his audience that he had selected this particular scripture passage because of his alarm over a decline in the customary Reformed practice of almsgiving: "The occasion which made way for this sermon is this: the Author being obliged to bestow some part of his ministry on the French church of Boston, until it would please God to provide for it, he was much surprised to observe that for many Sabbaths; this church contrary to its custom, extreamly neglected Alms toward the Poor, which our Discipline recommends at the conclusion of each exercise."[95] Not only should the church be generous to its own members, but French Protestant refugees in general were in dire straits, requiring relief from the society at large, Carré observed. This predicament was one common to the Huguenots' Camisard cousins, whose experience of persecutions were, at the time this sermon was preached, only just beginning. "The poor are the Treasures of Jesus Christ, he charges to his own account that which you bestow on them; and he will largely pay you the Interest another Day. If you advance some part of your Goods to the poor, he will Restore you an hundred-fold in the world to come," Carré reminded his readers.[96]

Carré's argument here was remarkably like that made by Bishop Compton to his London diocese on behalf of indigent Huguenot refugees there in 1686: "They who have no mite to give, have heart to pray; and this occasion requires, with an equal necessity, our Prayers for those who still lie in Misery and Irons, as it does our Benevolence for such as are escaped . . . Remember how it is written, 'He that hath pity upon the poor, lendeth unto the Lord.' "[97]

Carré explicated other aspects of the parable, and translated them into terms relevant to French Protestants. The Camisards felt that they fought in the *désert*, battled by the devil yet sustained by angels. They borrowed this motif from the Huguenots' experiences during the Wars of Religion, which were likened to those of the ancient Hebrews wandering in the wilderness during the Exodus.[98] Carré pointedly referred to God's word in the parable as "the Manna which the faithful that travel in the Desart of this World are fed with in this Inn."[99] In other parts of his explication, Carré employed code words or phrases common to French Protestants, constructing a network of references as a sort of Calvinist lexicon, one that also served the purpose of demonstrating to the Puritan population the orthodoxy of the French Protestants. For instance, Carré alluded to the parable of the talents—a favorite Huguenot scripture passage[100]—in his exposition of the parable of the Good Samaritan: "Of those servants that improved the Talents their Lord intrusted them withal, he caused them to enter into his joy."[101] Boldly, face to face with a Puritan congregation opposed to pneumatology,[102] Carré nonetheless heartily endorsed the workings of the Holy Spirit: "He recommends them to the Holy Ghost, in whose hands he left them . . . to comfort them . . . and to sanctifie them."[103]

But Carré showed himself of one mind with the Puritan congregation on the subject of free will. He urges his listeners to "quit [them]selves of these unjust and bold sentiments, Free will is but a chimera."[104] The apparent contradiction between this statement and the French Protestant commitment to freedom of conscience might be resolved through the realization that freedom of conscience is, for the Reformed, a matter of the Holy Spirit: the individual does not decide for himself; rather, the Holy Spirit indwells the believer and guides his decision.

Carré went quite far in legitimizing the Camisards' armed resistance to Louis XIV's dragoons, using the beaten man as a cipher for the Camisards: "They stripped him. But as *we* do not willingly permit the things we lawfully possess to be taken from us, so this man opposes them; he endeavors to repel violence by violence; he makes use of his utmost resistance . . . but . . . he falls wounded with many blows."[105] In narrating the story of the traveler's sufferings typologically, Carré read into it both Huguenot and Camisard experience, telling two stories simultaneously. At the same time, his phrases resonated with the Puritans' memory of their own past tribulations. And in decrying the *dragonnades*, Carré touched on the colonists' prevalent fear of a standing army. Absolutism and a standing army were construed as the yoked pair epitomizing the abuses of a French Catholic state whose agents, the Jesuits, were seeking dominion of the New World.[106]

Reminding his listeners that the Narragansett French colonists had recently and with a good will taken the oath of allegiance to the British Crown, but that they in no way intended to sacrifice or compromise their religious principles, Carré used this sermon to encourage the flock to stand firm in their Protestant faith. Further, Carré not only used the parable of the Good Samaritan to propound a theological lesson, but also to play politics, pitting the Huguenots and Puritans against the Jesuits.[107] He described a Jesuit priest figured as a doctrinally errant, satanic figure. "This is exactly the Tale of the . . . Jesuits. For Answer, But First, let me ask: Whether a man deadly wounded can heal himself? . . . He is dead [as] he knows not how to will to repent, this is a Moral Impotency."[108] Carré then attacked the other Catholic doctrine so abhorrent to Puritans, that of the intercession of the saints: "Do we then say with the Church of Rome, 'that the Saints and Martyrs by their works of Supererogation have made as it were an addition to the sufferings of Jesus Christ, and it is this surplus that the Lord here promises to compensate?' Answer, God forbid, Brethren, for that is to associate the creatures with the Creator."[109]

In this passage, Carré repudiated also the notion of salvation through works, abhorred by Puritans and French Protestants alike, thereby also adroitly signaling to the Puritan community that his fellow French Protestants were friends and coreligionists, not foes. He also upheld the strict Calvinist understanding that blasphemy was inherent in any attempt to join what is human with what is divine. This was a timely stance for Carré to adopt, since Cotton Mather had recently demonstrated some nascent ecumenism in the hopes of bringing more Protestants into the fold to join ranks against Catholicism.[110]

Carré's apologetic method consisted of honoring the integrity of the parable as biblical text through exegesis, while also opening that text out to speak to current circumstances through exposition: in short, Carré implemented the precepts of classical Calvinist preaching and hermeneutic technique. Carré explained his approach in this way: the passage is "an other sor[t] of Parabl[e], which humane wisdom cannot imitate, and which [has] a character wholly Divine[; it is] such as [is] founded upon some real fact . . . particular [contemporary] events which Providence has prepared, whereon to build Heavenly truths . . . I will show the literal Sense which is here propounded; on the other hand, I will discover the Mystical Sense here hidden."[111] This technique was similar to that practiced by lay Camisard and, later, by ordained Reformed preachers, and was also used in the process of selection of *inspiré* military leaders.

Though recalling a past marked by persecution, Carré called for a present awareness of obligation and gratitude: "God give us grace, that being animated by the example of this Samaritan, which we have this day set before our eyes, we may in all ways manifest our Charity towards our Neighbours, and even towards our most cruel enemies."[112] In the first phrase, the pronoun "us" drew Huguenot listeners as well as Puritan audience into the Camisard drama; with his subsequent use of "we," Carré deftly exhorted his Huguenot parishioners to live aright both with Huguenots and with Puritans.

He continued to involve his auditors in the scriptural drama, using the parable as a veiled plea for active charity for the Huguenot refugee community. He first remarked that all were in need of aid—"Sinners, consider your miserable condition, you are this man half dead, and stretcht out by the way"—and then reminded his hearers that "on the Last Day hardheartedness towards the distressed will be motive sufficient for Damnation."[113]

In his preface, Mather summarized these concerns of Carré's and urged his listeners to take steps to ameliorate the Huguenots' and Camisards' distress. He provided a personal example by pledging assistance to Carré and the small French community in exile, invoking as incentive the reasoning that the French Protestants espoused essentially the same beliefs and causes as did the Boston Puritans: "It is none of my Business here to Argue in defense of every particular Notion or Expression occurring here . . . All I shall observe is, that as 'tis the compassionate Samaritan Discoursed . . . on; so with the Bowels of a compassionate Samaritan, we ought here to reflect upon this dismal Persecution, which has driven this learned Person, and his Congregation hither."[114] Mather thus asserted, and maintained throughout, the worthy nature of the French Protestant cause. Mather's use of the pronoun "we" in the preface invited Bostonian readers—formerly unsure whether French Protestants were acceptable Protestants in Puritan eyes—to try to identify themselves with the French cause.

This "Prefatory Recommendation on the Sermon, with a brief account of the late French Persecution" further curried sympathy with the reader by offering a short history of the French Protestants' plight, characterizing their tribulations both as signs of the end-times and as tokens of Protestant affiliation, the Puritans having also come to the New World to flee persecution.[115]

It is worth noting that Mather's narrative in miniature antedated the 1708 publication of the history written by the Huguenot pastor and Camisard soldier Antoine Court, which is usually deemed the earliest and most complete account of the sufferings in the Cévennes. Mather's historical sketch was also published before Misson's collection of Camisard testimonials (1708). Thus, Mather's preface (1689) constitutes the first complete—and confessionally neutral, on the whole—historical summary of the persecutions of Huguenots in France, one also including an account of what had happened to the Camisards, to be written in English.

Translating the French Experience into New World Terms:
Mather's Prefaces to Carré

Mather played the role of translator between the Old World and New World experiences of the French Protestants whom he befriended. He constructed this role for himself. Other figures, such as the influential Benjamin Colman, also took on such roles of mediation. However, while Colman intervened against Jesuits and, later, on behalf of George Whitefield, Mather's advocacy on behalf of French Protestants is singular and noteworthy.[116]

In February 1694, Mather recounted how an angel appeared to him, announcing that he would, through his published work, stretch—in intellectual and theological stature—from America to Europe. The angel described this influence as Mather's "greatness . . . the Length of his Branches."[117] When signing himself at the end of his preface to Carré's *The Charitable Samaritan*, Mather used the term "translator" in referring to his role in mediating between the two strands, French and English, of the Reformed faith: "Farewell Reader, . . . now the Compassionate Samaritan, [preached in French, is known to you] by the Accurate Translations of an Ingenious Person, speaking English [who is] . . . Cotton Mather."[118]

Mather's account of Huguenot history and trials began, significantly, not with the persecutions of the sixteenth and early seventeenth centuries, but rather with the tribulations wreaked upon the Huguenot and Camisard population at the time of the Revocation, in the 1680s. This is interesting, since the Camisard plight might arguably have been less compelling to a Puritan audience, typically quizzical about "spiritism" and manifestations of religious sentiment. It would have been less problematic to present sympathetically just the more orderly and doctrinally oriented Huguenots to a Puritan audience. Nonetheless, Mather's account was not neutral, but rather showed a strong disposition toward the Camisards: "'Tis a Persecution which all the Cruelties and Butcheries perpetrated by the children of Cain, in former Ages, hardly equal; and the Characters of it, whether we consider the beginning of it with the Banishment of the Pastors . . . or whether we consider the various kinds of Barbary exercised by it upon the remaining Churches in Tortures."[119] Mather enumerated the various sorts of persecutions visited upon the Protestant population by the king, his dragoons, and Catholics in France:[120] "The poor Protestants in France found themselves loosing all sorts of Offices, until at length not so much as a Midwife of that Religion might be allowed . . . the new Converts were discharged from the payment of their Debts; and the Resolv'd Confessors might not sell their own Estates, to assist their escapes from the Storm now breaking on them . . . Parents [were] compelled to bear the Expences of a Popish Education for their own Children."[121]

Ironically, the very language in which Mather decried these atrocities seemed to mimic the sorts of torture that would be inflicted, with Mather's knowledge and consent, on the Salem witch suspects a few years later.[122] This similarity further underscores how Mather identified the French Protestants as Christians, while relegating the witchcraft suspects to beyond the pale, consigning them to the devil. Whatever the case, the dragoons' actions described by Mather were akin to the tests used at Salem: "These Tormentors [the dragoons] would hang up the poor People by their Feet, and making of great Smokes under them, would almost choak them. If then they would not sign an Abjuration, they tossed them to and fro into great Fires, until they were almost Roasted; and sometimes plunge them down into deep Wells, till they were half drowned there. They stript others Naked, and prick'd them with Pins and Bodkins, till they could endure no more."[123]

After describing the tribulations, Mather took a firm stand in defense of the victims. This advocacy role is consistent with ones taken up in other of Mather's pan-Protestant writings. Notably, in *Suspiria Vinctorum: Some Account of the Condition to Which the Protestant Interest in the World Is at This Day Reduced*, Mather observed that one mark designating a true Christian was that he not be part of "the church of Rome . . . [which is] resolved upon the Extermination of all the Christians upon Earth."[124] Though the Camisards were known for continually reiterating their loyalty to, and affection for, the very king who had ordered their slaughter, nonetheless, these pacifist people eventually were goaded beyond endurance by the Catholic clergy.[125] Their rationale for taking up arms was ultimately predicated on how they understood the notion of freedom of conscience, and Mather's reference to this justification marks the Camisards as his primary focus: "Let them know, 'twas the kings pleasure they should turn Roman Catholicks, and the poor people humbly replying, That they would gladly sacrifice their Lives and Estates in the Service of their king, but their Consciences were to be disposed of, by none but God alone."[126]

Finally, Mather made explicit the link between Huguenots and Camisards on the one hand, and Puritans on the other, describing how the former had arrived in New England as exiles from France, just as the latter had come earlier seeking a place for the freedom of religious expression denied them in England. Mather was not alone in his concern for the Camisards. Contemporary colonial opinion was much exercised on their behalf: "War between the Camisards and the French government forces trying to stamp out Protestant resistance once and for all . . . proved highly interesting to New Englanders. The prospect of a French Protestant remnant held considerable attraction, representing persecuted martyrs of the world Protestant cause."[127] John Campbell's *Boston Newsletter* regularly reported on "the Camisard revolt and the Huguenot persecutions," while John Danforth, pastor of the church in Dorchester, Massachusetts, told his congregation to "thank God they had not yet met the fate of the French Protestants."[128] Such sympathy stopped short of advocacy, however; Mather was alone in taking an active, pro-French Protestant stance.

In this way, Mather imported the narrative of an Old World time of trial[129] into the venue of the New World, where he hoped to see these fellow Protestants received positively and treated charitably: "Nevertheless, many Thousands of the Protestants, found a merciful Providence assisting of their Escape; and some of them have arrived in New-England, where before they came, there were Fastings and Prayers Employ'd for them, and since they came, they have met with some further kindness from such as know how to sympathize with their Brethren."[130] He urged his New World audience to provide succor to these Old World refugees: "In the mean time, as 'tis my Hope, that the English Churches will not fail in Respects to any that have endured hard things for their Faithfulness to the Son of God; So 'tis my Prayer, that the French may not lose what they have wrought; nor after their Prodigious Trials, come forth any other wise, than as Gold out of the Fire."[131]

After this initial, successful, Franco-American publishing venture, Mather used his influence to have another of Carré's tracts issued, in French, by the Boston publishing house of Samuel Green in 1690.[132] In this pamphlet, Mather and Carré formed common cause against the Jesuits. Carré's *Echantillon: De la doctrine que les Jésuites enségnent aus sauvages du Nouveau Monde* (Example of the Doctrine That the Jesuits Teach to the Savages of the New World) was important for several reasons.[133] It was the first publication in French to appear in the British colonies. It appeared because of Mather's literary midwifery. And it also made the case—certainly one already believed by the majority of the colonists—that the French were inciting the Indians to attack colonial encampments like the one at Deerfield, but it made the important distinction that such fomenters were Jesuits, thereby implying that French Protestants should be exonerated from any such charges.

Consequently, in the *Echantillon*, Carré proved to Mather's satisfaction that the French Protestants were the coreligionists—doctrinally and in their anti-Catholic zeal—of the Boston Puritans. To this end, the *Echantillon* is dedicated to the elders of the French Church in Boston: "A Messieurs les Anciens de l'Eglise Francoyse de Boston." Mather acknowledged this equal status of the two confessions in his preface, emphasizing his endorsement of the French cause by writing the preface in French himself.[134] In this preface, written in May 1690, Mather urged the members of the French Church to battle with the Puritans against the Jesuits: "It is likely that the present work will serve, along with so many others, to cause to be known just how much these people [the Jesuits] hold to a pernicious doctrine and have a lax morality."[135] It was crucial that all Protestants stand together against this scourge, newly transplanted to America: "How happy we should be, my dear brothers, if God were to use us as a means to help to destroy this infamous plague! . . . This will cause to be known how much that sect has a pernicious creed and blamable lack of morals . . . This will strengthen even further in your hearts the appropriate feelings of aversion that you feel toward this impure sect."[136] Mather also collaborated on the composition of the *Echantillon*: he supplied Carré with material taken from actual Jesuit documents that had fallen into his hands.

In the preface, Mather invoked the plagues and locusts in the ninth chapter of Revelation, the description of the Apocalypse, linking it with the hordes of Jesuits set loose to wreak havoc on the New World. He likened that destruction to the mayhem already inflicted on Huguenots and Camisards in the Old World, a seeming prefiguration of the end-times. Further, he reminded the French Protestants of the recent trials they had endured and how their perseverance had led them to the New World. The diaspora, he stated, now formed a distinctive part of their religious identity—one that made French Protestantism understandable to Puritans—and should not be forgotten: "I hope that this will confirm ever more in your hearts the righteous feelings of aversion that you have already experienced for this filthy Society [the Jesuits] and that, having abandoned all your worldly goods, your families and your country, you will now be even more ready to lose your life rather than compromise with the [Jesuit] communion."[137]

Mather subscribed, at least at this point, to the apocalyptic and millenarian vision of an impending toppling of the world order as delineated by the eminent Huguenot clergyman Pierre Jurieu.[138] Mather "looked for the fulfillment of prophecy, in the restoration of this persecuted people to their country; and the oracular divine [Mather] . . . did not hesitate to pronounce himself [in accord with Jurieu] on the subject."[139] Jurieu had been publishing prolifically from the Netherlands, where he had been driven into exile for his espousal of the Camisard cause.[140] Before Jurieu, Claude Brousson, a Reformed lawyer turned theologian, had made similar apocalyptic predictions linked with pronouncements against the Roman Catholic Church.[141] These two Huguenot thinkers reached a Continental and a transcontinental audience, as Mather's, and other clergymen's, knowledge of them attests.

Brousson, in particular, preached a message of revival, of hope in the face of persecution, that nursed the underground church back to health—albeit with minority status—in France.[142] Brousson had, as Walter Utt and Brian Strayer note, an "almost obsessive fascination with apocalyptic imagery and the . . . persecution of God's people in both the Old and New Testaments, something rarely heard outside the prophets of the Cévennes. Intrigued by the Apocalypse, Brousson borrowed its word pictures, prose, and prophetic timelines and projected them onto the landscape of seventeenth and eighteenth century Europe."[143] Brousson's approach was also one that Mather recommended as a survival strategy to Carré and the French refugees in Boston.

Ecumenical Mather

In the preface to Carré's *Echantillon*, Mather aimed at reaching two audiences: the Boston Protestants already present and the French Protestants composing the fledgling church. The preface thus functioned as an apologia for a new sort of Puritan ecumenism—both in what it said, and in the language in which it said it.[144] Mather's printer asserted that "it will manifest the Uniformity of the Doctrine of Protestants from the most distant places in the World; and that the great Traject of Sea which has a longtime separated us hinders not but that in the main we may have the same sentiments."[145] In a public and moving demonstration of his regard for the French Protestant community, for example, Mather invited Pastor Daillé to be one of the pallbearers at his wife's funeral.

In large part because of Mather's endeavors on behalf of his Huguenot associates, the Puritan establishment warmed to the French refugees, with both Increase and Cotton Mather providing housing and relief aid as well as permission for the French Protestants to assemble for worship "in the new schoolhouse," where they continued to convene for the next twenty-nine years.[146] Nevertheless, Puritans on the whole looked askance at some of the liturgical worship of the French Protestants, as well as their keeping of Christmas and Easter. This attitude signaled mere toleration rather than true equivalence.

Notwithstanding such cavils, Cotton Mather referred favorably on several occasions to the French Church as being the theological coreligionists of the Puritans, and joined his name to theirs.[147]

Characteristically, Mather and the Puritan establishment provided a norm of piety for polity; atypically, Mather found the French Protestants to be in conformity with this standard. This assessment effectively constituted a rediscovery of the virtues of French Protestantism on the part of British Protestants: during the Marian exile, many persecuted English Protestants had fled to Strasbourg and Geneva, where they found a church aligned with their beliefs. Back in England under Elizabeth I, they agitated for reform along the lines of Genevan piety.

Cotton Mather thus showed himself to be a particular type of Puritan—one who sympathized with religious enthusiasm.[148] In addition, while Mather's outreach to English-speaking Protestants has been extensively documented, now evident is the significance of the scope of Mather's interaction in this regard with French Protestants.[149] The collaboration of Mather and Carré on the *Echantillon* is a good example of such an alliance.[150] Mather adopted a surprisingly unhegemonic stance vis-à-vis the possibility that other professions of the Christian faith in the New World might not only be acceptable to, but actually consistent with, Puritan ideology. The lack of recognition for his sponsorship of French Protestants attests to an unrecognized Anglocentric bias in colonial scholarship.[151] Mather's largely unexplored French connection sheds light on aspects of his personality and faith, and provides an important missing piece to his portrait and to the ethnohistorical understanding of this era in colonial American history.

In 1725, Mather went even further in his espousal of the French cause, publishing anonymously a tract entitled *Une Grande Voix du Ciel à la France*; again writing in French, Mather spoke on behalf of his French Protestant coreligionists, supplying them with a voice (*voix*) in their own tongue. He called it in his diary "an Instrument in the French Tongue, that is calculated for the Awakening of the people there."[152] Then minister of the Old North Church, Mather called for the French abroad to rebel against their oppressive Catholic monarch. He deliberately posed in this way as the *porte-parole*, the interpreter and translator of, and the midwife to, the development of a distinctive French Protestant experiential idiom in the New World.

CHAPTER SEVEN

Elie Neau and French Protestant Pietism in Colonial New York

On August 20, 1697, Elie Neau, a prisoner for his faith, was forced into a gravelike cell. Air entered only through a tiny aperture; he could not walk or stand; and the hole was filled with excrement. Neau said that worms came from the walls and crawled along his body. Yet even in such circumstances, he did not despair: "My God mocks the attempts of my persecutors. I can hear His voice in my heart, telling me, as He told the prophet Isaiah, . . . 'Lift up your voice like a trumpet . . . and declare the riches of My mercy' . . . And I am utterly convinced that . . . God will cover me with His Providence even until the end."[1]

The Life of a Confesseur

Neau was born in Saintonge in 1662. He taught himself to read and to write. Although of fairly humble beginnings, as a young man he became a sailor, like many Rochelais, and eventually became quite a wealthy merchant, trading from his home port of La Rochelle across the Atlantic. He also traveled extensively in the south of France, where he came to know many Camisards. When the *dragonnades* began, he decided to go to the Americas and work as a sailor off the island of Hispaniola.

After the Revocation of the Edict of Nantes, he fled to Boston. There he became a naturalized British citizen. He met, and married, Suzanne Paré, a French refugee, in Boston in 1686. They settled in New York in 1690. By 1692, he had been given command of a merchant ship.

Shortly after the birth of his first son, while Neau was on a return voyage to London from New York in 1692, he was captured by a privateer belonging to the French navy. On being identified as a French Protestant, he was remanded to France, where he was sentenced to the galleys.[2] To be released, he would have had to sign an oath abjuring his Reformed faith: at the time, any criminal imprisoned for any act whatsoever could obtain release by signing such an abjuration.[3] Neau refused, in staunch Calvinist fashion quoting Mark 8:36 as his response: "What shall it profit a man, if he shall gain the whole world, and lose his own soul?"[4]

Put on trial "for having followed Jesus,"[5] Neau again refused to convert, and when told to choose between "death or the Mass,"[6] he chose "chains," invoking, as Camisards often did, the need to preserve his "conscience": "We must never obey or try to please men above what God asked of us . . . God alone has power over our souls, and our consciences are answerable only to Him."[7] Taken in irons to a galley at anchor in Marseille, he arrived on the day of Pentecost, a meaningful date for a man who was to become a "spiritist."

Neau spent the next several years chained to the ship, shoulder to shoulder with other galley slaves, whom he strove always to encourage and comfort, sharing the gospel through preaching, prayers, and song. His constant prayer was that God would grant him "pleasure in this pain, in oppression and persecution . . . for Your Name's sake . . . May Your love enable me to bear with joy the most cruel torture . . . May I find the way to glorify You through my suffering."[8] Neau found a paradoxical freedom in his bondage, stating that his chains liberated him: whereas before he had been bound by sin, in chains his opportunity to sin was felicitously denied. He said, "I understand now that true freedom consists in being freed from sin."[9] Shackled, he could be shaped "in conformity with Christ."[10]

Neau was eventually placed in a solitary confinement cell at Marseille for his steadfast refusal to abjure his faith. Known as the "galley preacher," he converted many by his ardor and his insistence on passive resistance, a tactic typical of the early stage of the Camisard experience, and one that distinguished him from the activist, militant piety of his coreligionists later in the Camisard uprising.[11]

Aware that many of the Reformed faith were saving their lives but losing their souls by abjuring, Neau, while still in solitary confinement, inveighed against such behavior and against Catholicism, citing many of the same "abuses" as those listed by Camisard coreligionists. He denounced, among other things, the veneration of the Virgin, the intercession of saints, the repetition of the Mass, and the blasphemous addition to the liturgy of ceremonies that were not scripturally derived: "I don't accept the errors of Rome, and I don't participate in its idolatrous worship . . . I'm no Papist; I keep my heart clean for God . . . They go to Mass, as if the Temple of Abominations and God's Temple were one and the same. They receive the 'so-called' Mass . . . and their lying preachers do not hesitate to come into the place where Christ is every day crucified yet again."[12]

It was specifically to vex the Protestants that "Mass was celebrated on board the galley ships; even on the galley ships of the pope the Mass was not celebrated, and in France it never had been before the Revocation, but only after

1685."[13] Because of Neau's firm convictions, willingness to preach the Gospel, and courageous, exemplary behavior, he converted many men on board the galley.

> His long-suffering patience in the face of all trials marvelously inspired all those who witnessed it. His pious Christian speeches drew the attention of the entire galley; the example of a saintly, religious life, accompanied by the kindness that is the true nature of Christianity, caused even the most hardened of scoundrels to admire him; his hatred for evil; his constant concern to convert evildoers and to inspire a holy life in the heart of the corrupt; caused . . . many to give their lives to God and convert . . . And this enraged the Chaplain of the Galley . . . because he could see in what contempt Neau held Rome.[14]

He labored in the heat and inhuman conditions of the galleys for six years, chained with 200 other *forçats*.[15] Neau's strong faith enabled him to endure despite the treatment that he and the other prisoners, mostly Camisards, received. Their treatment was especially inhumane: "The revolt in the Cévennes caused the intensity of punishments to be increased."[16]

A Catholic priest caused Neau to be placed in irons in solitary confinement on the ship.[17] Yet Neau continued his passive resistance, bellowing hymns and reciting psalms at the top of his lungs, earning him violent retaliation and frequent beatings.[18] Seeing himself as an illustration of 1 Corinthians 1:27—"God has chosen the weak things of the world," he reminded his fellow prisoners, "[in order] to put to shame the things which are mighty."[19]

On May 5, 1694, Neau was taken from the galley to prevent him from proselytizing and placed in solitary confinement on land, first in a high tower for several months, then in a tiny cell with no light. He was finally confined with three other men, again without light or anything to read or any writing materials. By what he called a miracle, Neau somehow came into possession of a Bible, which he succeeded in hiding from his jailers. According to Pastor Morin, a Reformed Walloon minister and Neau's faithful correspondent, in July 1696, "when he was brought in to the prison of the notorious Château d'Y[f], and in his cell there, God blinded those who inspected him so that they should not see this precious book which would henceforth so console him."[20]

The most formidable French prison of the time, the Château d'Yf, a tower built by François I in 1524 three kilometers off the coast of Marseille, was used for the first time as a prison in 1588, specifically to incarcerate "heretics." This was where most Camisards were sent, and this was where Neau was confined.[21] He endured six months of solitary confinement in a cell the size and shape of his body, was denied all light, and was forced to defecate beneath his own body. Neau survived by loudly singing hymns of praise all day long. He also shouted through the wall to other prisoners, exhorting them to remain strong in their faith: "The galley, the cells, the wood, the stone, everything conveys the suffering of our fellow believers. So why should we remain silent? Besides, should we not lift up, rejoice with, and console these brothers in setting before them such beautiful examples of [spiritual athletes] who emerge victorious from their trials?"[22]

Later, Neau was put with three Camisard prisoners in a lightless cell intended to house only one person. In later writings, Neau provided biographical sketches of his fellow Camisard prisoners, mentioning the piety of Pierre Lansonniére; some others "who converted to true religion";[23] and a young man of twenty-eight who was converted by another Camisard, Monsieur Carriére, and who "was so well thoroughly converted that he would never again turn to the Catholic church. They took his New Testament away from him . . . and persecuted me [for having given it to him.]"[24] Neau and the other prisoners practiced Camisard piety, which was communal, like that of the early Christian church; they shared the little that they possessed: "We had nothing privately owned, but rather put everything together for the common good."[25]

Neau was able occasionally to have letters smuggled out of prison for him, and also, infrequently, to receive response to them. While the fidelity of Pastor Morin, serving a Walloon congregation in exile in Beropzoom, did much to validate Neau's faith, it was really Neau's fervor, and almost mystical appreciation of the sacrificial nature of Christ's love, that invigorated the pastor and the churches among which he circulated Neau's missives.[26] Neau made extraordinary statements that attested to the strength of his conviction. He asserted that he was in prison by God's grace[27] and he denied prison's ability to restrain his faith.[28]

An important letter, dated November 5, 1696, to Pastor Morin provided a description of the sufferings inflicted on Neau and set the tone for the remainder of his imprisonment—and of his life after his release. In language reminiscent of the great Christian mystics of the *via negativa*, Neau, whom the prison guards were attempting to starve into recanting, fed on Christ's wounds and word: "This caused me to be sunk into an awareness of my own nothingness . . . Then I began to experience the effect of God's promises . . . I felt grace flowing over me; I felt bathed in a river of holy delights . . . God opened to me the five wounds of my Redeemer to bathe away in them the impurities of my soul."[29]

Neau's steadfastness continued to manifest itself. One letter from prison was triumphantly labeled "Du Camp du Seigneur ("From the Camp of the Lord")."[30] Even in confinement, Neau saw himself as participating in the fight for the Reformed faith, asserting that by "fighting against those who . . . would oppose my salvation, I serve in the true Christian militia."[31] Later, removed from solitary confinement, he named his fellow prisoners, calling the Christian society in their cell "the true Promised Land" ("la vraye Canaan"); they included Paul Ragatz, a Swiss, in chains for ten years for his faith; Antoine Capion, a Camisard from Montpellier; a forty-year-old minister from Switzerland; and Jean Mognier, another Camisard, a young man of twenty-six from the Cévennes who had been sent to the galleys for his refusal to recant, and then to prison.[32]

Endowed with great spiritual resources, Neau also proved capable of considerable practical action. He managed to find ways to procure a stub of candle and a bit of paper, and to send in secret a few letters to a church in Belgium whose pastor he knew. On November 11, 1695, for example, he wrote: "My sweet Jesus promises to render a hundredfold to those who forsake everything for the love of him. But I say, while praising him, that he gives even more to me, for he makes me prefer one moment of being with him to a longer, more peaceful life on earth without him. My prison has been wondrously changed into a place of liberty."[33]

On July 3, 1698, Neau's unwavering faith received its reward. He was pardoned by Louis XIV after the intercession of William III, the king of England, and released immediately. Nearly blind from the years he had spent in darkness—though he always invoked God's light and the illumination of the Holy Spirit in his letters[34]—Neau traveled to Marseille to reunite with Camisard fellow believers, then to Orange, where he was greeted by a multitude of coreligionists celebrating his release: "The gathering of such a large flock of the faithful filled him with such joy . . . Neau mingled his joy with that shared by the faithful. And all that could be heard was prayers of thanksgiving and pious discourses concerning the great miracles that God had worked."[35] From Orange, Neau went to Lyons, "where he found a remnant [of believers] who received him most warmly";[36] then, leaving France "as if leaving cruel Egypt"[37] and entering Switzerland, he found in Geneva "another Canaan, flowing with the milk and honey of the Gospel."[38] Neau was welcomed by the Reformed ministers of Geneva.[39]

As though to claim the Continent for Calvinism through the physical imprint of his foot, Neau then journeyed to several of the evangelical Swiss cantons, spending some time in Bern, where he pleaded for help for his fellows languishing in prison.[40] He embarked on a preaching and proselytizing tour of Europe, obtaining personal audiences with William III to petition for the release of fellow believers still in prison. In a letter to Neau dated September 10, 1696, Ragatz, writing on behalf of himself and the other two Camisards still incarcerated, declared his faith in Neau to plead their case: "Only those who have been truly illumined by saving grace, who have truly been made participants in the action of the Holy Spirit, and who have truly tasted that sweetness of the

Good News [can help us] . . . You are Lazarus called forth from the tomb."[41] By calling Neau "illuminé," Ragatz recognized the Huguenot Neau as one of the Camisards' own, one who had received the "light of saving grace" like other Camisard inspirés. Neau was ultimately effective in obtaining the release of Ragatz and the other Camisard prisoners.

Neau was hailed as a model and a hero by other French Protestants. His example was explicitly invoked by other Protestant galley slaves. Notably, a band of such men penned a document to regulate their conduct and maintain their faith in the time of trial. Entitled "Règlements faits sur les galères de France par les Confesseurs qui souffrent pour la vérité de l'Evangile," the text, penned in 1699 and signed primarily with Camisard patronyms (Serres, Domouyn, Pelecuer, Valette, Allix, Bancillon, Peraud, Masseton, Maurin, Gonin, Lardant), offered a pledge of "mutual support and encouragement," referring to how "l'illustre Monsieur Elie Neau," recently freed from confinement, had proselytized other galley slaves. The document included, among other guidelines, a provision for ministering to fellow French Protestant galley slaves about to die.[42]

Neau continued to play a role as public advocate for persecuted French Protestants, leaving France for Holland. In September 1697, he informed William III, who was paying a diplomatic visit there, of the plight of his fellow Camisards still in prison. Neau went to London next, and then sailed for New York, where he was reunited with his wife and two children, one of whom had been a mere infant when his father was sent to the galleys. There, he was acclaimed by the French Church of New York as a model confesseur of the Reformed faith: "You did not hide; you did not swerve; you never changed your faith . . . You loudly declared without fear or equivocation that you would have no religion but that of Jesus Christ . . . You are an example of the efficaciousness of grace."[43]

In 1705 Elie Neau was "conformed" to the Church of England in America. The piety of the church he attended was Reformed, close to that of his Calvinist roots, its Anglican liturgy notwithstanding.[44]

"Camisard" Cantiques

During his incarceration, Neau, despite having no pen or paper, had composed a book of spiritual poetry and songs. These cantiques—called by Walloon pastor Morin "testimonials of faith"—were eventually published as the Histoire abbregée des souffrances du sieur Elie Neau (1701).[45] Cotton Mather translated Neau's spiritual songs and cantiques from French to English, and published them together with one of Neau's letters from prison to his wife under the title A Present from a Farr Countrie. Mather regarded Neau as a model Christian. In his preface, Mather exhorted readers to model their piety after Neau's. He published Neau's works in English in 1698, before the French original appeared in print. It is likely that Mather issued Neau's work first in English because the climate in the colonies was not then propitious for publication in French.

Mather himself seems to have penned poetry similar in idiom to Neau's: "While I was lying on the Couch in the Dusk of the Evening I extempore composed the following Hymn, which I then sang unto the Lord: . . . 'I will not any Creature love / But in the love of Thee Above.'" "I deigned rather pietie than poetry in these lines," Mather continued, concerned to justify his writing theologically.[46]

Neau began the account of his tribulations at approximately age thirty-eight. The published version included his narrative, letters from correspondents, copies of his responses, and a concluding body of *cantiques* that he wrote to praise God even in the midst of his trials. Many phrases in Neau's *cantiques* recalled *The Song of Solomon*. John Calvin refused to write a commentary on this biblical book, his objection being that its language was too sensual and mystical, and therefore unsuitable for Christian meditation. It is therefore striking that the Huguenot Neau adopted such an idiom. This choice bolsters the case for Camisard influence on his piety.

Illiterate until early adulthood, Neau taught himself to read and write so that he could draft biblical meditations and compose hymns. While imprisoned with Camisard confessors, Neau was much compelled by their testimonies. Neau's own spiritual expression itself took on an ecstatic tenor similar in tone both to Camisard prophecy and to the raptures recounted in Mather's journals. Mather may have been a sympathetic first audience in part because he had himself composed spiritual songs as a young man.

Neau's Camisard sympathies can be heard distinctly in his *cantiques*: several of these spiritual songs praise the power of the Holy Spirit, such as his "Oraison au Saint Esprit, sur le chant du Pseaume 42." Neau embodied the Camisard strand of Calvinism in urging passive resistance and a mystical acceptance of God's Providence, a willed absorption of the believer into the overflowing fullness of the Spirit:

Come, Holy Spirit, whom I adore,
In your love, please, me absorb . . .
Plunge into your immensity
All my [small] capacity,
And may I in your fullness
Find there all my surcease.[47]

Neau's text is a masterpiece of mystical literature that also provides a wealth of documentation on the experiences of galley slaves. His collection echoes Camisard themes: poverty, suffering, exaltation of the lowest, Christ found in affliction. These all evoked the helpless Camisard peasant sustaining himself—

and his community—through fervent lay enthusiasm, and contrasted with the rational exposition of doctrine propounded through an institutional church, an approach more characteristic of Huguenots.

An engraving entitled *Elias Neau in the Dungeon*, published in London in 1749 to accompany a brief biography of Neau and a selection of his writing, adds evidence to the case for Camisard influence.[48] The illustration appeared in a tract entitled *A Short Account of the Life and Sufferings of Elie Neau*.[49] It is significant that the title made no effort to discern between Huguenot and Camisard, speaking only of "French Protestants," communicating thereby the powerful sympathy that the Huguenot Neau had for the Camisard experience.

In this image, Neau prayerfully and patiently abides in a tiny, bleak prison cell. Through the slats of the barred door stream rays of light that appear to provide consolation and spiritual illumination. Neau's bare feet, shoeless like those of the impoverished and ill-clad Camisards, stretch toward the door as though he were about to embark on an interior, spiritual journey. He wears a "heretic's hat" derisively adorned with a dancing devil, but his proud, patriarch-like bearded face shows only serenity in the face of adversity. His hands are joined in prayer. The illustration accurately encapsulates what Neau himself had to say about his prison experience: "I beg you to try to imagine what kind of life a man can have in a cell with no light but that which comes through the crack in the door; my window had been blocked up . . . Everyone was forbidden to speak to us . . . There was no fire, no candle . . . But I tell you that deprived of the light of the sun, we nonetheless had the rays of the sun of grace shining brilliantly in our hearts . . . What more can I say? I was in prison by the Grace of God."[50] The iconography of the image "support[s] the . . . millenial [*sic*] program of the . . . French Prophets."[51]

In his writing, Neau's accents were like those of the Camisard prophets who spoke in tongues upon receiving the gift of the spirit. His tone was almost rhapsodic, moving toward a willed and willing dissolution of the self in God: "May my spirit, my heart and my body be entirely dedicated to [God], and may He utterly subjugate my interior and my exterior to His will."[52] He further beseeched God, "O come make your dwelling in my soul and confirm me in your love, so that I may say day and night, 'I am with my beloved.' "[53] Like his Camisard fellow prisoners, he protected his freedom of conscience[54] so that he could glorify Christ in the correct way.[55] Also like the Camisard prophets, Neau was evangelical, urging no delay in repentance and conversion: "As you can see, my dear sister, my goal is to wrest your soul out of the arms of death. Come out of the tomb of your sins. Do not put your repentance off until tomorrow."[56] Neau found that more grace was granted as tribulations increased: "Suffering, rather than exhausting my courage, only made it increase. Grace always filled my heart with zeal and love."[57] And he discerned everywhere God's sheltering hand, extolling "the care that God's providence surrounds me with."[58]

Neau's was a life of exemplary piety. His publisher voiced the hope that "God willing, your example and your chains will contribute in some way to God working out his saving act [in the hearts of others]."[59] Thanks to Mather's midwifery, Neau's writing circulated throughout the colonies and on the Continent.[60] Consequently, Neau had an extensive influence on Huguenot congregations in the New World,[61] forging "links between intensely examined personal suffering and the receipt of God's grace" and fostering a "flowering of refugee piety that grew in the wake of [his] prison experience."[62]

Neau in the New World

The French Protestant refugees who came to the New World to seek religious freedom, freedom of conscience, and protection from persecution played a major role in shaping colonial America. In New York City in particular they contributed greatly to the development of governmental, social, and economic structures, and to shaping an ideology for the growing nation. Neau was one of the most important of the New York Huguenots. His writings "marked a renewal of Protestant piety through the Camisard metaphor in both America and Europe in the 1690s."[63] His personal involvement in matters of Protestant piety was extensive, formative for the faith of others, and influential: "Neau's immense importance for understanding the intense period of piety and revival among Huguenots in New York's French Church in the 1690s and the great significance of his work to influence the spiritual and material condition of the city's African slaves in the violent context of rebellion and reprisal in the early eighteenth century [must be acknowledged]."[64]

Neau was responsible for the revival of Protestant piety in the Middle Colonies, especially New York, at this time. Neau later attended an Anglican church,[65] where he had his daughter Suzanne baptized, an affiliation not uncommon at the time, since the Anglican Church had been in many quarters sympathetic to Reformed Protestantism and had espoused doctrines such as predestination and election. Neau was involved with many prominent social and political figures as well as religious leaders. He maintained a correspondence with Gabriel Bernon and served with him in the Society for the Propagation of the Gospel; he was also, of course, a friend of and publishing collaborator with Cotton Mather.[66] He began preaching to slaves in his role as catechist for the SPG.[67]

However, despite the warm reception that Huguenots gave Neau, their ardor cooled when he began to attend Anglican services in 1704.[68] Neau was convinced that this was the only way to secure the financial assistance and moral support of the Society for Promoting Christian Knowledge (SPCK), an Anglican body. Along with this new affiliation, Neau began to work to try to bring about some sort of collaboration among all the churches of New York; he was an early and ardent ecumenist.[69] At the same time, faithful to his French Protestant beliefs, Neau formed, and continued to participate in, a predominantly Huguenot Wednesday Devotional Society.[70]

The SPCK's support was necessary for Neau to fulfill his dream of opening a school for African slaves.[71] He caused a small chapel to be constructed on the upper floor of his own house, and there he taught black and Indian slaves as well as poor whites. This school has been deemed "the first rescue work in New York" and the "first school in America."[72] Neau identified with the plight of these indentured servants and slaves because of his ordeal as a galley slave, and believed that it was his Christian mission to perform this outreach, which he did with great success.[73] There was a significant riot of black slaves in New York in 1712, and whites threatened to kill Neau for his advocacy of their education and humane treatment. He weathered the trial, however, and persisted in his activities until the day he died.

In his will, Neau continued to be a faithful supporter of the Camisards, who had inspired him, providing, even after his death, for the perpetuation of the moral precepts he had learned as a galley slave.[74] He left $100 for the poor, $50 for the new pastor, Daniel Bondet, $50 for the pastor of the Church of Saint-Esprit, and $250 to keep in print fifty-two poems that he had written in French.

"A Habitation Elsewhere"

Huguenots, Camisards, and the

Transatlantic Experience

The case of the Cévennes Camisards is a neglected historical component of both European and colonial American narratives, one that warrants telling. Through the addition of this French dimension, the customary portrait of Protestantism in this period becomes more nuanced and complete. This inclusion enables scholars now to explore more fully the relationship between Huguenots and Camisards and to trace their impact on European and, especially, early American culture. Three influential French Protestant exiles provide focal case studies for informing and enlarging our understanding of the New World experience. Thanks to their presence and voices, scholars who had been limited to a sketched profile of our nascent nation can now see a complete face, thoroughly fleshed out, that incorporates the French dimension and delineates Cotton Mather's French connection.

The piety and prophecy of French Protestants profoundly influenced the culture, religiosity, and polity of Europe and the New World. Their belief system intersected in dialogue with Puritanism and prepared the ideological content (freedom of speech, freedom of conscience) for Enlightenment understandings of the appropriate relationship between church and state. French Protestantism contributed theologically, aesthetically, and socially to the pre-Revolutionary colonial context.

Huguenots and Camisards: Common Ancestry, Changed Circumstances

During the latter half of the sixteenth century, the Wars of Religion convulsed France as Protestants, influenced by the teachings of Martin Luther and organized by the administrative genius of John Calvin, tore themselves away from their former Catholic adherence. They had come to believe Roman Catholicism to be unscriptural. The king and others in positions of power increasingly perceived these French Protestants, or Huguenots, to be a threat. Although part of the body politic, Huguenots embodied what was viewed as a form of "possession": they represented the demon that lurked at the heart of the nation-state. Soon, official policy was aimed at extirpating French Protestants. Royal troops under Henri II and Henri III were deployed against a significant por-tion of the king's own subjects, committing atrocities in the name of Christ (and king). As civil war divided France, John Calvin, who had fled to Geneva, devised a coherent way to organize Calvinists in Switzerland, training some of them as pastors to be sent secretly to France, there to nurture covertly an ecclesiological counterculture despite the systematic persecution being waged against French Calvinists.

From the beginning, the hallmark of the Huguenots was the seriousness with which they received and interpreted scripture. Their reading of the Bible was often very sophisticated, and the debates in which they engaged among themselves often relied on rational discourse that deployed "proof texts" and counterarguments based on scriptural loci, imitating the meticulous structure of a lawyer's brief. This legalistic and rationalistic frame of mind would reach its apogee in Reformed Protestantism in the New World a couple of centuries later, and still characterizes some strands of modern Protestant thought. The Huguenots thus offer a form of scriptural dependence—and, for the Camisards, reliance on scriptural literalism—associated with adherence to the virtue of freedom of conscience, a stance resulting in much humanitarian and reformist work on their part once they found a haven in the New World.

Henri IV finally quelled the religious hostilities, at least on the surface, by forswearing his Protestant faith in order to appease predominantly Catholic Paris and thus win the allegiance of the majority of the French; he promulgated the Edict of Nantes in 1598. This arrangement was, at best, one of grudging and very limited toleration. While unofficial persecution continued, more than lip service was now accorded to Protestant subjects, who experienced unprec-edented liberty in which to celebrate their faith. This continued, for the most part, throughout the reign of Louis XIII. However, Louis XIV, urged on by his morganatic wife Madame de Maintenon and by his minister Richelieu, as well as by the very powerful group of Jesuit advisors at the court, came to view Protestants as unorthodox and undesirable. Particularly worrisome to him was the establishment of the Calvinist state of William of Orange after the Peace of Ryswick. As early as 1685, concerned that his French Protestant subjects might leave the country and support a Calvinist regime against him, Louis XIV issued orders forbidding Huguenot emigration. Pushed by Catholic clergy and espe-cially by Jesuit hard-liners, he further mandated conversion to Catholicism, revoking the Edict of Nantes in 1685 with the Edict of Fontainebleau in 1698.

Despite the prohibition against leaving France, many Huguenots on the west-ern seaboard profited from their proximity to the English Channel and fled to London, taking with them their wealth and their expertise as skilled craftsmen and merchants. Others scattered to the Low Countries, Belgium, Switzerland, and elsewhere, such as the island of Martinique.

In the southeast of France, long a Huguenot bastion, the socioeconomic plight of French Protestants was somewhat different. Unlike many Huguenots elsewhere in France, the southeastern Huguenots were not usually noble or bourgeois. The Camisards thus evidenced an experiential as well as a geographical distinction from other Huguenots. In addition, their history after the time of the Cévennes War (1701–1705) had a slightly different storyline from that of the Huguenots, although both started as Calvinists with the same sort of ecclesiastical formation. While there were some differences engendered by the dire straits in which Camisards found themselves, the preponderance of Camisard piety manifested a faithful Calvinist theological understanding. A heightened form of pietistic religious expression developed among the Camisards, however, in response to a climate of severe persecution and their geographical isolation from the rest of France, Geneva, and the world.

The distinctive experience of the Huguenots' Camisard "cousins" became more apparent when several thousand Huguenot refugees went to the New World. In England, Huguenots from the earlier "First Refuge," during the 1610s and 1620s, had already established cohesive French Protestant institutions known as the "Stranger Churches." Thus, for those later Huguenots who managed to flee to England, churches like the Threadneedle Church in London were already there to receive them, practicing piety along the lines of the Calvinist consistory model with which the Huguenots had been acculturated. Not much changed for these emigrants. They were even able to maintain membership on the rolls of the dominant Anglican Church while being active members in their own French Church, a "successful straddling of French and English worlds . . . [that] did not necessarily entail for these immigrants and their children a concomitant abandonment of the French church and the community it represented."[1] Similarly, in the Low Countries, well-established French or Walloon churches existed already, complete with relief programs and a recognizable Calvinist order of service: "The Protestants who fled from France to the northern Netherlands found there not only a society prone to accept them as brothers of the same faith, but also a fully developed system of assistance, accustomed to help persecuted co-religionists, and indeed an organized Reformed church using the same language and liturgy, and working with similar institutions as in their homeland."[2] Huguenots in the Low Countries had to adapt to a new geographical location, but not a significantly changed religious, or even social, context.

The case was somewhat different for those Huguenots, and the few surviving Camisards, who eventually came to the British colonies in North America. No French church had yet been established there, and those that were built up struggled mightily to maintain a toehold in, for instance, Puritan Boston. Most of these churches did not survive beyond a generation.

New World, New Models

When attempting to analyze how Huguenots in the New World adapted to their surroundings while still struggling to maintain their confessional distinctiveness—the very reason for their immigration—a good starting point is to aver that the refugees developed a theology of exile. However, it is also useful to describe the actual mechanisms by which the Huguenots maintained their identity. Religious identity remained significant for Huguenots in exile; cultural identity, while a factor, was subordinate to it. To one who had been reared in a faith system in which right believing was the standard for salvation (and heterodoxy meant damnation), cultural identity alone did not suffice. Even the notion of "freedom of conscience," so dear to both Huguenots and Camisards, derived from their understanding of their faith: they were obliged to render ultimate obedience to God alone—and not to caesar or worldly authorities. Therefore, it is imperative to understand how the Huguenots used the paradigm of Camisard experience—the perseverance of religious identity in the midst of dire deprivation of the institutional resources designed precisely to enable such perpetuation—in their changed, New World context.

For Huguenots in the New World, a strategy of adaptation was required that was, in some ways, different from what was needed in England or the Netherlands. This strategy was also different from those used by sixteenth-century Huguenots during the Wars of Religion. During the earlier period under the Edict of Nantes, nominal parity had existed between Catholics and Protestants, with, for instance, the existence of judicial *chambres mi-parties* (bipartisan courts); in places like Dieppe and La Rochelle, the Huguenot population was actually at times the majority population. However, in the British colonies, French Protestants experienced what it meant to be a minority. They then could turn to the model of the Camisard experience for survival tactics—for the Camisards had been a persecuted minority.

Consequently, in the New World, the more traditionally Calvinist Huguenot refugees borrowed the paradigm that their Camisard cousins had enacted out of desperation. Deprived of clergy and the institutional means of worship, as the Camisards had been, and finding themselves in a distinctly anti-French environment, they resorted to what sociolinguists have called a strategy of code shifting. Code shifting enables the negotiation of two different worlds in the same space. The language or way of behaving most immediately needed is accessed and adapted to circumstances.

Huguenots adopted the Camisard strategy of speaking one way to the authorities and another way to family, one way to strangers on the street and another way to coreligionists. They adapted by reviving the Camisard ploy of intensely personal and individualistic religious observance, primarily in private: when no church is present and few ministers are available, the household becomes the locus of piety, and the individual believer its practitioner. Raymond Mentzer has shown that "an insistence on social discipline—the meticulous reform and supervision of all aspects of communal life—was as important to the Reformation as traditional considerations such as the rethinking of theological positions or the revision of prayer and the liturgy."[3]

This was the standard that persisted in London and in the refugee congregations in the Netherlands. But although it was initially the experience of the Camisards, it did not remain so: their church structures were demolished and their instruments for social control destroyed. In their absence, the Camisards substituted a more intensely personalistic piety and a more military model of governance as they threw themselves into guerrilla fighting against the king's troops. In a context of ethnic cleansing, they placed the need to experience signs and wonders over concerns for exerting social control. Prophets either led their fellow laymen into battle or acted as channels for words of reassurance from the Holy Spirit; social control could hardly be a priority when actual physical survival was threatened.

While some Huguenots in the New World preserved their faith but assimilated through marriage or by church membership in other denominations, most often Anglican, this does not mean that their religious identity was no longer important for these refugees. Their writings and life choices show, in fact, that religious identity remained a very important factor for them, but that they preserved it in more underground or internalized ways. They were then able to integrate into the dominant culture but still retain their identity before God.

In this way, the Camisard strategy of covert worship and personal, ecstatic piety from the periphery, rather distrusted by the more rule-bound continental Calvinists such as those in Geneva and London, became the paradigm for the survival and perpetuation of French Protestant identity by and for Huguenots in the New World. It is therefore especially important to examine the Camisard experience in detail, since they were first Huguenots, conformed to the institutional Calvinist church, then forced to become lay leaders and preachers and inspired individuals. And just as that model was being eradicated from Western Europe, their Huguenot cousins who had looked rather askance at Camisard enthusiasm adopted some of its techniques in a play for self-preservation. This adaptation had profound, long-lasting ramifications:

Huguenots helped achieve religious pluralism in America . . . In America, there would be a religion for every person and a person for every religion. The individual, not the state, made spiritual choices. And the individual might create a religion when no acceptable alternative seemed available . . .

. . . Indeed it could be said that the capacity of American religion for . . . pluralism, and experimentation followed the history of colonial Huguenots writ large.[4]

While the French Protestant experience stretched both literally and metaphorically "from a far country," finding its roots in France as well as in the kingdom of heaven, ultimately, the Camisard expedient seemed a very *American* choice.

NOTES

Introduction. Camisards and Huguenots

The epigraph may be translated this way: "That which is both the greatest strength and the greatest weakness of men of the [Protestant] Religion is the large number of fugitives who fled abroad."

1. Between 1680 and 1695, more than 160,000 French Protestants fled programmatic genocide in France, arriving in America and settling primarily in New York, Charleston, and Massachusetts, but also in smaller concentrations in numerous other parts of the colonies.

2. Gwynn, *Huguenot Heritage*, 2; see his chapter entitled "The Process of Assimilation."

3. Kamil, *Fortress of the Soul*; Cosmos, *Huguenot Prophecy*; Sparks and Van Ruymbeke, *Memory and Identity*; Vigne and Littleton, *From Strangers to Citizens*.

4. "La révolte camisarde, dans son originalité, peu de gens en ont parlé. Révolte populaire de style traditionnel, mais nimbée de la religiosité protestante, elle mêle dans un vaste mouvement des paysans, des artisans ruraux, des artisans urbains et des petits commerçants" (Garrison, *L'Edit de Nantes*, 267). [Very few have spoken of the Camisard rebellion in terms of its originality. A popular rebellion of traditional style, its Protestant character distinguished it, and it also drew together a wide and diverse group of peasants, rural and urban workers, and small shopkeepers.]

5. A forthcoming book by Caroline Lougee Chappell uses testimonials given by Huguenots who escaped to America when they were affiliating with new churches there, and Van Ruymbeke has worked on testimonials coming out of the London Threadneedle Church as well as some testimonials taken in South Carolina from Huguenots who fled there.

6. An additional worthwhile source on the French prophets is Garrett, *Spirit Possession and Religion*. See also these primary sources: *An Account of the French Prophets and their Pretended Inspirations*; *An Account of the Present Condition of the Protestants in the Palatinate*; *The English and French Prophets mad or bewitcht*. Jon Butler provided me with these references and much other guidance.

7. Randall Balmer observes that one "distinctive" of Methodism was precisely that it devised an apparatus by which to survive nineteenth-century industrialism (in conversation with the author, May 2006).

8. There are New World parallels to this strategy too. Among the early colonial Dutch, Frelinghuysen and the "New Lights" adopted a pietistic worship that rejected the Old World ecclesiastical apparatus. The Dutch New Light colonists, like the Camisards, chose their leaders according to spiritual criteria.

9. "Proceedings of the General Assembly held for the Colony of Rhode Island and Providence Plantation, at Providence, the 3d day of November, 1716.... Gabriel Bernon, having exhibited a petition before this Assembly, wherein were divers foul charges

against Capt. John Eldredge, an assistant of this colony; and the matter being duly debated, the said Capt. John Eldredge was deemed innocent of the slanders . . .

"The Assembly do order the said Gabriel Bernon to sign two acknowledgements; the one, for his causelessly charging Capt. Eldredge, and the other for contemptuously and disorderly behaving himself before the said Assembly . . .

"I, Gabriel Bernon, do hereby acknowledge myself to have causelessly charged Capt. John Eldredge . . . and that I am heartily sorry for the same, and desire him to forgive me my fault in so doing . . . Gabriel Bernon, November 2d, 1716." Bartlett, *Records of Rhode Island*, 213–15.

10. See Noll, *Rise of Evangelicalism*, 24.

11. See Balmer, *Perfect Babel of Confusion*, 208; see also Cohen, "Elias Neau," and Hewitt, "New York's Black Episcopalians."

12. Porterfield, *Feminine Spirituality in America*.

13. Godbeer, *Escaping Salem*.

14. Lovelace, *American Pietism of Cotton Mather*, 32.

15. There is no mention by Lovelace at all of Mather's involvement with the French, yet his involvement is a matter of historical record; see Lovelace, *American Pietism of Cotton Mather*.

16. Stein, *Shaker Experience*, 5.

17. "Il n'y a point de paroisse qui n'ait été bien nettoyée." Abbé Basville, quoted in the Jesuit Meynior's *De l'exécution de l'édit de Nantes dans le bas Languedoc* (1662), which describes a programmatic strategy to "eat up the adversary" ["grignoter l'adversaire"].

18. Balmer, *Mine Eyes Have Seen*.

19. See Balmer, *Thy Kingdom Come*.

20. See the works by Randall Balmer and Mark Noll listed in the bibliography for discussions of the development and evolution of the American evangelical subculture.

Chapter One. Crisis in the Cévennes

A version of this chapter appeared under the title "Reforming Calvinism" in *Fides et Historia*.

1. "Trouva avant hier dix ou douze hommes ensemble dont un lisoit la Bible et quelques uns se baignoient dans une rivière. Les Miquelets tirèrent un peu de trop loin . . . et en blessèrent deux, entr'autres celui qui tenoit la Bible; et comme c'étoit un endroit près d'un bois dans les rochers, ils se sauvèrent" (quoted in the preface to Bonbonnoux, *Mémoires*, 3).

2. Bonbonnoux, *Mémoires*, 3.

3. Garrison, *L'Edit de Nantes*, 269.

4. "Le vide intense d'un champ religieux, la privation d'identité de tout un peuple pour lequel le protestantisme était culture, ethnique, organisation sociale et politique. Dire aussi que ces gens viennent de subir les dragons, les temples brûlés ou livrés aux flammes, toute une immense blessure/traumatisme qui a coupé court le fil de leur histoire" (ibid., 266).

5. Baum, *Mémoires*, 7–8.

6. Garrison, L'Edit de Nantes, 191.

7. "Je te dis mon enfant" (Jacques Mazel, quoted in Misson, Le Théâtre sacré des Cévennes [1707], part I, 79).

8. "De la part de Dieu" (Bost, Mémoires inédits, 5–6).

9. "Partout où cet Esprit de Dieu était répandu, les personnes qui le recevaient et ceux qui fréquentaient ces personnes-là devenaient soudainement gens de bien; ceux même dont la vie avait été auparavant déréglée" (ibid., 79).

10. While much work remains to be done on the dragonnades, some very helpful information is provided by Labrousse, "Calvinism in France."

11. Louis XIV had hoped in this way to put an end to Reformed worship by denying Protestants worship sites. This tactic, however, underscores his (and other Catholics') ignorance of Protestant piety, for as the temples were burned to the ground, small "ateliers," or Bible studies, sprang up in homes and throughout the community. Piety went underground.

12. The measures did not affect the Camisards exclusively: for instance, a copy of Claude Brousson's sermon attesting to the depredations of the dragoons, penned in 1692, has been catalogued among the private effects of a Cévennol family. See Cosmos, Huguenot Prophecy, 41.

13. See the story of Gabriel Bernon in the present study for an example of a Huguenot who fled to England.

14. "The Camisard insurrection of the first decade of the eighteenth century . . . tied up a complete French army under Marshal de Montrevel, even though the Camisards received little external assistance" (Gwynn, Huguenot Heritage, 150).

15. The term "Huguenot" is used for Calvinists in France. "Calvinists" can refer either to those French who left for Switzerland and practiced Protestantism according to Calvin's prototype there, or to second-generation Protestants—in England or on the Continent—following Calvin.

16. For prayer practices, see Hugues Villars, Correspondance, cited in Crété, Les Camisards, 201.

17. See Crété, Les Camisards, 164.

18. Although the doctrine of predestination is present in Augustine and can be found in Calvin's Institutes, it took Beza, Calvin's successor, to really systematize it; see Coats, Subverting the System, chapter 1.

19. "Ce n'est pas le grand nombre qui vous doit délivrer, ou délivrer l'Eglise. C'est le bras du Tout-Puissant, qui peut, qui fait délivrer, et qui le fait mieux faire avec un petit nombre qu'avec un plus grand, afin qu'à lui en soit toute la gloire" (Court, L'Histoire des troubles des Cévennes, 473–76).

20. In the preface to Elie Neau's Histoire abbrégée, his publisher states that the inspirational autobiography is "plein du langage de Canaan" (ii). The "langue de Canaan" is, effectively, an applied typology, the understanding that scripture is relevant to present circumstances (that God's word is always in dialogue with his people) and can be applied, as such, in an instructive and illuminating fashion.

21. Two Protestant museums known as the Musées du désert narrate the Camisard history through a collection of artifacts: the Musée du protestantisme in La Rochelle,

which displays artifacts from Huguenots during the Wars of Religion but which also includes some Camisard exhibits, and the Musée du désert, in the Cévennes, which displays objects used in the Camisard uprising.

22. "L'inspiration de la conscience" (Vauban, *Mémoire pour le Rappel*, 15).

23. Calvin had considerable investment in maintaining civic order, as was demonstrated by the Amy Perrin controversy and the burning of Michael Servetus. His work to structure and institutionalize the church in Geneva, solidified by followers such as Beza and Goulard, had long been complete by the time of the Camisard rebellion.

24. See Peter Iver Kaufman's thoughtful explanation of how even divine-right kings could forfeit, in the eyes of their Calvinist subjects, the right to be deemed "authorities" if they did not act in accordance with divine will, which was always subject to interpretation by any interested party (*Redeeming Politics*, 11–13).

25. On Laporte (active with a preaching ministry circa 1702), see Crété, *Les Camisards*, 94.

26. "Grignoter l'adversaire" (Meynior, quoted in Ducasse, *La Guerre des Camisards*, 25).

27. "Fuïr la rencontre du Curé, & l'entrée de l'Eglise" (from a sermon delivered in July 1702, quoted in Court, *L'Histoire des troubles des Cévennes*, 43).

28. "Ce ne sont que de misérables prédicants, cardeurs ou paysans, qui n'ont pas le sens commun . . . des gens fols et légers . . . qui persistent à affronter la mort sans nécessité" (Basville, *Mémoires*, quoted in Ducasse, *La Guerre des Camisards*, 27).

29. "Sortir de Babylone" (the Camisard strategy: flee, hide) contrasts with "bâtir les murs de Jérusalem" (the Huguenot strategy: build, construct). See Randall, *Building Codes*. For Jurieu, see *Lettres pastorales* of 1686.

30. "On les fera boire à long traicts, ou . . . on les mène en Amérique" (Demerez, *Mémoires*, quoted in Ducasse, *La Guerre des Camisards*, 72). This reference to America marks the beginning of a transcontinental connection for the Camisards.

31. It is significant that a young girl was first, since the Catholic Church admitted of no such involvement by women. The Camisard influence on John Wesley and Methodism begins here: Wesley encouraged female preachers (see Chilcote, *She Offered Them Christ*).

32. This is a demonstration of the availability of spiritual gifts, akin to the protodemocratic distribution of gifts among Quakers and Shakers: "From Cévennes in 1689, the exiled Camisards went forth over Europe and visited England in 1706. Here they were known as the French Prophets. Out of rhapsody and ecstatic emotion grew lives of purity and uprightness. The Quaker Church, a parallel movement, was remarkable for stillness before God till moved by the power of the Spirit. Some who were especially subject to spiritual influence upon the external being were called in derision 'Shaking Quakers' or 'Shakers'" (White and Taylor, *Shakerism*, 14). Camisards influenced such perceptions among Moravians and early Methodists also.

33. This myth persisted into the early twentieth century, as Knox's *Enthusiasm* demonstrates. Cilette Blanc also analyzes, then debunks, this story as Catholic propaganda ("Genève et les origines").

34. Cosmos, *Huguenot Prophecy*, 32–35.

35. See ibid., 50–51.

36. "Privés de la douceur évangélique, d'un culte régulier, de sermons ordonnés, d'une religion sensible mais raisonnable, les Cévennols vont se ruer dans l'illuminisme" (Brousson, *Relation*, quoted in Ducasse, *La Guerre des Camisards*, 56).

37. Sometimes, literacy was a basis for leadership; those who could read had greater access to scripture, which the Camisards respected. For instance, Rolland, a charismatic Camisard leader, carried a worn Bible with him, a precious and rare possession. Michelet recounted how this Bible was found after Rolland's death: "The Bible still had very visible wear marks and fingerprints from being often consulted. These marks were especially evident on pages that talked about God's anger at Nineveh and Babylon [for their sin]" (Michelet, cited by Ducasse, *La Guerre des Camisards*, 138). ["Elle porte encore très visibles l'usure et la marque des doigts rudes qui l'ont feuilletée. Les traces apparaissent surtout au bas des pages qui appellent l'ire de Dieu sur Ninive et Babylone."]

38. Misson, *Le Théâtre sacré des Cévennes* (1707), part I, 86.

39. "Inspirations . . . ont changé nos Agneaux en lions [et] nous ont suscitez, nous, la faiblesse mesme, pour mettre un frein puissant, à une armée de plus de vingt mille hommes d'élite" (testimony of Marion, cited in Misson, *Le Théâtre sacré des Cévennes* [1707], part I, 81).

40. "C'est là que le Tout-Puissant a fait des choses grandes . . . C'est là le terrible creuset où la verité & la fidelité des Saints Inspirez a esté esprouvée . . . lors mesmes qu'ils avoient les os brisez sur les rouës, ou que les flammes avoient déjà dévoré leur chair" (ibid., 81–82).

41. The majority suffered the latter fate, because of the constraints on flight already mentioned. This estimate appears inflated, but the figure is the one cited by Court (*L'Histoire des troubles des Cévennes*, 39).

42. "Jusques ici, les Protestans avoient souffert ces persecutions avec une patience . . . [et] se laissoient égorger . . . [ils n'en purent plus] (ibid., 38).

43. "Selon la loi du talion" (ibid., 74).

44. "Le jardin étoit l'Eglise; & les gros boeufs noirs, les Prêtres qui la dévoroient" (Mazel, quoted in ibid., 75).

45. "Mazel's story was . . . essential for an understanding of the origins of the war and the cause for which the Camisards fought in the *désert*. His portrayal of them as a kind of apocalyptic force of Christian soldiers who had been summoned to discharge the wrath of God, gave substance to the *inspirés*' Cévennol past" (Cosmos, *Huguenot Prophecy*, 104).

46. Abraham Mazel, one of the original Camisard leaders and one of the few to survive, ultimately left in disgust for London, revolted by Rolland's compromises. He attempted to revive the rebellion first from abroad, then again in the Cévennes after Rolland's fall from power.

47. "Chez lui, la politique a tué le mystique" (Ducasse, *La Guerre des Camisards*, 165).

48. Court, *L'Histoire des troubles des Cévennes*, 93.

49. Ibid., 99.

50. "L'ordre de Dieu . . . d'aller secourir [ses] Fréres" (Cavalier, quoted in ibid., 108).

51. "La Religion dans laquelle ils estoient nés, devoit leur être plus précieuse que la vie, & qu'il falloit exposer celle ci, pour se procurer le libre exercice de celle là" (Cavalier, quoted in ibid., 109).

52. "Loin de [les effrayer], on anima [les Camisards] de plus en plus, & l'on augmenta le nombre de Mécontens" (ibid., 114).

53. The plight of Génolhac was emblematic of terrible trauma: it was three times taken by the king's troops, and three times taken back and sacked.

54. This had happened only one other time in French history, when Innocent IX unleashed the northern Catholic nobles under Simon de Montfort against the southern Cathar heretics, launching an inquisition that eradicated the Cathars, or Albigensians, from Languedoc. In both cases, the Catholic Church deemed the targeted groups heretical; in both cases, the political interests of the ruling authorities were well served by such an assessment.

55. Enlightenment figures, greatly alarmed at this treatment of a peer, published the *Ecrits pour établir la necessité de secourir les Protestans des Cévennes*. Salgas spent thirteen years in the galleys, dying months after his release at the age of eighty. Camisards were treated worse than other galley slaves: "If the Huguenots were treated more severely than other galley slaves, Camisards were treated the worst of all" (Ducasse, *La Guerre des Camisards*, 203). ["Si les huguenots sont traités plus rigoureusement que les [autres] galériens, les Cévenols sont les plus mal traités [de tous]."]

56. Both tracts are mentioned in Dedieu, *Le rôle politique*.

57. Gédéon Laporte, quoted by Pin, *Un chef camisard*, 106n2.

58. "Celle-ci, clandestine, parfois dispersée par les troupes royales, possède le label du calvinisme bon teint, elle convient donc aux exigences de raison des protestants notables ou petits-bourgeois qui viendront là chercher les sacrements et écouter les prêches" (Garrison, *L'Edit de Nantes*, 268). ["The [Camisard worship assemblies], clandestine, sometimes broken up by the king's troops, were every bit as Calvinist as the Calvinist worship services; they had to be, to meet the demands of the bourgeoisie and Protestant bigwigs who came there to receive the sacraments and to listen to sermons."].

59. Tobie Rocayrol, quoted in Thomas, *Un agent des alliés*, 22–23.

60. The Camisards had female prophets. Calvin had tolerated female preachers for several years before finally forbidding the influential Huguenot street preacher Marie Dentières to preach in Geneva. See Katharina Wilson, *Women Writers of the Renaissance*, 260–69. Similarly, Jonathan Edwards capitalized on the enthusiastic piety of Phoebe, a young "inspired" girl in Northampton, Massachusetts, at the time of the Great Awakening.

61. "Vive Dieu et notre bon Roy! Fin du clergé!" (Antoine Court, folder 635, Manuscrit de Calvisson, fols. 24–25 and 27–29, Bibliothèque du protestantisme français, Paris).

62. Bonbonnoux served as a "minister of the Desert" ("pasteur du Désert") under the guidance of Antoine Court (*Mémoires*, 3). His autobiographical paraphrase of Luther reads: "Me voici. Je ne puis autrement. Que Dieu me soit en aide!" (*Mémoires*, i).

63. Since it was not possible to be baptized or married with any legal recognition unless the ceremony was Catholic, this sort of "nicodemist" lip-service conformity was fairly common.

64. The reference to Bonbonnoux is found in Rolland's correspondence, which is housed in the Bibliothèque de Genève in the papers of Antoine Court.

65. "Pour la gloire de Dieu et mon salut" (Bonbonnoux, *Mémoires*, 9).

66. "Nous priasmes Dieu et le jour et la nuit. Nous chantasmes des psaumes, nous lûmes l'Ecriture Sainte; et un jeune garçon . . . [de] dix-sept années, nous adressoit tous les jours une exhortation ou un [*sic*] espèce de sermon tiré de passages de l'Ecriture Sainte et qu'il accompagnoit de ses réflexions . . . notre dévotion était telle que j'étois ravi en admiration" (ibid., 11).

67. "Les exercices de piété estoient fréquens parmi nous. Nous avions des lecteurs . . . et surtout des prédicateurs . . . le peuple venoit de toute part pour les entendre. Bien souvent nous avions deux exhortations et prédications par jour. Nos courses étaient continuelles, rarement nous séjournions deux jours dans un même endroit. Les réformez des lieux circonvoisins où nous campions nous apportoient des vivres" (ibid., 14).

68. "Avant que de paroître devant les troupes, le sieur Daire, jeune prédicateur d'environ trente ans, nous exhorta avec beaucoup de zèle au combat et à la mort . . . Au chant du psaume LIe, entonné par le nommé Adam (soixante ans, cordonnier) . . . mon zèle étoit . . . grand" (ibid., 12–14).

69. "Peut-être que la chose ne paroîtra pas de même à tout le monde, mais elle nous paroissoit ainsi à nous, et nous la mîmes bien entre les sujets de nos actions de grâce" (ibid., 70).

70. "Dieu . . . les aveugla" (ibid., 73).

71. "Il le fit en effet . . . le soir même . . . c'étoit un songe . . . extraordinaire" (ibid., 75).

72. "Ce fut un miracle comme je peus me cacher" (ibid., 90). For an understanding of how Camisards discerned and interpreted miraculous occurrences, see Mullin, *Miracles and the Religious Imagination*, 18–20.

73. "Après souper, nous nous rendîmes publiquement au Temple de ce lieu, qui n'avoit pas été démoli . . . où nous fimes un exercice de Piété accompagné du chant des Psaumes et de la Prédication" (Bonbonnoux, *Mémoires*, 36).

74. " 'Tous nos prédicateurs sont morts ou rendus,' nous dit Claris tout attendri, 'que ferons-nous?'—Dieu y pourvoira, répliquai-je . . . Et cette réponse faite . . . donna occasion à Claris, en sortant un ABC de sa poche, de nous dire: 'Amis, allons étudier. Nous serons encore des ministres.' Quelle proposition pour des hommes qui ne savaient pas lire! . . . je dois vous dire néanmoins que . . . trois [d'entre nous] ont prêché l'Evangile dont par la grâce de Dieu, j'ai été du nombre" (ibid., 56).

75. "Le phanatisme du Réformé visionnaire" (ibid., 107).

76. "J'entends par là . . . de ne s'être pas rendus et d'avoir soutenus la foi" (ibid., 77).

77. "L'inspiration fut malheureusement fausse pour ce prophète" (ibid., 96).

78. "Ma soeur en Christ, je ne prends pas à honte l'Evangile de Jésus-Christ. C'est la puissance de Dieu" (ibid., 15).

79. "Ainsi le ministre de Jésus-Christ marche où Dieu l'appelle et regarde toutes choses comme de la fiente: Il méprise les biens et les aises de cette vie et il met sa confiance en Dieu en disant humblement, mais avec une haute assurance, 'l'Eternel est mon roc assuré'" (ibid.).

80. "C'est le courage que le Seigneur m'inspiroit qui m'a fait entrer tant de fois avec mes livres dans les bourgs et dans les villes; quelquesfois je les tirois de mon petit sac pour les remettre dans mes poches et dans mon sein; quelquesfois les enveloppant dans mon mouchoir, je les couvrois avec des herbes et les portois ensuite à la main en forme de salade . . . J'ai passé et repassé avec mes livres, j'ai été même arrêté avec quelques-uns, sans que l'ennemi me les aye découvers et sans qu'ils m'ayent jamais exposé à rien de fâcheux" (ibid., 111–12).

81. "Vingt-sept années et environ sept mois que j'ai vécu dans le désert" (ibid., 10). ["Twenty-seven years and seven months that I spent in the desert."]

82. Baum, *Mémoires*, 71.

83. "Le feu et le fer" (ibid., 2).

84. "Tout abandonner" (ibid.).

85. Depending on the social class to which a Camisard belonged, he might or might not be literate. Corteiz appears to have come from a bourgeois family. As farmers, the majority of Camisards were poorly schooled, even analphabetic.

86. "Rebut" (Baum, *Mémoires*, 10).

87. "Et tout à coup je me trouvais rempli de courage, et je parlai avec beaucoup de fermeté de la parole de Dieu. Dès lors je fus ardemment requis par les voisins de notre village" (ibid., 11).

88. Ibid., 7.

89. "Dieu retira la colonne de sa protection" (ibid., 8).

90. "Prétendus prophètes" (ibid., 26).

91. Ibid., 12.

92. "Je fis tous mes efforts pour l[e] détourner. M[on]sieu[r] me répondi[t] que l'Esprit de Dieu n'était pas menteur, et qu'il l[ui] avait déclaré que Dieu l['Javait chois[i] pour délivrer son Israël de la puissance de ces oppresseurs, que la victoire l[ui] était pleinement assurée" (ibid., 26).

93. "La nouvelle . . . m'affligea, mais je regardai cet événement comme tous les autres dirigés par la bonne providence" (ibid.).

94. "Je pris donc la liberté de leur aller représenter que tuer les prêtres, brûler les églises, cela n'était ni de la doctrine de l'Evangile, ni de la pratique des premiers chrétiens" (ibid., 12).

95. "Pour obéir à Jésus-Christ, qui nous dit, 'quand on vous persécutera dans un lieu, allez dans un autre'" (ibid., 5).

96. Many of the later Resistance fighters against the German occupation in World War II hid out in the maquis and were Protestants.

97. "Les Cévennes, dont la plupart était tombée en indifférence de religion, commencèrent à se réveiller, par le moyen de la prédication de l'Evangile" (ibid., 24).

98. "Ordre dans nos églises naissantes" (ibid., 28).

99. "Quelques articles convenables . . . à cette nouvelle discipline" (ibid.).

100. Ibid., 38.

101. He called prophets and preachers "those who without ordination pour out their lives in sacrifice, to uphold truth . . . and the purity of faith" (ibid., 2–3). ["Qui sans ordination mirent leur vie en aspersion du sacrifice, pour le soutien de la vérité . . . et la pureté de la foi."]

102. "Alors la vérité commença à prendre force pour triompher de l'erreur; alors le zèle du peuple sa ranima, la religion se réveilla, la foi se fortifia et toutes choses commencèrent de prendre un bon train; on vit en peu de temps augmenter le nombre de prédicateurs" (ibid., 32).

103. "Un merveilleux effet de l'assistance de Dieu" (ibid., 41).

104. "C'est ainsi que les églises se fortifièrent dans nos montagnes et que les prêtres perdaient toute espérance de voir jamais les Réformés dans la communion de l'Eglise romaine" (ibid., 52).

105. The papers of his successor as leader of the Reformed Church in France, Paul Rabaut, are housed in the library of the city of Geneva, in the papers of Antoine Court.

106. The confessional tone is much like that found in two martyrological collections published in Geneva, Jean Crespin's *Histoire des martyrs* and Theodore Beza's *Icones, vrais pourtraicts des hommes illustres,* underscoring yet another affiliation between Camisards and Huguenots. For the distinction between Catholic hagiography (Jacob Voragine's *Golden Legend,* for example) and Protestant "martyrological narratives," and the different purposes for which they were used, see Coats, *(Em)bodying the Word.*

Chapter Two. Survival Strategies

1. Charles Bost, in *Mémoires inédits,* saw prophecy as representing a new stage in Protestant resistance in Lower Languedoc; Emmanuel Le Roy Ladurie, in *Les paysans de Languedoc,* mentioned a link between prophetic pronouncement and the developing notion of freedom of conscience; Solange Deyon, in "La Résistance protestante desert," talked about the "desert" as providing an opportunity for Reformed believers to begin to regenerate their faith through prophecy in the wake of the devastation of institutional church structures; Daniel Vidal described prophetic imagery and its applications in *Le Malheur et son prophète.* By producing prophets from within their own ranks in response to a lack of ministers, the Camisards were arguably the best of Protestants, since the "priesthood of all believers" recognizes a vocation in daily life, rather than requiring an ordained clergy.

2. Cosmos, *Huguenot Prophecy,* 57.

3. Robert Wilson, *Prophecy and Society,* 22. "[After 1670] the king [strengthened] provincial rulers by dominating the areas most vulnerable to Protestantism and popular rebellions. The wars of the Camisards were ample proof that king and province would now be united against . . . divisiveness from below" (Beik, *Absolutism and Society,* 326 and 328). See also Bercé, *Croquants et nu-pieds,* 117–18.

4. "As described by . . . witnesses, the act of prophesying was characterized by intelligible, coherent discourse in French. It was not, however, the language in which inspired youths and adults expressed themselves when not in an altered state of consciousness.

" . . . Witnesses . . . distinguish[ed] between the French spoken by persons under inspiration and the languages commonly spoken by the inhabitants of the region . . . Prior to inspiration, these persons had not previously been known to speak in any language other than what they referred to as the *patois* of their province" (Cosmos, *Huguenot Prophecy*, 75).

5. Robert Wilson, *Prophecy and Society*, 3.

6. Ibid., 4.

7. An occasional Huguenot sympathized with the Camisards' plight, but generally this concern was expressed from a distance. Elie Neau, the Huguenot galley slave who wrote mystical songs and poetry, came into contact with several Camisards during his period of incarceration, and is perhaps the best example of a Huguenot who was touched by their plight and moved by their steadfast faith.

8. See Cosmos, *Huguenot Prophecy*, 105.

9. Fléchier, *Lettres choisies*, 1:377.

10. The term *nouveaux convertis* was used to refer to Protestants throughout France who had abjured their faith.

11. Briggs, *Communities of Belief*, 229.

12. "Un predicant, un homme sans étude, crut avoir une vision et entendre une voix qui lui disait, 'Va consoler mon peuple'" (Jurieu, *Lettres pastorales*, [letter of October 15, 1686] 1:27A).

13. This vital component of social process is underscored by Vidal (*Le Malheur et son prophète*, 1).

14. Jurieu, *L'Accomplissement des prophéties*, 5.

15. Jurieu's millennial speculations predated the war in the Cévennes by several years, but were certainly influenced by the troubled tenor of the times there. Further, Jurieu, in another attempt to encourage Huguenots to view Camisards as their brethren, interpreted the "slaying of the witnesses" in the book of Revelation to symbolize the persecution of French Calvinists in general, not just Camisards (*L'Accomplissement des prophéties*, 31).

16. "It is in this way that the first Christians and the first Reformers sowed the Gospel in the midst of paganism and anti-Christian sentiment" (Jurieu, *Lettres pastorales*, 2:29). ["C'est ainsi que les premiers chrestiens & premiers Reformateurs ont planté l'Evangile dans le Paganisme & dans l'antichristianisme."]

17. "A nos freres qui gemissent sous la captivité de Babylone."

18. "The *Pastoral Letters* were much appreciated by the people, not only in France but throughout the areas where Camisards had fled for refuge . . . Jurieu allies himself with 'humble folk' . . . by the hope that he gives them" (introduction to Jurieu, *Lettres pastorales*, 1:lii). ["*Les Pastorales* étaient très appréciées du 'peuple,' non seulement en France, mais au Refuge . . . Jurieu s'allie avec 'les simples' . . . [par] l'espoir qu'il leur donnait."]

19. "Lues et goutées par les simples . . . avec autant de fruit que par les autres" (Jurieu, *Lettres pastorales*, [letter of April 4, 1688] 2:24B).

20. Apocalyptic predictions were fairly common in the late seventeenth century, and churchmen spent a great deal of time attempting to calculate the date of the end

of the world, following the tradition running from the early Christian church—when apocalyptic thought was orthodoxy—with Tertullian, Eusebius of Caesarea, Hippolytus, and Lactantius, through the Middle Ages, with Joachim of Fiore and Nicholas of Cusa, and then Servetus and Comenius in the sixteenth century. Thus, Jurieu was in good company, and he had impeccable Reformed credentials. Jurieu's text for apocalyptic manifestations were, primarily, Revelation 20:1–20, Isaiah 11:6–9, Isaiah 2:4, Isaiah 41:18–19, Isaiah 55:12–13, and the book of Ezekiel.

21. "Il faut que cette persécution soit la dernière . . . [c'est] le même message que celui que l'auteur de l'Apocalypse addressait" (Jurieu, *L'Accomplissement des prophéties*, 19).

22. "Comme on a dessein de faire entrer dans ces lettres les principaux actes de nos Confesseurs & Martyrs: ceux qui en pourraient scavoir quelque chose de fort certain, prendront la peine de nous le faire scavoir" (Jurieu, *Lettres pastorales*, 1:1).

23. Figures are from *Lettres pastorales*: 1:56 (letter of September 1, 1686); 2:151 (letter of June 1, 1688); and 3:88B (letter of February 1, 1689). The figures may refer collectively to persons from the southern regions of France, notably Languedoc, Dauphiné, the Vivarais, and the Cévennes; the 200,000 emigrants were from all provinces of France. It is estimated that rates of emigration from the Cévennes were low.

24. The more staid Huguenots were, on the whole, not inclined to be persuaded. They were concerned about the disorderly consequences of Camisard "enthusiasm": "The *Pastoral Letters* were much less appreciated by the good Huguenot folk" (Jurieu, *Lettres pastorales*, introduction, 1:li). ["*Les Pastorales* . . . étaient beaucoup moins [appréciées] par les 'honnêtes gens' du Refuge."]

25. "Dieu doit sauver son peuple . . . C'est rappeller ainsi aux huguenots défaillants en France leur élection individuelle et collective, leur identité de minorité, séparée des autres hommes, privilégiée et persécutée" (ibid., 1:279 [letter of October 15, 1686]).

26. "Chants & Voix qui ont été entendus dans les airs en divers lieux" (ibid., 1:385).

27. He does also offer an anthropological or psychological explanation for some of the manifestations: "On the one hand, it could be the result of an imagination overheated by violent persecutions; on the other hand, it could be due to zeal . . . [and other] contagious feelings" (ibid., 1:384). ["Ça pourrait être l'effet d'une imagination échauffée par la violence de la persécution d'une part, et par le zèle d'autre part."] And he affirms the possibility of such "sentiments contagieux" being shared by the *inspirés*; nonetheless, such causality comes only late in the day—in his final letters—and does not diminish his estimation of the authenticity of the prophesying.

28. "Nous avons laissé leurs Assemblées au coeur de l'hiver. Et nous avons vu que malgré les rigueurs de la saison, les précipices dont les chemins sont bordés, et les ténèbres de la nuit, ces fidèles ne laissoient pas de se trouver dans les lieux dont ils convenoient pour prier Dieu ensemble" (Jurieu, *Lettres pastorales*, 4:17).

29. "En quoi il ne faut pas vous imaginer qu'ils ayent commis aucune irrégularité. Car il est content que la véritable vocation dépend du peuple, & du choix des assemblées" (ibid.).

30. "La mission d'un Pasteur par l'autre n'est qu'une forme . . . dont on se peut passer dans des cas de nécessité" (ibid.). The Camisards did indeed operate by a sort of

popularly devised theocracy: "God let them know his will through the agency of inspired ministers whose orders [the people] followed to the letter" (Jurieu, introduction to *L'Accomplissement des prophéties*, 2). ["Dieu les instruira de ses volontez par des ministres inspirés dont ils suivront exactement les ordres."]

31. "Mechans contes" (Jurieu, *Lettres pastorales*, 1:48).

32. "Milles superstitions" (ibid., 1:49).

33. Ibid., 1:25.

34. "Rien ne se fait sans Dieu. Est-il possible que Dieu se soit tellement caché derrière les créatures, & sous le voile des causes secondes, que jamais il ne veuille tirer un peu le rideau?" (ibid., 1:49).

35. "Des temps que les Ecrivains sacrés écrivoient, il y avoit de tout cela" (ibid., 1:50).

36. "Dieu accorda à Gédéon une figure dans la nature" (ibid., 1:50).

37. "Ezéchias en reçut une dans le soleil" (ibid., 1:51).

38. "C'est une merveille qui vaut bien la peine qu'on y fasse attention. Nous croirions être bien ingrats à la bonté Divine, si nous supprimions un aussi éclatant témoignage de son approbation" (ibid., 1:49).

39. "Je declare que Monsieur Bazin le cadet de la Ville d'Orthez en Béarn, m'a dit que se promenant avec quelqu'un de ses amis l'après midy, auprès de la ville d'Orthez, il ouït des Voix qui chantoient les Pseaumes . . . Cela arriva quelques mois avant l'interdiction de nostre Temple" (ibid., 1:52).

40. "Fait a Amsterdam le 23 novembre 1686, signé, Magendie ci devant Ministre" (ibid., 1:53).

41. See, for example, the opening words of the quotation in note 35 above.

42. "Mesme à l'heure que je vous écris, j'entend cette plainte" (ibid., 1:55).

43. "Je luy dis, Monsieur, si les hommes se taisent, les pierres meme parleront" (ibid., 1:53).

44. "Nous ne pouvons seulement douter, que ce ne soit des troupes d'Anges que Dieu nous envoie pour notre consolation, pour nous assurer que Dieu ne nous a pas tout a fait abandonez, & que notre délivrance approche" (ibid., 1:55).

45. "Rempli[r] ce pauvre peuple affligé d'une joye, & d'une consolation extraordinaire" (ibid., 1:52).

46. "Dieu s'est fait des bouches au milieu des airs . . . Il vous fait un grand changement de vie, pour vous rendre dignes de recevoir Dieu . . . le temps de votre délivrance est près, mais il ne viendra pas, que celui de votre répentance ne soit venu . . . que l'esprit de piété & de dévotion ne soit rentré en vous" (ibid., 1:56).

47. "Ce n'est qu'une femme [dira-t-on] mais c'est une femme qui rapporte une chose arrivée en public & dont elle a pour témoins avec elle plusieurs centaines de personnes" (ibid., 1:53).

48. "Mademoiselle de Vebron . . . a toujours été de la Religion Réformée & Dieu l'a préservée jusqu'ici de la chute générale" (ibid., 1:55).

49. "Nous bénîmes Dieu de la grâce qu'il nous faisoit de nous admonester de notre devoir par ces voix célestes, qui chantoient mélodieusement les hymnes sacrez" (ibid., 1:53).

50. "La même chose est arrivée dans les Cévennes" (ibid., 1:55).

51. "Il faut vous assembler entre vous le plus souvent que vous pourrez; lire ensemble l'Ecriture... Il faut vous consoler mutuellement par de bonnes prières... et sermons... Il faut enfin imiter le zèle de nos frères du Languedoc" (ibid., 4:16; emphasis added).

52. "Je vous ay fait cette histoire de la vigueur que nos frères de Languedoc ont eu de continuer leurs assemblées... & de s'exposer par là au martyre & à la mort, dans la vue de vous persuader ce que je vous ay prouvé dans... cette lettre... que vous ne devez pas... all[er] dans l'Eglise Papiste" (ibid., 4:32).

Chapter Three. *The Testimonials*

Georgia Cosmos's *Huguenot Prophecy and Clandestine Worship in the Eighteenth Century: The Sacred Theatre of the Cévennes* is the only monograph to treat *Le Théâtre sacré des Cévennes* in full. See also Jean-Pierre Richardot's introduction to the third edition; he treats the development of the prophetic phenomenon among the Camisards as a response to Louis XIV's repressive policy aimed at eliminating French Protestantism. Other works on Huguenot prophecy and the clandestine *culte* include Daniel Vidal, *Le Malheur et son prophète*.

1. Misson, *Le Théâtre sacré des Cévennes* (1707), part I, 65.

2. Esprit Fléchier, a Catholic polemicist and the bishop of Nîmes, was one of the severest critics of the "Petits prophètes". See Fléchier, *Lettres choisies*, 1:352, 358.

3. Jurieu, *Lettres pastorales*, 3, letters 3, 4, 62, and 82.

4. "Peut-on parler ici de légende? Il est fort probable... que des cas isolés, colportés de bouche à l'oreille ou par des missives recopiées avec plus ou moins de véracité... devinrent des généralités" (Crété, *Les Camisards*, 61).

5. "Ce sont nos Inspirations qui nous ont mis au coeur de quitter nos proches, & ce que nous avions de plus cher au Monde, pour suivre Jesus Christ... Ce sont elles qui ont donné à nos vrais Inspirez, le zèle de Dieu, & de la Religion pure: l'horreur pour l'Idolatrie. Ça esté uniquement par les Inspirations & par le redoublement de leurs ordres, que nous avons commencé nostre sainte guerre. Un petit nombre de jeunes gens simples, sans éducation, & sans expérience, comment auroient-ils fait tant de choses, s'ils n'avoient pas eu le secours du Ciel?" (Misson, "Témoignage d'Elie Marion," *Le Théâtre sacré des Cévennes* [1707], part I, 88–89).

6. "Le prophétisme ne s'arrête pas à la fin de la guerre, lorsque les derniers insurgés se sont rendus; au contre, il se transporte Outre-Manche, par l'intermédiaire... d'Elie Marion, Durand Fage et Jean Cavalier de Sauve... ils font des disciples aussi bien parmi des protestants français réfugiés à Londres que parmi les Anglais" (Misson, citing the testimony of Elie Marion, ibid., 81).

7. Schwartz, *French Prophets*, 54. Another factor influencing Huguenots' attitudes toward the Camisards was which London church they attended. After the Restoration, Charles II had required that the Savoy Church observe Anglican ritual and answer to the bishop of London. Therefore, two models for the expression of Huguenot piety—one

conformist, one reformed—coexisted in England at the time, and the 50,000 or more French refugees divided themselves between the two forms of church polity.

8. Marion was to foment a great furor, prompting sporadic uprisings throughout the Cévennes until 1712, particularly in the region of the Vivarais, where Isabeau Vincent had prophesied several years before; see Schwartz, *French Prophets*, 28.

9. Their prophecies were recorded by Nicolas Fatio du Duillier, Jean Daudé, and Charles Portales. These three self-appointed secretaries were socially prominent and well connected, enhancing the French Prophets' access to audience; Daudé was a lawyer, Portales a lawyer's son, and Fatio the son of a well-placed Huguenot family from Geneva and a friend of Sir Isaac Newton. For more on this, see Schwartz, *French Prophets*, 69–74.

10. Elie Neau was active in Saumur; see Chapter Six.

11. Schwartz, *French Prophets*, 42.

12. Quoted in ibid.

13. Considerable publishing activity attests to the impact of the Camisard cause on the English mind-set at the time. Among such tracts are D'Auborn, *The French Convert*.

14. "The potential power of the French Prophets lay in their unusual ability to attract millenarians of all persuasions and from every ethos. Fear of this power, as well as of the original ethos of the Camisards, was a major factor in the English reception of the inspirés" (Schwartz, *French Prophets*, 54).

15. Charles Weiss, *French Protestant Refugees*, 1:248–49.

16. Cosmos, *Huguenot Prophecy*, 14.

17. "The Protestant churches in France had been rent by divisions over the issues of grace and predestination . . . Doctrinal differences emerged once again in the comparative freedom of exile. Orthodox ministers felt that matters were becoming serious when . . . meetings of the Cévennes 'prophets' created a major stir in London in 1706–1707" (Gwynn, *Huguenot Heritage*, 105).

18. For a more detailed background on the responses of the Threadneedle and Savoy churches, see Cosmos, *Huguenot Prophecy*, 19–21.

19. "French refugee churches were divided into two groups . . . 'those which retained that form of worship and church government which was in accordance with the discipline of the Reformed Church of France, commonly called non-conformist churches, and those which adopted the French translation of the English liturgy'" (Cosmos, *Huguenot Prophecy*, 14, quoting scholar George Beeman).

20. Quoted in Schwartz, *French Prophets*, 80. The original text is Rawlinson MSS C. 984, 242–242v and ff., housed at the Bodleian Library.

21. Quoted in Schwartz, *French Prophets*.

22. Schwartz notes that "the narrative comes full circle now, for as the French Prophets quickened the prophetic and millenarian impulses on the continent, they took back with them to England the idioms of continental pietism" (ibid., 190).

23. Misson, *Le Théâtre sacré des Cévennes* (1707), part I, 4.

24. Cosmos, *Huguenot Prophecy*, 3–4.

25. Cosmos notes that "of all those who gave depositions it was Mathieu Boissier who established the Cévennes as a place of sacred significance for a religious community. It was from his narrative that Misson drew the phrase which inspired the title under which the depositions were published collectively in London in 1707. The idea of locating good and evil forces in specific places is represented by this witness through spatial symbols which define the boundaries of the region of the Cévennes and the three adjoining provinces of Dauphiné, Vivarais and the Velay" (*Huguenot Prophecy*, 33).

26. Misson, *Le Théâtre sacré des Cévennes* (1707), iii.

27. Ibid.

28. "Des Imposteurs & des Blasphémateurs publics, sans avoir allégué aucune sorte de Preuve" (Misson, quoting from the sermon in "Avis," ibid., vii).

29. "Tesmoins oculaires" (Misson, "Au lecteur," ibid., i).

30. "Tous ont prêté serment" (ibid., iii).

31. "Solemnellement jurées devant le Magistrat"—"solemnly sworn before the judge" (ibid., i).

32. Cosmos, response to a review by Monahan.

33. They were translated by a Mr. Lacy, who was opposed to the Camisard cause but who later, through his contact with the testimonials, became convinced of their sincerity, thus proving the worth of Misson's project.

34. The Huguenot poet Agrippa d'Aubigné recalls this tribulation in "Les Misères."

35. "J'ai souvent assisté à des assemblées que nos pauvres Protestans persécutez faisoient dans des lieux écartez, pour prier Dieu ensemble, selon l'ancienne maniere de nos Eglises de France" (Dalgone, quoted in Misson, *Le Théâtre sacré des Cévennes* [1707], part I, 80).

36. "Vous serez bien heureuse quand on vous aura injuriez & persecutez, & quand on aura dit mauvaise parole contre vous en mentant. Ejouissez-vous, & vous égayez, car vôtre Salaire est grand aux Cieux. Ainsi ont-ils persécuté les Prophets qui ont été avant vous" (ibid., i).

37. "Ce sont de simples Récits, des Faits naïvement racontez, & juridiquement attestez. Lisez, & considerez bien tout, & tirez-vous mêmes les Conséquences" (ibid.).

38. "Quand une vérité est établie sur des fondemens solides, rien ne la peut ébranler" (ibid., iii).

39. Ibid., iv.

40. "Si des personnes . . . ont quelque chose de serieux & de raisonnable à objecter, pour l'éclaircissement de la vérité, je recevrai volontiers leurs Argumens en petit volume, ecrits & signez de leur main" (ibid., iii).

41. "Des Témoins d'élite, des Personnes dont la Foi & la fidélité ont été extraordinairement éprouvées" (ibid., iv).

42. "Les pieux Catholiques, comme l'Auteur des Mémoires du Marquis de Guiscard, & Mr de Brueys" (ibid., iii).

43. "Des Extraits de livres"; "des lettres écrites de la propre main des Auteurs"; "des Dépositions renduës à Londres . . . par vingt-six bons Témoins, qui ont vû & entendu les choses qu'ils rapportent" (ibid., v).

44. "Qui . . . a été présent lors que la grande partie de ces Témoignages ont été reçûs" (ibid., vi).

45. "La Méthode constante a été de représenter fortement aux Déposans, combien ils devoient être circonspects, pour ne rien avancer dont ils ne fussent parfaitement assurez . . . & sur des choses qu'ils promettoient de jurer solennellement" (ibid., vi).

46. "Un gentilhomme Anglois, de beaucoup de mérite, & qui entend bien nôtre langue, a travaillé de concert avec moi . . . [à] sa Traduction" (ibid., v).

47. "Les diverses choses qui sont exposées dans ce Livre . . . contiennent ensemble une trés-solide justification des Personnes à qui on livre un [*sic*] Guerre si horrible & si tyrannique" (ibid., vi–vii; emphasis added).

48. Catholic authorities called the Camisard rebellion "Satan's strategy to reignite in France Calvin's heresy, formerly almost extinguished" ["une ruse de Sathan, pour rallumer en France l'hérésie de Calvin presque éteinte"] (testimony of David Flotard in ibid., 62).

49. "Je suis de ces Esprits . . . qui croyent de bonne foi que la main de Dieu n'est pas raccourcie: que comme elle a fait des miracles autrefois, elle en peut faire encore aujourd'hui" (ibid., 2).

50. "De près, & avec un Microscope, pour ainsi dire" (Misson, *Meslange*, ii–iii).

51. "La SAGESSE SOUVERAINE gouverne le Monde qu'elle a créé . . . cette Providence adorable . . . paraît avoir une grande part . . . dans ces opérations surprenantes" (ibid.).

52. "Leur état a des circonstances si miraculeuses qu'il ne se peut imaginer rien de plus desraisonnable, que de penser à les mettre au rang des Malades, et des Fanatiques" (Misson, *Le Théâtre sacré des Cévennes* [1707], ii).

53. One Catholic account, that of M. de Brueys, calls them "the dregs of the common folk" ("la lie du Peuple"; quoted in ibid., 8), and derides "these poor benighted fools who think themselves divinely inspired" ("ces pauvres Insensez [qui] croyoient estre effectivement inspirez du S. Esprit," 6).

54. "Je n'ai . . . aucune honte . . . de . . . témoigner . . . Je sçais, moi qui écris ceci . . . Je sçais avec certitude qu'ils sont Innocens" (ibid., ii–iv).

55. "Le Dessein général du Théâtre est de vous faire voir, contre . . . les fausses Idées de la bruyante Multitude folle & aveugle, qu'il est reellement vrai, que depuis environ six Ans, il y a eu, dans les Cevennes, un fort grand nombre de Personnes, de tout âge & des deux sexes, qui ont été, & qui sont présentement encore, dans un état tout semblable à celui d'Elie Marion, de Jean Cavalier, & de Durand Fage" (ibid., i).

56. Georgia Cosmos notes that, her study excepted, to date "little use has been made of the texts of the *Théâtre sacré* by historians of Reformed religion in France during this period" (*Huguenot Prophecy*, 8).

57. "Jean Cabanel d'Anduse est venu declarer à la Compagnie . . . qu'il n'a jamais crû que les prétendus inspirez fussent de véritables Prophètes" (quoted in Misson, *Le Théâtre sacré des Cévennes* [1707], part II, 17).

58. "Prétenduë[s] Déposition[s] . . . fausse[s], supposée[s] & faite[s] à plaisir, par des Imposteurs, pour favoriser lesdits prétendues prophetes" (quoted in ibid., part II, 18).

59. "Ainsi ils mettoient dans leurs Inspirations ce qu'ils apprenoient en particulier, & vouloient faire passer cela pour des Revelations du Saint Esprit" (quoted in ibid., part II, 24).

60. "L'on n'a pû trouver qu'une femme de ce nom-là. Elle a declaré, que la Déclaration est une piece entierement supposée" (quoted in ibid., part II, 26).

61. "Les Ennemis de ces Innocens leur imputent des Abominations, pour les perdre. Ils les accusent de n'être pas Chrétiens & de haïr les ministres de l'Evangile [mais les Camisards] . . . protestent solennellement encore, qu'ils croyent en Dieu, Père, Fils & Saint Esprit, & que l'Espérance de leur salut est uniquement fondée, sans équivoque, sur le Merite, & sur la satisfaction de Jesus Christ . . . ils aiment et vénèrent les bons Ministres. Ils déclarent aussi qu'ils sont Pauvres . . . ils ont foulé aux pieds les Richesses iniques, pour porter la Croix du Seigneur" (Misson, *Le Théâtre sacré des Cévennes* [1707], v).

62. "Impostures," "fanatisme," "ruses de Sathan," or "yvresse" (Flotard's testimony, quoted in Misson, *Le Théâtre sacré des Cévennes* [1707], 62).

63. "Bonne foy" (from *Examen du Théâtre sacré*, quoted in Misson, *Le Théâtre sacré des Cévennes* [1707], part II, 5).

64. *Examen du Théâtre sacré*, quoted in ibid., part II, 5.

65. "[C'est l'Enthousiasme . . . [de] personnes du plus bas ordre" (*Examen du Théâtre sacré*, quoted in ibid., part II, 10).

66. "Ont prêté serment" (*Examen du Théâtre sacré*, quoted in ibid., part II, 10).

67. "Je fais ici une remarque, qui doit servir pour tout le *Théâtre sacré*; c'est qu'on a plus de soin du beau François que de la vérité. Toutes les Dépositions paroissent estre du même Auteur . . . ce sont la plupart des gens qui savent à peine parler, & on les fait tous parler avec . . . [de l'] éloquence . . . dont ils sont entierement incapables" (*Examen du Théâtre sacré*, quoted in ibid., part II, 14–15).

68. Misson, *Le Théâtre sacré des Cévennes* (1707), part I, 7.

69. "L'Auteur de ce Meslange, croyez-moi, je vous prie, cher Lecteur, est un des hommes du Monde le plus débarassé de toute sorte de préjugé. C'est un Ennemi déclaré des fausses idées de la multitude" (Misson, "Le libraire," in "Avis au lecteur," *Le Théâtre sacré des Cévennes* [1707], part III, i).

70. "Son principe étant que le moyen de bien conduire sa raison, dans la recherche de la vérité, est de commencer par établir distinctement tous les faits, avant que de nier, ou d'affirmer" (*Meslange*, quoted in Misson, *Le Théâtre sacré des Cévennes* [1707], part III, iii).

71. "L'Apologie du Sage, n'est pas destinée à servir de Digue, contre le Torrent débordé de la Multitude aveugle & méchante: Elle est pour ceux qui sont dignes de son Estime" (*Meslange*, quoted in Misson, *Le Théâtre sacré des Cévennes* [1707], part III, 69).

72. "Et, au reste, chacun doit sçavoir que toutes ces merceilles qu'il a plû à Dieu de faire éclater, depuis le commencement du Siècle, dans le théâtre sacré des Cévennes & sur les frontieres du Païs de Roüergue, sont de la mesme nature dans toutes les circonstances, que celles qui ont fait tant bruit . . . dans nostre Daufiné, dans le Vivarez, & dans le Vellay. Provinces qui, au sentiment de quelques uns, font partie des Cévennes"

(testimony of Mathieu Boissier, quoted in Misson, *Le Théâtre sacré des Cévennes* [1707], part I, 13; emphasis added).

73. Cosmos, *Huguenot Prophecy*, 119.

74. "Estre saisi de l'Esprit"; "recevoir des Graces"; "recevoir l'Inspiration"; "l'Ecstase" (Misson, *Le Théâtre sacré des Cévennes* [1707], passim).

75. "Tous ceux que j'ai vus dans l'Ecstase, parloient François, mieux qu'il [*sic*] ne l'auroient pu faire, hors de l'Ecstase" (testimony of Castanet, quoted in ibid., 21).

76. "Que ce n'étoit pas lui qui parloit; mais que c'estoit l'Esprit de Dieu qui parloient par sa bouche" (testimony of Mazel, quoted in ibid., 24).

77. "J'ai entendu dire, à plusieurs de ceux qui venoient de parler dans l'Ecstase, qu'ils ne pouvoient pas repeter les choses qu'ils avoient dites" (testimony of Castanet, quoted in ibid., 20). This is another leitmotif. Jacques Mazel makes a similar observation: "I asked several [who had just spoken while in ecstasy] if they could repeat the things they had said in their Paroxysm, who replied, they could not do it" (26). ["J'ai demandé à plusieurs de ceux qui venoient de parler dans l'Inspiration, s'ils pourroient bien dire, une seconde fois, ce qu'ils avoient prononcé pendant l'Ecstase, & ils m'ont répondu qu'ils ne le pouvoient pas faire."]

78. "Il citoit, à propos, des passages de l'Ecriture, comme s'il avoit seû la Bible par coeur. Je suis assuré qu'il ne savoit [même] pas lire" (testimony of Claude Arnassan, quoted in ibid., 31).

79. Misson, *Le Théâtre sacré des Cévennes* (1707), iii.

80. There is a similarity with Quakers and Shakers; although the Shakers insisted on differentiating men's from women's work, women could, and did, prophesy just as did men.

81. "Mais mon petit raisonnement ne se porta pas plus loin qu'à soupçonner que ces gens-là pourroient bien estre quelque espéce des Devins ... j'aurois voulu estre à dix lieuës de là" (testimony of Jean Cavalier, quoted in Misson, *Le Théâtre sacré des Cévennes* [1707], part I, 37).

82. Ibid., 31.

83. "Après que sur l'examen que nous avons fait de ces gens-là; nous avons été convaincus qu'ils ne sont pas ce qu'ils prétendent être. Vingt théâtres sacrez n'en feroient pas des Anges de lumière" (quoted in Misson, *Le Théâtre sacré des Cévennes* [1707], part II, 3).

84. "[Elle] parloit en Prédicateur" (testimony of Boissier, quoted in Misson, *Le Théâtre sacré des Cévennes* [1707], part I, 9).

85. "Pria Dieu ... qu'il déliast sa langue, afin qu'elle pût annoncer sa Parole" (ibid.).

86. "Je croyois entendre quelque Ange tant estoient belles les Paroles qui sortoient de sa bouche ... il y avoit quelque chose en elle qui n'estoit pas humain" (ibid., 10).

87. "Que je crois pouvoir & devoir appeller des Miracles" (ibid., 13).

88. "Dans l'Inspiration" (testimony of Vernet, quoted in Misson, *Le Théâtre sacré des Cévennes* [1707], part I, 14).

89. "Ce qui me causa une grande surprise ... car jamais elle n'avoit essayé de dire un mot en ce langage" (ibid.).

90. "Les plus grandes agitations ... étoient de la Poitrine" (ibid.).

91. Ibid.

92. "Il arriva un jour dans une des Assemblées, que plusieurs Inspirez commençoient à parler ensemble, de sorte que l'un de ceux de la Compagnie dit à quelques uns, 'Taisez-vous, de la part de Dieu'; et ils cessérent de parler ensemble, mais en suite, ils parlèrent l'un apres l'autre" (testimony of Castanet, quoted in Misson, *Le Théâtre sacré des Cévennes* [1707], part I, 21).

93. "Quittoient incontinent toutes sortes de libertinage . . . Quelques-uns qui avoit esté débauchez, devinrent d'abord sages, & pieux" (testimony of Cabanel, quoted in ibid., 26).

94. "Il parût une Lumiere en l'air, comme une grosse Etoile, qui s'avança vers le lieu où étoit l'Assemblée" (testimony of Arnassan, quoted in ibid., 28).

95. "Des feux ou des Lumieres en Ciel, pendant la nuit, pour éblouïr des ennemis" (testimony of Du Bois, quoted in ibid., 32).

96. "Une espece d'étoile, qui venoit se poser sur le lieu où étoit ce que je cherchais" (testimony of Bruguier, quoted in ibid., 38).

97. "Je commençai à avoir une toute autre opinion de ces personnes-là" (testimony of Cavalier, quoted in Misson, *Le Théâtre sacré des Cévennes* [1707], part I, 39).

98. "Satan ne pouvoit pas . . . glorifier le Nom de Dieu" (ibid., 41).

99. "Ne crain point, je suis avec vous [les Camisards] . . . je veux mettre ma parole en ta bouche" (ibid., 42).

100. "Un Dimanche matin, comme je faisois le [*sic*] priere dans la maison de mon Pere, je tombois dans une Ecstase extraordinaire, & Dieu m'ouvrit la bouche. Pendant trois fois ving-quatre heures, je fus toujours [en ecstase]" (ibid., 43).

101. "La main de Dieu me frapoit son vent, mais ma langue ne se délioit point; il est vrai que sa Grace me consoloit d'ailleurs, car j'obéissois avec plaisir à l'Esprit intérieur qui me portoit toujours à l'invoquer. Je ne me souciai plus de mes Jeux, & de mes Divertissemens ordinaires, & sur tout, je me sentis une veritable haine partout cet attirail du Culte public des Papistes, & pour toute cette farce de Messe" (ibid., 42).

102. "Mes yeux devinrent des fontaines de larmes" (ibid., 41).

103. "Aussitost apres que la predication fut finie, je sentis comme un coup de marteau qui frapa fortement ma poitrine. Et il me sembla que ce coup excita un feu . . . Cela me mit dans une espèce de défaillance, qui me fit tomber. Je me relevais aussitost . . . je fus frapé d'un second coup, avec un redoublement de chaleur . . . un troisiesme coup me brisa la poitrine, & me mit tout en feu . . . & puis je tombai soudainement dans des agitations de la teste & du corps" (ibid.).

104. Ibid., 42.

105. "J'estois ravi quand il disoit que les plus petits, & les plus simples estoient d'un grand prix devant Dieu" (ibid., 40).

106. Ibid., 41.

107. "Il y avoit . . . une certaine pauvre idiote . . . quand on me dit qu'elle preschoit . . . je n'en crus rien du tout . . . Cependant elle s'aquitoit de tout cela miraculeusement bien. Cette Asnesse de Balaam avoit une bouche d'or, quand l'Intelligence Céleste la faisoit parler . . . C'estoit un torrent d'Eloquence; c'estoit un prodige . . . elle devenoit

une créature toute nouvelle, étant transformée en un grand Prédicateur . . . il y avoit là dedans du miraculeux" (testimony of Caladon, quoted in Misson, *Le Théâtre sacré des Cévennes* [1707], part I, 101).

108. "Neuf mois de sanglots, & d'agitations sans parole" (testimony of Cavalier, quoted in ibid., 42).

109. See the "born again" account at the beginning of John Bunyan's *Grace Abounding to the Chief of Sinners*, for example.

110. For an example of Cavalier's emotional rhetoric, see Misson, *Le Théâtre sacré des Cévennes* [1707], part I, 43.

111. "Et declare solennellement, & sans équivoque, par cet Acte public, & sous le serment que je fais devant Dieu, que je ne suis point l'Auteur des Agitations que je soufre dans mes Ecstases. Que ce n'est point moi . . . mais que je suis meû par une Force qui est au dessus de moi" (testimony of Cavalier, quoted in ibid., 44).

112. "J'estois bien heureux de m'estre trouvé parmi ceux que Dieu avoit rappellez, pour estre rassasiez de sa Grace . . . ainsi de mettre sa parole en ma bouche" (ibid., 42).

113. Ibid., 50.

114. Ibid., 64.

115. "J'avois esté . . . forcé . . . de mon enfance, à fréquenter les Messes" (testimony of Marion, quoted in Misson, *Le Théâtre sacré des Cévennes* [1707], part I, 82).

116. "Superstitieuse . . . Plus j'y pensai, plus j'en fus choqué. Je n'avois point leû la Sainte Ecriture, mais mon sens commun se souleveoit contre toutes les folies" (ibid.).

117. "Après que j'eus assisté à quelques Assemblées où plusieurs de ces Inspirez parlèrent d'une maniere plus forte & plus pathétique que je ne le pourrois exprimer, je me sentis frappé au coeur par la puissance irrésistible du langage Divin" (ibid.).

118. "Une joye secrette;"—"un sentiment intérieur de la Grace de Dieu"; "un certain feu occupoit toute ma poitrine, & me causoit une sorte d'oppression qui me faisoit jetter de forts grans soupirs. Mon corps estoit un peu renversé, & je demeurai un gros quart d'heure en cet estat" (ibid., 83).

119. "Le premier jour de l'année 1703, comme nous estions retirez, la Famille, & quelques Parens, pour passer une partie de la Journée, en prieres & autres exercices de piété . . . je sentis tout d'un coup une grande chaleur qui me saisit le coeur, & qui se répandoit partout le dedans de mon corps . . . une Puissance à laquelle je ne pûs résister d'avantage, s'empara tout-à-fait de moi . . . Dieu me frappoit, & m'encourageoit tout ensemble . . . mon Créateur m'eust fait un coeur nouveau . . . Il plût à Dieu de délier ma langue & de mettre sa parole en ma bouche" (ibid., 84–85).

120. "Ce mesme Esprit de Sagesse & de Grace, me déclara aussi qu'il falloit que je prisse les Armes . . . pour la Cause de Dieu . . . je m'enroll[ai] dans une troupe de Soldats Chrestiens" (ibid., 86).

121. "Joint aux Camisars" (ibid., 90).

122. Ibid., 94.

123. "Je suis François Protestant, échapé de la grande Tribulation . . . contraint de [me] réfugier dans [un] Païs de seureté" (ibid., 92).

124. Ibid.

125. "Ennemis Papistes & . . . sa prière [les] exposoit à de grands dangers" (testimony of Chauvain, quoted in Misson, *Le Théâtre sacré des Cévennes* [1707], part I, 93).

126. Ibid., 106.

127. "Elle n'avoit jamais fait que garder des Brebis" (ibid., 107).

128. "Comme il l'a fait" (ibid.).

129. Testimony of Charras, quoted in Misson, *Le Théâtre sacré des Cévennes* [1707], part I, 16.

130. "Grande joye" (ibid., 17).

131. "Elle s'abandonne à l'Esprit, qui la guidoit si bien . . . la Voix intérieure" (ibid., 16).

132. "Des chants des Pseaumes qui ont esté entendus en beaucoup d'endroits, comme venant du haut des airs . . . cette Divine Mélodie, en plein jour . . . dans des lieux écartez de maison, où il n'y avoit ni bois, ni creux de rochers, & où, en un mot, il estoit impossible que quelqu'un fut caché" (testimony of Marion, quoted in Misson, *Le Théâtre sacré des Cévennes* [1707], part I, 90).

133. Ibid., 91.

134. "Dieu faisoit tant d'autres merveilles au milieu de nous" (testimony of Mary Rouviere, quoted in Misson, *Le Théâtre sacré des Cévennes* [1707], part I, 104).

135. "Il nous sembloit, que c'estoit des fruits assez excellens des saintes Inspirations" (testimony of Caladon, quoted in ibid., 99).

136. Cosmos, *Huguenot Prophecy*, 78–79.

137. "Une lumiere tombant du Ciel, comme une fusée" (testimony of Fage, quoted in Misson, *Le Théâtre sacré des Cévennes* [1707], part I, 61).

138. "L'Esprit a esté repandu sur quantité de petits Enfans . . . il plaisoit à Dieu de faire annoncer ses merveilles, par la bouche de ces Innocens" (ibid., 104).

139. Ibid., 105.

140. "Devions-nous attaquer l'Ennemi? Etions-nous poursuivis? La nuit nous Surprendra-t-elle? Craignions-nous les embuscades? Arrivoit-il quelque accident? Falloit-il marquer le lieu d'une Assemblée? Nous nous mettions d'abord en prieres . . . Aussitost . . . l'Esprit nous répondoit, & l'Inspiration nous guidoit en tout" (ibid., 69).

141. "Toutes les divers cruautez que l'on exerçoit contre les Inspirés, ne faisoit qu'augmenter leur zele" (ibid., 122).

142. Quoted in Misson, *Le Théâtre sacré des Cévennes* [1707], part I, 141.

143. "Histoire[s] miraculeuse[s]" (Misson, *Le Théâtre sacré des Cévennes* [1707], part I, 140).

144. "Je vous dirai d'abord que ce qui me faisoit aimer les Camisards, & ce qui m'obligeoit aussi à sacrfer ma Personne & mon Bien pour eux, c'étoit le zéle et la Piété qu'ils avoient. Il faudroit être entièrement aveugle, pour ne pas voir que c'est la Main de Dieu qui les a soutenus" (ibid.).

145. "L'Eternel est nôtre Retraite, & le Rocher de nôtre Refuge" (testimonies of Marion, Cavalier, and Fage, quoted in ibid., 123).

Chapter Four. "From a Farr Countrie"

1. Garrison, *L'Edit de Nantes*, 272.

2. Garrison provides detailed statistics for Camisard and Huguenot emigration, especially immigration figures for England, Holland, Geneva, Germany (notably Frankfurt), but none for the Americas; see *L'Edit de Nantes*, 270–72.

3. *Report of a French Protestant*, 25.

4. Kamil, *Fortress of the Soul*, 755. See also Van Ruymbeke and Sparks, *Memory and Identity*.

5. Butler, *Huguenots in America*, 1.

6. Ibid., 2.

7. Butler examines three areas: Boston, South Carolina, and New York City. In the case of Boston, he finds "an extraordinary pattern of intermarriage with the English . . . exogamy . . . [being] a major 'indicator' of assimilation that destroyed refugee cohesion" (*The Huguenots*, 81).

8. "Un mouvement semblable anglicanise ceux qui ont choisi l'Angleterre" (Garrison, *L'Edit de Nantes*, 272). ["A similar development anglicanized those who chose to go to England."]

9. "Recent scholarship suggests that the region, once thought to have been 'monolithically' Puritan, was in fact settled intermittently by diverse groups of migrants, not only from a variety of East Anglian settlements, but from all over Europe and America" (Kamil, *Fortress of the Soul*, 711). See also Archer, "New England Mosaic."

10. "A process of Anglo-French creolization was active in the cultural and material life of New York City and the Long Island Sound region" (Kamil, *Fortress of the Soul*, 744). He finds "material manifestation[s] of the interactive and competitive discourses of cultural convergence, quotation, and creolization whereby different regional cultures communicated their perception of difference to themselves and others" (749).

11. Nicodemus was a Pharisee who came to see Jesus by night (John 3). See Randall, *Building Codes*, for a discussion of the uses of Nicodemism by Calvinist architects during the Wars of Religion in France; "hi[d] in plain sight" (Kamil, *Fortress of the Soul*, 711).

12. However, he finds the source of this pietistic orientation in the writings of Bernard Palissy, famed sixteenth-century Huguenot potter and preacher, as well as in the mystical and pietistic beliefs propagated by Jacob Boehme or Henry Melchior Muhlenberg a bit later in the 1730s. Kamil (*Fortress of the Soul*, 123) finds that the latter influence even resulted in an alliance between Huguenot "spiritualists" and Quakers on Long Island.

13. Kamil interprets a variety of material artifacts from the period. His methodological framework derives from philosophical discourse and especially from types of paratheological thinking such as alchemy and Rosicrucianism.

14. See Kamil, *Fortress of the Soul*, 318, 477, and 478.

15. William Penn had studied with Moyse Amyraut at the French Protestant Academy in Saumur from 1663–1664; already well disposed to the Huguenot cause, he published French-language announcements encouraging Huguenot settlement in Pennsylvania

(Butler, *Huguenots in America*, 53). Butler notes "a potentially important Huguenot influence on William Penn" and the Quakers (ibid.). Regarding French Protestants in the southern colonies: "In the history of the Huguenot settlement in early America, South Carolina occupies a particular place" (Van Ruymbeke, *From New Babylon to Eden*, xv).

16. "The St. Denis enthusiasts' violent, gory, and apocalyptic message based on the premise of an angry or revengeful God, their anticlericalism, and their claim to read signs denote a clear influence from the French Prophets" (ibid., 143). The Dutartre incident was set off by Moravian missionaries distributing tracts having to do with the French Prophets' revivalism.

17. Van Ruymbeke, *From New Babylon to Eden*, 224.

18. Kamil speaks, for instance, of "an improvisational cultural style" on their part (*Fortress of the Soul*, 815).

19. Butler, *Huguenots in America*, 99.

20. Balmer, *Perfect Babel of Confusion*, 112.

21. "Forced out into the Atlantic world, Huguenot craftsmen sought to form new social and economic identities through artisanal interaction. Long experience in crafting heresy at the French court, the core of French absolutism, had revealed that skill in manipulating the material languages of concealment and display was absolutely necessary to maintain a semblance of cultural equilibrium amid the asymmetries of the New World" (Kamil, *Fortress of the Soul*, 754).

22. Elie Neau, Gabriel Bernon, and Ezéchiel Carré did not in any significant way alter their faith perspective when they engaged in cross-denominational cooperation, but rather stood firm while using these interactions for their commercial benefit and social advancement. Their theology did not change in a climate of what Kamil calls religious "pluralistic interaction" (*Fortress of the Soul*, 796). See, for example, Carré's forthright professions of faith in his sermons, or Neau's impassioned pleas, based on his understanding of Christianity, for the education of African American slaves.

23. On this, see, for example, Kingdon, "Pourquoi les réfugiés."

24. They were akin to the Quakers—who mirrored aspects of Camisard piety—in most ways except their sometime militancy, and to Shakers, who acknowledge the Camisards as ancestors. So, for example, when Henry Melchior Muhlenberg reproached the Camisards for having lost their faith when they went over to a less pietistic denomination, he was shortsighted in his assessment.

25. "Those of the [Camisard] prophets who survived were dispersed when peace came, or earlier still. Some of them made their way to Germany . . . The refugees from the Cévennes helped to arouse the spirit of enthusiasm which gave birth to the Moravian brethren and so, indirectly, to the Methodist movement . . . They went to Bristol . . . They were still in evidence in that neighborhood when the early preaching of Wesleyanism began to arouse symptoms more spontaneous and hardly less sensational than theirs. But their lasting success was at Manchester, where they converted the . . . Quakeress Ann Lee. She it was who emigrated to America, and there founded a sect [called] . . . the Shakers" (Knox, *Enthusiasm*, 365–71).

26. Benoît, *Durand, Marie*.

27. Three Camisard pastors in exile, Court, Roger, and Corteiz, ordained Pierre Durand by the laying on of hands in Geneva on May 17, 1726.

28. Court, *L'Histoire des troubles des Cévennes*, 110.

29. "Il eut la joie de extirper [la prophécie] de sa province . . . Plus encore que la persécution, le prophétisme faisait courir, par ses excès, les plus grands dangers à la Réforme" (Benoît, *Durand, Marie*, 19).

30. Kamil, *Fortress of the Soul*, 796.

31. Ibid., 755.

32. Thomas Kidd details the Lutheran Pietist strand that influenced Increase Mather and the influence of Philipp Jakob Spener, Jean de Labadie, and Theodorus Frelinghuysen (see the chapter "Soul-Satisfying Sealings of God's Love," in Kidd, *Great Awakening*). Increase Mather in 1708 called the movement of Pietism "the New Reformation . . . in Germany" (quoted in ibid., 25). In addition, "Huguenot descendants . . . were important in early Methodism, and Vincent Perronet, a close associate of the Wesleys, was styled the Methodist 'archbishop' . . . There is [also] a significant connection between the Huguenots and the Oxford Movement [with] . . . Edward Bouverie Pusey" (Gwynn, *Huguenot Heritage*, 86). See also Randall, " 'Loosening the Stays,' " 29n4.

33. Kidd, *Great Awakening*, 168.

34. Ibid., 163.

35. Butler observes, for instance, that "European historians have for some time analyzed and appreciated [Elie] Neau's work, while American historians have been unaware of its existence" (*Huguenots in America*, 165).

36. Kidd's important study of the Great Awakening does not go back that far, but such affiliations appear probable, even obvious, given Neau's renown in evangelical and abolitionist circles; see the chapter "Ethiopia Shall Stretch Out Her Hands" in *Great Awakening*.

37. Quoted in Kidd, *Great Awakening*, 215–16.

38. Appropriately, Cotton Mather's translation of some of Neau's prison writings was published under the title *A Present From a Farr Countrie*.

39. See Barnes and Barnes, *Genealogies of Rhode Island*, 487.

40. Lovelace, *American Pietism of Cotton Mather*, 5.

41. For Bernon and the Society for the Propagation of the Gospel in Foreign Parts, see Barnes and Barnes, *Genealogies of Rhode Island*, 487.

42. Lovelace, *American Pietism of Cotton Mather*, 8.

Chapter Five. Protestant and Profiteer

1. The title of this section—"Everyone That Hath Forsaken Houses"—is the Bible verse (Matthew 19:29) inscribed on Bernon's headstone.

2. Such concern for the needy had been typical of Calvinism since John Calvin established a social welfare system in sixteenth-century Geneva; see Kaufmann, *Redeeming Politics*. Bernon also voiced unexpected sympathy for Quakerism, deeming part of the cohort of scripturally literate figures in Providence "Protestant Quakers . . . [who] make

their application to read the Holy Scriptures and are very well able to give an account of their faith" (quoted in Weeden, *Early Rhode Island*, 208) and referring to "Wm. Wilkinson, the greatest preacher among the Quakers"; he also expressed admiration for several Anabaptists, among them Winsor, James Brown, and Hakin (quoted in ibid., 208–9).

3. More traditional Calvinists felt that revelation was "closed": signs and wonders had been granted to the early Christian church by God for encouragement but were now no longer commonplace, and such manifestations as speaking in tongues were not considered desirable.

4. Bernon to the SPG, April 7, 1724, quoted in Updike, *Episcopal Church in Narragansett*, 60.

5. Fosdick, *French Blood in America*, 143.

6. See the Centre des Archives d'Outre-Mer, La Rochelle, seriesC-11A, vol. 8, folio 288, letter from Governor Denonville to the minister, 1686.

7. Quoted in Fosdick, *French Blood in America*, 143; emphasis in the original.

8. Some sources indicate that the brothers' efforts were successful; others recount the story of the wine cask. For an example of the former, see Fosdick, *French Blood in America*, 144.

9. *Report of a French Protestant*, 26.

10. Cited in Reaman, *Trail of the Huguenots*, 110.

11. Carpenter and Holmes, *South County Studies*, 38.

12. Fosdick, *French Blood in America*, 145.

13. "Gabriel Bernon was Foremost Layman of His Day in R. I.," an article in the *Providence Journal* (1938) by J. Earl Clauson, characterizes Bernon's venture in this way: "It occurred to him to a do a bit of land speculating and a good turn to fellow exiles . . . [in] Oxford, Massachusetts."

14. *The Oxford Settlement*, 136; this is a report found in the Bernon Papers in the Rhode Island Historical Society, Providence.

15. Butler, *Huguenots in America*, 126.

16. *The Oxford Settlement*, 137.

17. As for Bernon's economic prominence: "There was scarcely a branch of colonial traffic to which the versatile Frenchman did not turn his hand" (Baird, *History of the Huguenot Emigration*, 220). Bernon's correspondence is preserved in the Gabriel Bernon Manuscript Collection, Bernon Papers. For instance, there is a letter dated September 1, 1722, from Bernon to James Honeyman regarding the appointment of a minister to the Providence church, and a copy of a letter dated October 4, 1722, from Bernon to Francis Nicholson, of South Carolina, soliciting funds to build a church in Providence. Bernon's first letter to the French Church of New York appears to have been written on March 25, 1699.

18. This reached beyond the French Protestant community to include a wider circle of Protestant denominations: several letters in the Bernon Papers attest to his role in the SPG (see Bernon Papers, scrapbook, 72–73).

19. Meschinet, *Les Protestants rochelais*, 4.

20. Bernon Papers, folder 18.

21. Ibid., folder 20.

22. Kamil mentions Benjamin Faneuil, a prominent merchant in the Boston area (*Fortress of the Soul*, 116). Faneuil was a major investor in Bernon's New Oxford project.

23. Butler, *Huguenots in America*, 66.

24. "The Leislerians had strong economic and cultural interests in Westchester and would have been sympathetic to families with French connections. Jacob Leisler had powerful ties with New York's Huguenot community. His father was Jacob Victorian Leisler, a French Reformed minister in Frankfurt am Main, so Jacob the Younger spoke French and German interchangeably and shared a strong internationalist religious perspective with New York's French refugee community. Indeed, it was Jacob who organized the settlement at New Rochelle between 1687 and 1689, and made certain it was named after La Rochelle" (Kamil, *Fortress of the Soul*, 803).

25. "Unlike the wayward clergy and the affluent merchants and landowners who had, in the Leislerians' view, sold out to the English and the popish James II, the Leislerians saw themselves as people who had stoutly resisted Anglicization and therefore, unlike the clergy, were the true heirs of Dutch religion" (Balmer, *Perfect Babel of Confusion*, 47).

26. Maynard, *The Huguenot Church of New York*, 93.

27. Bellomont was "a Whig who had openly supported the Leislerians back in England" (Balmer, *Perfect Babel of Confusion*, 48). He "approved the exhumation of Leisler and Milborne, calling their execution ' . . . violent cruell and arbitrary' " (ibid.).

28. "The *Boston Gazette* . . . reported that the Jesuits seemed to be taking over the court of France . . . Newspapers' and sermons' constant refrain of Catholic persecution of Protestants in Europe warned New Englanders that they could be next, should they fail to be vigilant and pious" (Kidd, *Protestant Interest*, 109).

29. It was claimed that letters had been found, written in French, saying that if the French fleet came over, it could take New York City without trouble. Elie Neau was one of the Committee that the Church of Saint-Esprit formed to prove that these assertions were slanderous and unfounded. These rumors were dispelled by Lord Cornbury who investigated the matter and then exonerated the French community (Maynard, *Huguenot Church of New York*, 119).

30. "The threat posed by Catholicism became most immediate to New Englanders in time of war, especially during [Jesuit] Father Rale's War of 1722–25. New Englanders had heard for years about the threat of world Catholicism against the international Protestant movement" (Kidd, *Protestant Interest*, 168).

31. "New Englanders also used the perceived threat of Jacobitism as a way to present themselves as unquestionably loyal British Protestants" (ibid.).

32. This may not have been an idle threat: a mere ten years earlier, many of the lower-class Dutch Leislerians had packed up their belongings and moved off in a huff to New Jersey, leaving Manhattan to their more moneyed Dutch Reformed collaborators.

33. Reaman asserts this as support for the claim that many on the *Mayflower* were Huguenots (see *Trail of the Huguenots*, 23).

34. The date of his actual conversion is not sure. However, in 1699, Bernon petitioned to establish an Anglican church in Newport, Rhode Island, so if he did not actually

convert at the time of his naturalization as a British subject, it is probable that he had done so by this date of this request.

35. These poems were important to Neau; in his will, he left the sum of $250, his largest financial bequest, for their continued publication.

36. Maynard, *Huguenot Church of New York*, 94.

37. In the Bernon archives can be found at least two letters documenting their correspondence, one from Bernon to "Elias Neau" dated June 5, 1701, and another dated September 30, 1701.

38. Balmer, *Perfect Babel of Confusion*, 49.

39. The successor to Peyret after his death in 1704 was Jacques Laborie, a pastor trained in Zurich who was active in an Anglican missionary society before coming to America and who, responding to the same trends and pressures as had Bernon, began to apply pressure on the Huguenot Church to conform to Anglicanism when he began his tenure there. Although it resisted, the Church did finally become Anglican in 1802 (Wiley, *French Church of Saint-Esprit*).

40. This is how John Calvin (and not the *tyrannomachs*) interpreted scripture.

41. Quoted in Balmer, *Perfect Babel of Confusion*, 38. Bernon was already a naturalized British citizen, but he would have sympathized with the Dutch clergy's strategy, at least as concerned means.

42. The story deviates from the paradigm that Balmer delineated for the Dutch in the Middle Colonies, for the Huguenot pastors, who were not paid by the Crown but merely accepted subsidies from it, safeguarded their independence to some degree. The mercantile-clerical alliance present in the case of the Dutch was not in evidence here. Increasingly, however, under continued political pressure and urging toward social conformity, the French begin to conform to the Dutch model. The episode related by Maynard may have been a "hold out" case in which the French resisted adaptation and conformity.

43. Bartlett, *Records of Rhode Island*, 213–15.

44. His obituary describes Bernon as "courteous, honest and kind . . . and le[aving] a good name among his acquaintances" (quoted in Clauson, "Gabriel Bernon was Foremost Layman," *Providence Journal*, 1938).

45. Fosdick, *French Blood in America*, 147.

46. Ibid.

47. Ibid.

48. Quoted in ibid., 148.

49. Born in 1685, Berkeley lived in Ireland, Rhode Island, and London, England. He was consecrated bishop in 1732 in Ireland. He died at Oxford in 1753. He was a prolific author and theologian and a proponent of "theological idealism," which comported well with Reformed distrust of the material world and which advocated self-knowing through an examination of one's standing before the Lord, ideas with which Bernon was sympathetic.

50. On this, see Moorman, *Anglican Spiritual Tradition*, especially the prologue, 15–17, and 24–30.

51. Ibid., 32. An additional factor was the ongoing influence of the of the revised Book of Common Prayer (1552), whose doctrines were more in line with Reformed theology: "Cranmer's friends were Calvinists . . . [or] Marian exiles" (ibid., 39).

52. "After his death, among Bernon's personal effects was numbered a book of Psalms, said to have been given to him by a fellow prisoner back in France, and which Bernon had kept in memory of that comrade and of that tribulation" (Austin, *Genealogical Dictionary of Rhode Island*, 21; emphasis added).

53. Epitaph on the tombstone of Gabriel Bernon, St. John's Church, Providence, Rhode Island.

54. Quoted in Updike, *Episcopal Church in Narragansett*, 61.

55. Barnes and Barnes, *Genealogies of Rhode Island*, 486; emphasis added.

Chapter Six. Cotton Mather, Ezéchiel Carré, and the French Connection

The epigraph is quoted in Wendell, *Cotton Mather*, 50.

1. Silverman, *Life and Times of Mather*, 302.

2. "The great tradition of Puritanism he fought so passionately to defend had in it the seeds of a grim, untruthful formalism, which has made it seem to many men of later times a gloomy delusion, fruitful only of limitation and of cant. Those who see in it only or chiefly this, forget what even to Cotton Mather himself was its greatest truth[:] . . . to the Puritans, . . . the infinite mercy of God, with free grace mitigating his infinite justice, gave every living man the chance and the hope of finding in himself the signs of eternal salvation" (Wendell, *Cotton Mather*, 302).

3. Ibid., 109–10.

4. Ibid., 49.

5. Lovelace, *American Pietism of Cotton Mather*.

6. On Mather's suspicions of the French, see for example, Levin, *Cotton Mather*, 61. Among other malevolent acts ascribed to the French, they were blamed for fomenting uprisings by Native Americans: "Boston was having its troubles. As Cotton Mather wrote: 'New England was miserably briared in the perplexities of an Indian war; and the savages in the east part of the country, issuing out from their inaccessible swamps, had for many months made their cruel depredations upon the poor English planters, and surprized many of the plantations on the frontiers into ruin.' Their depredations were laid to the influence of the French" (Boas and Boas, *Cotton Mather*, 85).

7. Kamil refers briefly to Mather's acquaintance with a French refugee: "In 1698, Cotton Mather reached for a broader Protestant audience and published, in Boston, a single lengthy letter to [Elias] Neau's wife, which he translated into English and called *A Present from a Farr Country*" (*Fortress of the Soul*, 402).

8. The most important biography to date, which won a Pulitzer Prize, is Silverman, *Life and Times of Mather*.

9. We saw this in the Gabriel Bernon and the Lord Bellomont issue (see Chapter Five).

10. It is instructive to glance at the indices of the Wendell, Levin, and Silverman biographies. There are five references in Wendell, and they have to do with the politicized notion that French Catholics posed a threat to Boston; he also mentions "French refugees" but not French Protestants. Silverman includes a few references to the French and Indian wars, one to France, and two mentions of "Protestants persecuted in France." Levin has nine references, most of which are taken up with the French and Indian wars. None of the biographers appears to have examined Mather's relationship to Ezéchiel Carré, and none has done anything with Mather's prefaces to Carré's published tracts. There are no index listings for Camisards or Huguenots.

11. Mather quoted in Wendell, *Cotton Mather*, 35.

12. Diary of Cotton Mather, quoted in Wendell, *Cotton Mather*, 68.

13. It is not uncommon for scholars to misidentify Camisards as typical Huguenots. They were Calvinists, but their experience took a different direction because of different circumstances, so their own "distinctives" also need recognition. One should never assume an exact identity between these two groups of French Protestants.

14. Kamil calls this attitude an "eschatology of waiting" (*Fortress of the Soul*, 821, 831). Camisards impatiently awaited the millennium, believing their tribulations to be signs of the fast-approaching Apocalypse. Again, the beliefs and affiliations are not always clear-cut, since the groups influenced each other. There were many Huguenots who shared the Camisard sensibility, however.

15. Many Huguenots were active in the scientific community and were more skeptical of signs and wonders, while Camisards eagerly construed such miraculous phenomena as revelations of God's will.

16. Wendell, *Cotton Mather*, 136.

17. Silverman, *Life and Times of Mather*, 93.

18. "Mather found inspiration in Halle [and in the Camisard and Huguenot experiences] for a more positive evangelical concern for the spiritual and social well-being of Boston . . . He was working consciously to help bring in the premillennial awakening which his eschatology led him to expect in the 1730s . . . a remarkable outpouring of the Holy Spirit. Mather—like the other main figures in the Puritan/Pietist stream—was firmly dedicated to the goal of ecumenical union among evangelical Protestants" (Lovelace, *American Pietism of Cotton Mather*, 8).

19. Ibid., 57. Among these figures were Francke, Anthony William Boehme, and Bartholomew Ziegenbalg. Lovelace traces Mather's pietism exclusively to Germany, overlooking the Camisard influence on the Pietists (see 35–38).

20. Silverman, *Life and Times of Mather*, 302; emphasis added.

21. Lovelace, *American Pietism of Cotton Mather*, 32.

22. The quaking and twitching that characterized early converts to Wesley's theology seem to have been borrowed from the Camisards.

23. Among such Huguenots was Elie Neau, discussed in Chapter Seven.

24. Wendell, *Cotton Mather*, 60, 68. Wendell is working from Mather's diaries.

25. See ibid., 53.

26. Ibid., 29. The influence of those around Cotton Mather was always a significant factor in the development of his theological perspectives, and this was also to be the case in his relations with Ezéchiel Carré and other French Protestant refugees.

27. Silverman, *Life and Times of Mather*, 123; emphasis added.

28. See Mullin, *Miracles and the Religious Imagination*, 25.

29. Knox, *Enthusiasm*, 134.

30. Wendell, *Cotton Mather*, 109. Mather was fervent in his attempts to be worthy of spiritual gifts: "[And so that] those Divels may be cast out by Fasting and prayer, sett apart a Day of Secret prayers with fasting on the occasion of each of them: to Deprecate my own guilitness therein, and supplicate for such Effusions of the Spirit from on High, as may Redress, Remove, and Banish such Distempers from the place" (quoted in ibid., 63).

31. "The role of the prophets during the war was a singular one. They did not lead the troops, but each commando seems to have had its own military chaplain (as it were) whose voice could be more potent than that of the leader himself . . . it was the prophets who decreed whether prisoners should or should not be spared; they sometimes gave the signal for the opening of a battle and prophesied its event, not always with accuracy" (Knox, *Enthusiasm*, 364–65).

32. Kidd, *Great Awakening*, quoting Mather, 5.

33. For the later manifestations, see Wendell, *Cotton Mather*, 206.

34. Ibid., 25.

35. Ibid., 27.

36. This is not to say that there were not other contemporary Puritans who described experiences like Mather's. The similarity with the Camisard descriptions simply suggests another line of influence.

37. Quoted in Silverman, *Life and Times of Mather*, 196.

38. From Cotton Mather's diary entry for June 15, 1699: "This Day, as I was (may I not say?) in the Spirit, it was in a powerful Manner assured me from Heaven, that my Father shall one Day be carried unto England: and that he shall there glorify the Lord Jesus Christ: and that the Particular Faith which had introduced it, shall be at last made a manner of wonderful Glory and Service unto the Lord" (quoted in Boas and Boas, *Cotton Mather*, 141).

39. Mather, quoted in Silverman, *Life and Times of Mather*, 43.

40. Mather's diary for August 28, 1698, quoted in Wendell, *Cotton Mather*, 167.

41. See Caldwell, *Puritan Conversion Narrative*, 24.

42. It could be found earlier, in the first generation of Huguenots to be persecuted, during the sixteenth-century Wars of Religion. But even Théodore de Bèze or Agrippa d'Aubigné, while speaking of spiritual phenomena, was much more likely to avoid subjective statements or highly emotional turns of phrase, and to scaffold his writing on biblical references rather than a description of phenomena experienced by the individual believer; see Coats, *Subverting the System*.

43. A similar vocabulary was used to describe the sorts of angelic visitations recorded by the Huguenot Elias Boudinot (see Kidd, *Great Awakening*, 33).

44. Mather, *Grounds and Ends*, 160.

45. Caldwell describes this attitude as one of "suspicion, even animosity, toward the possibilities of language itself. Words must be handled very gingerly . . . If only the language of individual saints could be kept absolutely under control . . . 'For want of such a Rule,' see what social and psychological havoc . . . may follow" (*Puritan Conversion Narrative*, 102–3).

46. Manuscript records of Second Church, Massachusetts Historical Society, Mather Papers, Reel 4B, fr. 0249.

47. As both Pierre Jurieu and François Misson documented; see Chapters Two and Three.

48. Cotton Mather, diary for 1685, quoted in Wendell, *Cotton Mather*, 64.

49. "I used secret prayer, not confining myself to Forms in it" (Mather, *Corderius Americanus* [1708], quoted in Wendell, *Cotton Mather*, 33).

50. Quoted in Boas and Boas, *Cotton Mather*, 141; emphasis added.

51. He wrote in support of many causes. Mather could always be counted on by the ministers and magistrates to pen provisions. When others declined to write about the witchcraft trials, Mather readily acquiesced, even though he was not present at them. Mather's baroque style, larded with italics, hyperbole, ejaculations, Latinisms, and scriptural citations, was bombastically delivered—and much dissimilar from the Calvinist "plain style."

52. Mentioned in Wendell, *Cotton Mather*, 68.

53. By espousing this ideological stance in this way, Mather deviates from the customary portrait of him as austere and buttoned-down. Such apparent contradictions may seem to illustrate, but in fact belie, Silverman's characterization of Mather as "ambidexter." Many of Mather's contemporaries called him this. The phrase signifies the professing of one stance while acting in a contrary way, and experiencing great ambivalence over the taking and holding of positions.

54. Wendell, *Cotton Mather*, 53.

55. Levin, *Cotton Mather*, 102.

56. Gywnn, *Huguenot Heritage*, 137.

57. See Silverman, *Life and Times of Mather*, 198, 199. He seemed also to want to develop a transcontinental ecumenism (among Protestants); see Lovelace, *American Pietism of Cotton Mather*, 34, 63.

58. Quoted in Silverman, *Life and Times of Mather*, 234.

59. Ibid., 241.

60. Kidd, *Great Awakening*, 93–94.

61. "Ezéchiel Carré, a minister from Chatelerault in Poitou, France. Came with Pierre Berthon de Marigny to Narragansett Colony RI 1681–1685. 45 families in this colony" (Reaman, *Trail of the Huguenots*, 213).

62. This was a disputed claim, although the plantation had been awarded to Rhode Island Colony by the king. It is not clear whether the Huguenots approached individual proprietors, the representatives of Narragansett in the Dominion of New England, or the colonial government.

63. Kamil mentions Carré: "Ezeckiel [*sic*] Carré, a Huguenot minister, a native of the Ile de Ré . . . emigrated in 1686 with twenty-five other French families to the short-lived settlement of Frenchtown in East Greenwich, Rhode Island" (*Fortress of the Soul*, 743).

64. *Report of a French Protestant*, 19.

65. For the settlers' hope to attract "above 500 French families" to join them, see Baird, *History of the Huguenot Emigration*, 299.

66. From the diary of Dr. Ayrault, quoted in ibid.

67. "Lord Bellomont to the Lords of Trade, November 28, 1700," quoted in Maynard, *Huguenot Church of New York*, 104.

68. Ibid., 302. The New England colonies were subsumed under one government (Dudley and Andros) in 1684–1688.

69. Maynard, *Huguenot Church of New York*, 103.

70. From the diary of Dr. Ayrault, quoted in Baird, *History of the Huguenot Emigration*, 308.

71. *Report of a French Protestant*, 10.

72. Baird suggested that the earliest cell of a French church in Boston may have been gathered by Pierre Daillé shortly after coming to the colonies in 1682 (*History of the Huguenot Emigration*, 220). Baird also believed that Daillé was sent to Boston at the urging of the bishop of London through the Society for the Propagation of the Gospel in Foreign Parts.

73. For establishing the church in a former schoolhouse, see Massachusetts Archives (Oxford), vol. IXXXI, 472. Bondet was also the pastor with whom Gabriel Bernon founded New Oxford, Massachusetts, as a "refugee" town; Carré was a cousin of Bernon's.

74. *Report of a French Protestant*, 36.

75. "I can assure you that I have passed Winters in Languedoc more severe than this one" (ibid., 33).

76. Ibid., 30.

77. Ibid., iv–v.

78. Reaman, *Trail of the Huguenots*, 158.

79. John E. Latourette, "Another Latourette Fable: The Rhode Island Colony," www.latourette.net/rhodeisland.html.

80. Manuel, *James Bowdoin*, 45.

81. Blaikie, *Presbyterianism in New England*, 32.

82. Mather, preface to Carré, *Charitable Samaritan*, 4; emphasis added. For more on the radical preaching of the French Prophets, the best source is Schwartz, *French Prophets*.

83. Among others, they claimed the ability to raise the dead.

84. Indeed, Bellomont, governor of the New York colony, refused to grant naturalization to any Frenchman who could not prove that he was Protestant.

85. Carré, *Charitable Samaritan*, "Advertisement," a3.

86. Ibid.

87. Mather, preface to Carré, *Charitable Samaritan*, a2.

88. Baird, *History of the Huguenot Emigration*, 303.

89. Ibid., 305.

90. Mather, preface to Carré, *Charitable Samaritan*, 1.

91. The anonymous author of the *Report of a French Protestant* called the New World the "Land of Exile" (v).

92. Carré, *Charitable Samaritan*, 15.

93. Quoted in Baird, *History of the Huguenot Emigration*, 306.

94. Carré, *Charitable Samaritan*, 15.

95. Ibid., "Advertisement," A1. This practice, first normalized by John Calvin in Geneva, has remained a part of Reformed piety.

96. Ibid., 25.

97. Bishop Compton Papers, Library of the French Church of London, Soho Square, document dated April 2, 1686.

98. See Coats, *Subverting the System*, especially 83–85 on "election and expression."

99. Carré, *Charitable Samaritan*, 15.

100. Ibid., 17; see Randall, *Building Codes*, especially Chapter 3 on Bernard Palissy's Calvinist explication of the parable of the talents and its broader significance for Huguenots in general.

101. Carré, *Charitable Samaritan*, 8.

102. This concern to operate not from emotion but rather from rational principles was reinforced by contemporary science, to the point that "the more precise formulation of celestial mechanics and the other triumphs of the scientific revolution did create skepticism . . . and discredited Spirit" (Silverman, *Life and Times of Mather*, 93).

103. Carré, *Charitable Samaritan*, 12.

104. Ibid., 17.

105. Ibid., 5; emphasis added. This passage may counter Kamil's thesis that southwestern Huguenots—of which Carré was one—practiced passive resistance.

106. Gwynn, *Huguenot Heritage*, 137.

107. "What then? Hath a Sinner any ability for Grace? Shall we say that man in his Natural Corruption then is not Dead in Sin . . . but he is wounded, he is but half dead" (Carré, *Charitable Samaritan*, 12).

108. Ibid.

109. Ibid., 16.

110. Middlekauff, *The Mathers*, 215.

111. Carré, *Charitable Samaritan*, 3.

112. Ibid., 3–4.

113. Ibid., 20, 24.

114. Mather, preface to Carré, *Charitable Samaritan*, 1.

115. Such millenarianism had been in the air since the beginning of the century and earlier, and some Puritans, such as Joseph Mede Richard Baxter, espoused these beliefs. Cotton Mather wrote defending his beliefs in *Wonders of the Invisible World* (1692) and preached at least one apocalyptic sermon (following the Andover conversions) early in his career. He also at one point speculated that the Salem witchcraft manifestations

might be harbingers of the end-times (Silverman, *Life and Time of Mather*, 107). Mather also read and admired the prolific and influential millenarian theorist Pierre Jurieu.

116. Kidd, *Protestant Interest*, 29–30.

117. Mather, quoted in Silverman, *Life and Times of Mather*, 129.

118. Mather, preface to Carré, *Charitable Samaritan*, 4. As already noted, Nehemiah Walker was the actual translator, yet Mather chose to call himself the "translator" in the preface, perhaps recalling the Latin sense of "trahere," in which a product is carried across from one place—France—to another—the colonies.

119. Mather, preface to Carré, *Charitable Samaritan*, 2.

120. Ibid., 3.

121. Ibid., 2.

122. Perhaps this is more evidence of what Silverman calls Mather's "ambidextrous" nature.

123. Mather, preface Carré, *Charitable Samaritan*, 3. For Mather's account of the Salem witch trials, see his *Memorable Providences*.

124. Quoted in Kidd, *Protestant Interest*, 70.

125. This was also the case with Huguenots. Van Ruymbeke showed that the Huguenots appealed incessantly to the Edict of Nantes and, in so doing, defined themselves de facto as loyal subjects of the Crown ("Minority Survival," in *Memory and Identity*, 4). This stance was more surprising—and even heroic—when taken by the Camisards after the *dragonnades* began; they have been described as "more loyalist than the King, exhibiting the 'patience of a Huguenot'" (Utt and Strayer, *Bellicose Dove*, 1).

126. Mather, *Suspiria victorum*, 129. Similar protestations are found in Misson's collection of Camisard testimonials.

127. Kidd, *Protestant Interest*, 62.

128. Ibid., 62, 63.

129. Mather describes the dragoons "using wherewithal the thousand other Cruelties, which none but the wit of Divels could have invented for them. And if none of these things brought the Protestants to Renounce the Truth of the Lord Jesus, they were cast into horrible Dungeons, where they pined away to Death" (preface to Carré, *Charitable Samaritan*, 3).

130. Ibid., 4.

131. Ibid.

132. See Haefeli and Stanwood, "Jesuits, Huguenots, and the Apocalypse."

133. Mather's venture into French echoed Camisard glossolalia.

134. Carré, *Echantillon*, A3.

135. "Il est vray semblable toujours que ceci servira avec tant d'autres écrits faits sur pareil sujet à faire connetre combien ces gens là ont une Doctrine pernicieuse et une Morale relâchée" (Carré, *Echantillon*, A3).

136. "Que nous serions heureus, mes chers freres, si Dieu se servait de nôtre [*sic*] moyen pour aider à détruire ces villains inféctes!... ceci servira... à faire connetrè combien ces gens là ont une Doctrine pernicieuse et une Morale relâchée... cela

confirmera de plus en plus en vos coeurs les justes mouvemens d'aversion que vous avez . . . pour cette impure Société" (Mather, preface to Carré, *Echantillon*, A2).

137. "J'espere que cela confirmera de plus en plus en vos coeurs les justes mouvemens d'aversion que vous avez jusqu'á present pour cette impure Société et quanques avoir abandonné vos biens vos Parens et votre Patrie vous serez encore prets à abandonner votre vie plutot que dentrer dans la communion dont ils font á present la partie la plus considerable" (ibid., A2–A3). Mather's statement showed his awareness that some French Protestants had initially capitulated—and converted to Catholicism to escape persecution in France.

138. In this, Mather also echoed the thought of renowned Calvinist clergyman and lawyer Claude Brousson, who had preached in Nîmes in the 1660s and whose thought was influential, some decades later, in the development of a coherent ideology for the Camisard cause. He blamed "the Society of Jesus and the Company for the Propagation of the Faith [an arch-Catholic group formed by Louis XIV] for making Protestantism 'odious' [and] defended the Reformation as necessary to restore doctrinal purity and religious freedom in France" (Utt and Strayer, *Bellicose Dove*, 10).

139. Baird, *History of the Huguenot Emigration*, 230.

140. "The opinion had been broached, in Protestant Europe, that the great persecution in France was the theme of Apocalyptic vision, and that the suffering Huguenots were symbolized in the book of Revelation by the Two Witnesses clothed in sackcloth, slain in the street of the great city" (ibid.).

141. Brousson's dates are 1647–1698. Born in Nîmes, a cradle area for Camisard enthusiasm, he vigorously attempted to defend the rights of French Protestants in France despite strong contemporary (Catholic) attempts to undermine the status of the Edict of Nantes. The "Bons Catholiques" called the Huguenots "enemies of the State", a charge that Brousson persistently sought to deny through the mechanism of the law courts as well as through his preaching (Utt and Strayer, *Bellicose Dove*, 6).

142. "What proved essential to the survival of Protestantism in France was the mystique of resistance and recovery associated with Claude Brousson—the 'bellicose dove'—and the underground lay preachers in the critical time just after the Revocation" (ibid., 4). For the minority status (*fait minoritaire*) of the French Protestant community, both in France and in exile, see Van Ruymbeke, *Memory and Identity*, 2.

143. Utt and Strayer, *Bellicose Dove*, 118.

144. This insight comes from Randall Balmer (personal communication).

145. Printer's notice, ("Advertisement"), Carré, *Echantillon*.

146. Baird, *History of the Huguenot Emigration*, 221.

147. Baird acknowledges that this endorsement was somewhat unusual (ibid., 229). Baird is the only scholar to have noticed that Mather joined forces with the French Protestants.

148. The incipit to Carré's *Echantillon* also introduced and framed Mather's French preface: it urged the need to attend to the workings of the Holy Spirit ("Esprouvès les Esprits s'ils sont de Dieu. 1 Jean 4.1," Carré, *Echantillon*, 1).

149. Silverman, *Life and Times of Mather*, 145. Silverman notes, for instance, that Mather "sought a rapprochement with English Protestants" for this reason, and suggests "ecumenical tendencies that had long existed within Puritanism (Richard Baxter was a pioneer ecumenist) [on which Mather may have drawn in his awareness of] . . . the need for allies in the raging struggle against Catholic Europe" (79).

150. Some scholars flatly deny such an ecumenical attitude on Mather's part; Middlekauff, among others, speaks of any such endorsements of toleration on Mather's part during the 1690s as "undoubtedly insincere" (*The Mathers*, 28).

151. Not only the French have suffered from such neglect. Henry Selyns, the prominent Dutch Reformed minister in New York, is not mentioned in Silverman's study either. I owe this observation to Balmer, who rectified the oversight in *A Perfect Babel of Confusion*.

152. Quoted in Rice, "Cotton Mather Speaks," 198.

Chapter Seven. *Elie Neau and French Protestant Pietism in Colonial New York*

1. "L'Eternel se moque d'eux. Il me semble que j'entens sa voix dans le fonds de mon coeur, qui me dit comme à son Prophète Esaye: 'Parle haut . . . Eleve ta voix comme une trompette . . . declare . . . les richesses de ma misericorde . . .' Et je suis tres persuadé que . . . [Dieu] étendra sa providence sur moi jusqu'à la fin" (Neau, *Histoire abbrégée*, 151–53).

2. Zysberg, *Les Galériens*, 8.

3. Ibid., 19.

4. "Que profitera-t-il à l'homme s'il gagne tout le monde, et qu'il fasse perte de son âme, ou que donnera l'homme pour récompense de son âme?" (Neau, *Histoire abbrégée*, 8).

5. "Pour avoir obéi à Jésus" (ibid., 10).

6. A customary formula: "la mort ou la Messe" (ibid., 12).

7. Ibid., 13.

8. "Que . . . je prends plaisir dans les angoisses, et dans les oppressions pour ton glorieux Nom . . . que ton amour me fasse supporter avec joye les peines les plus cruelles, qui me sont infligées par ton amour . . . [que je trouve] tous les moyens de te glorifier dans mes souffrances" (ibid., 15–22).

9. Ibid., 52.

10. Ibid., 53.

11. Kamil has suggested that some of the Huguenot experience in the Saintonge region in the 1680s was similar to early Camisard experience, and that passive resistance was not unknown in that region among Huguenots: "Neau . . . endured a period of . . . quietist contemplation that recalled sixteenth-century Saintongeais experiences" (*Fortress of the Soul*, 402).

12. "Je n'épouse point les erreurs de l'Eglise Romaine; je ne participe point à son culte idolâtre. Et . . . je ne suis point Papiste, je conserve mon coeur à Dieu . . . Ils vont à la Messe, comme si le Temple des Idoles, & le Temple de Dieu étoient la même chose, ils

assistent au prétendu sacrifice de la Messe . . . leurs Prédicateurs de mensonge . . . ils n'ont plus d'horreur pour entrer dans les lieux où Christ est de nouveau crucifié" (Neau, *Histoire abbrégée*, 63–65).

13. Zysberg, *Les Galériens*, 11.

14. "La patience avec laquelle il souffroit toutes ces épreuves, édifia merveilleusement tous ceux qui en furent témoins. Ses discours pieux et chrétiens lui attiroient l'attention de toute la chiourme; l'exemple qu'il donnoit d'une vie sainte & religieuse, accompagné d'une douceur qui est le caractere du Christianisme, le firent admirer des plus scélérats, l'horreur qu'il avoit pour le mal, le soin qu'il prenoit de convertir les errants & d'inspirer la sainteté aux corrompus, firent qu'il y en eut d'entr'eux . . . en effet il y en eût qui donnerent gloire à Dieu en se convertissant. Et c'est ce qui irrita si fort l'Aumônier de la Galere contre Neau . . . parce qu'il voyoit d'ailleurs l'aversion invincible que nôtre Confesseur avoit pour le Culte Romain" (Neau, *Histoire abbrégée*, 79; Neau is talking about himself in the third person).

15. Tournier, *Les galères de France*, 45. For more on this experience, see Zysberg, *Les Galériens*.

16. "La guerre des Camisards fit remonter le niveau des sentences" (ibid., 64).

17. Neau called the Jesuits "gens cruels et barbares" ("cruel barbarians") and characterized them in this way: "In their zeal to persecute, they were especially tough on those who had been sentenced to the galleys because of their religion. And since those would neither listen nor understand what [the Jesuits] were preaching to them, the Jesuits told them that they were there to try to save them. Upon hearing that, [one of the Camisards] said to [the Jesuits]: 'Physician, heal thyself'" (Neau, *Histoire abbrégée*, 125). ["Ces zelez . . . s'attachoient principalement à ceux qui souffroient sur les Galeres pour cause de Religion. Et comme ceux ci ne vouloient ni les ouïr, ni les entendre, les Jésuites leur dirent qu'ils étoient là pour travailler à leur conversion. Sur quoi quelqu'un leur dit, 'Medecin gueri [*sic*] toi toi-mesme.'"]

18. A customary phrase heralding another beating was the sadistic remark "Let's go make a Huguenot salad," the comment reflecting the practice of rubbing salt and vinegar into a prisoner's flesh after it had been beaten raw; this practice was called the *bastonnade*.

19. "Dieu a choisi . . . les choses foibles de ce monde pour rendre confuses les fortes" (Neau, *Histoire abbrégée*, 124).

20. "En entrant dans le Château d'Y, & dans ses cachots, Dieu aveugla les inspecteurs du Confesseur pour qu'ils ne vissent pas c[e] precieux livr[e] qui allai[t] desormais causer un redoublement d'etude & de consolation à ce cher prisonnier" (ibid., 106).

21. Tournier, *Les galères de France*, 52.

22. "Les Galeres, les cachots, le bois, la pierre, tout parle des souffrances de nos Confesseurs: Et pourquoi nous tairions-nous plus long-temps? De plus ne faut-il pas édifier, réjouïr et consoler ses frères en leur mettant devant les yeux de si beaus exemples que ceux qui nous viennent de ces heureux athletes qui sortent victorieux du combat?" (Neau, *Histoire abbrégée*, iii).

23. Ibid., iii.

24. "Fut si bien converti . . . qu'il ne seroit jamais de l'Eglise Romaine. On lui fit ôter le Nouveau Testament qu'il avoit. Cela fut le sujet d'une nouvelle persecution contre moi" (ibid., 191); the last part is implied.

25. "Nous ne possedons rien en particulier qui ne soit mis avec joye en commun" (ibid., 117).

26. The body of Neau's letters thus served, remarkably, the same purpose as had many of the Apostle Paul's letters from prison: to invigorate and encourage the Christian community.

27. "Je suis dedans par la grace de Dieu" (Neau to Messieurs le Boiteux in Amsterdam, in *Histoire abbrégée*, 110).

28. "I am . . . confined in a very small space, but only my body is imprisoned; my faith is free" (ibid., 131). ["Je suis . . . renfermé dans un petit coin, mais par bonheur il n'y a que mon corps de renfermé, ma foi ne l'est point."]

29. "Cela me fit absorber dans mon néant . . . Dan ce tems là je commençai d'éprouver l'effet des promesses de mon Dieu . . . Je me vis comblé de graces & absorbé dans un fleuve de chastes delices . . . Dieu m'ouvrit les cinq playes de mon Redempteur pour laver les impuretez de mon ame" (Neau to Morin, in *Histoire abbrégée*, 147).

30. Neau, *Histoire abbrégée*, 162.

31. "Combatt[ant] avec constance les ennemis de mon salut qui s'opposent à ma course . . . je me range sous l'étendart de la vraye milice chrétienne" (ibid., 170).

32. Ibid., 183.

33. "Mon adorable Jesus promet le centuple à ceux qui abandonnent tout pour l'amour de lui. Mais je dis en le benissant, qu'il m'en donne beaucoup d'avantage, car il me fait preferer un moment en le possedant, à une vie plus longue & la plus tranquille sur la terre sans lui. Ma prison est admirablement convertie en un lieu de liberté" (ibid., 102).

34. "My eyesight is like that of an owl, due to the splendor of the Sun, which I have not seen in so long" (Neau to Morin, July 4, 1698, in *Histoire abbrégée*, 200). ["J'ai la vûë comme les chöuettes, à cause de l'éclat de la splendeur du Soleil, qu'il y a long-tems que je n'avois pas vû."]

35. "Le relevement de ce grand troupeau lui avoit fait trop de joye . . . il [alla] mêler sa joye à celle de tant de Fideles. Aussi n'entendoit on là que des actions de graces à Dieu, ou des entretiens pieux sur les merveilles que Dieu avoit faites" (Neau, *Histoire abbrégée*, 201).

36. "Où il trouva un reste de freres charitables qui le recûrent fort humainement" (ibid., 202).

37. "Il sortit de France comme d'une cruelle Egypte" (ibid.).

38. Ibid., 203.

39. This was in marked contrast to the treatment some of the other Camisards were awarded. Neau said that "the pastors and professors received [me] with incredible tenderness, giving thanks to God, and blessing God for this marvelous deliverance" (ibid., 202). ["Messieurs les Pasteurs, & les Professeurs [me] reçurent avec des tendresses incroyables, rendans graces à Dieu, & le benissans pour cette merveilleuse delivrance."]

40. Ibid., 204. He especially spoke on Ragatz's behalf. The two were to sustain a lengthy correspondence. Bern was known for its willingness to give aid to Calvinists, having already sent money and supplies on many occasions into France and the Piedmont.

41. "Il n'y a que ceux qui ont été véritablement illuminez des lumieres de la grace salutaire . . . qui ont été veritablement faits participans du S. Esprit, & qui ont veritablement goûté les douceurs de la bonne Parole [peuvent nous aider] . . . [vous êtes] Lazare retiré hors du Sepulchre" (Ragatz to Neau, in ibid., 244).

42. Included in Tournier, *Les galères de France*, appendix 7, 261–76.

43. "Vous ne vous êtes point caché; vous n'avez point biaisé, ni varié le moins du monde, lorsqu'il s'est agi de rendre raison de vôtre foi . . . vous avez hautement déclaré sans déguisement & sans détour que vous n'aviez d'autre Religion que celle que Jesus-Christ nous a revelée . . . [vous offrez] un exemple de ce que peut la grace" (French Church of New York to Neau, September 28, 1696 [while Neau was still in prison], in Neau, *Histoire abbrégée*, 213–14).

44. "The church was undoubtedly Protestant" (Maynard, *Huguenot Church of New York*, 93).

45. Morin termed them "autant de témoignages des saintes & pieuses occupations de cet âme fidèle dans le fonds de ses cachots" ("testimonials of the holy occupations of this faithful soul while deep in his cell"); quoted in Neau, *Histoire abbrégée*, 190.

46. Quoted in Wendell, *Cotton Mather*, 55.

47. "Viens Saint Esprit que j'adore, / M'absorber dans ton amour . . . / Plonge en ton immensité / Toute ma capacité / Et que dans ta plénitude / J'y trouve ma quiétude" (Neau, Cantique V, *Histoire abbrégée*, 259).

48. Morin and Jacobi, *Life and Sufferings of Neau*. Kamil includes a reproduction of this engraving, but interprets it rather differently, discerning alchemical, "Palissian," and neo-Rosicrucian symbolism in it (*Fortress of the Soul*, 403). There is a simpler and more evident equation to be drawn: an exact equivalence between what Neau says and how the engraver illustrates his text. Everything that Neau describes is faithfully and literally rendered by the illustrator.

49. The text, first published in 1689 (and reissued in 1749), was essentially a reprise of the text that Mather had translated and caused to be published in Boston in 1698. The engraving appeared only in the 1749 edition; see Kamil, *Fortress of the Soul*, 402.

50. "Je vous prie de penser la vie qu'un homme peut mener dans un cachot sans lumière qu'au travers la porte; on a maçonné ma fenêtre . . . deffense à personne de nous parler . . . sans feu, sans chandelle . . . Mais si je vous dis qu'au defaut de la lumière du soleil de la nature, le soleil de la grace fait briller ses divines rayons dans nos coeurs . . . que diriez-vous? Je suis dedans par la grace de Dieu" (Neau, *Histoire abbrégée*, 110).

51. Kamil, *Fortress of the Soul*, 402.

52. Neau, *Histoire abbrégée*, 18.

53. "O viens donc faire ta demeure dans mon ame, pour m'affirmer dans ton amour, en sorte que je dise nuit & jour, 'je suis à mon bien-aimé'" (ibid., 17–18).

54. Ibid., 69.

55. Ibid., 63–65.

56. "Voilà, ma chère soeur ... je vise à arracher vôtre âme d'entre les bras de la mort ... sortez du tombeau de vos péchez ... Ne remettez pas au lendemain à vous repentir" (ibid., 141).

57. Ibid.

58. "Le soin que la providence de Dieu a de moi" (ibid., 173).

59. "Et Dieu veuille que vôtre exemple, & vos liens, contribuent en quelque façon à une oeuvre si salutaire" (ibid., 55).

60. In 1696, the Quaker printer William Bradford also published Neau's letters from prison in French (as *A Treasury of consolations*). See also Kamil, *Fortress of the Soul*, 402.

61. Maynard, *Huguenot Church of New York*, 92.

62. Butler, *Huguenots in America*, 76, 160.

63. Ibid., 71.

64. Kamil, *Fortress of the Soul*, 402.

65. Nonetheless, the factors for such decisions, and their consequences, deserve more programmatic examination, since, as Butler observes, Neau's "influence among most New York Huguenots [ended] because [of his] conformity to the Church of England" (*Huguenots in America*, 162). The Camisard spirit comported with Anglican theology and ecclesiology; see Moorman, *Anglican Spiritual Tradition*.

66. "The legendary Elias Neau had launched this distinct congregation in 1704 under the auspices of the Society for the Propagation of the Gospel in Foreign Parts (SPG), the newly created missionary arm of the Church of England, which was designed to bring the Anglican faith to the colonies' slaves and Native Americans. Neau was an unlikely person for the post, having arrived in New York in 1691 as a French Protestant (a Huguenot) fleeing the enforcement of the Roman Catholic faith in his native land. He was not, therefore, an Anglican (though he had been granted British citizenship by this time) nor was he ordained. Yet the SPG forced his appointment on Trinity's rector, the Rev. William Vesey, overcoming one objection by requiring Neau to join the Church of England. The SPG also agreed to pay his salary" (Townsend, *Faith in Their Own Color*, 14).

67. There are letters in the Bernon archives to and from the SPG as well as correspondence with Neau. David Humphreys was the secretary who wrote on behalf of the SPG.

68. Neau's conversion to Anglicanism may have been prophetic, since in 1803 the French Protestant churches voted to accept the denominational authority of the American Episcopal church—formerly Anglican. The Huguenot church in New York was renamed at this time the Church of Saint-Esprit.

69. Maynard, *Huguenot Church of New York*, 92.

70. Ibid., 93.

71. Another similarity between Mather and Neau was that Mather published in 1693 a tract entitled *Rules for the Society of Negroes*, attesting to his concern for inculcating Christian principles and for educating, if not manumitting, his slaves. While Neau was not in Boston at the date of Mather's publication of some of Neau's writings—he had taken up residence as a merchant trader in New York in 1690 after having emigrated

in 1688—the two may later have had correspondence concerning their shared attitudes toward the treatment of slaves.

72. Maynard, *Huguenot Church of New York*, 93.

73. "Neau was not immediately successful, as he had to overcome slaveowners' concerns that making Christians of slaves might be construed as making them legally free. Neau and Vesey set this obstacle aside by persuading the British governor to obtain an act confirming the status of slaves as such after baptism" (Townsend, *Faith in Their Own Color*, 15).

74. "More than the taking of sides in the political life of New York, and even its economic life, this story of Elie Naud [*sic*] represents the Huguenot spirit. Across the haze of centuries, [the] ancestors are now only names, but we know the Book they read, the psalms they sang, the faith they believed, and we know them to have been good men and true, French of course, and that gave to their religious life a certain characteristic" (Maynard, *Huguenot Church of New York*, 94).

Conclusion. "A Habitation Elsewhere"

1. Littleton, "Acculturation and the French Church," 97.

2. Frijhoff, "Uncertain Brotherhood," 132.

3. Mentzer, "Sociability and Culpability," 45.

4. Butler, "Huguenots and the Immigrant Experience," 200–201.

BIBLIOGRAPHY

An Account of the French Prophets and their Pretended Inspirations. London, 1708.

An Account of the Present Condition of the Protestants in the Palatinate James [sic], 2nd. ed. London, 1699.

Adams, Geoffrey. *The Huguenots and French Opinion, 1685–1787: The Enlightenment Debate on Toleration.* Waterloo, Ontario: Wilfrid Laurier University Press, 1991.

Archer, Richard. "New England Mosaic: A Demographic Analysis for the Seventeenth Century." *William and Mary Quarterly* 47, no. 4 (October 1990): 17–28.

Aubigné, Théodore-Agrippa d'. "Les Misères." In *Oeuvres,* edited by Henri Weber. Paris: Gallimard, 1969.

Austin, John Osborne. *The Genealogical Dictionary of Rhode Island: Comprising Three Generations of Settlers Who Came before 1690.* Albany, N.Y.: Munsell's Sons, 1887.

Bacquet, Christian. "Prophétisme montaniste, prophétisme cévenol, essai de mise en parallèle." HOREB, May 2, 1986.

Baird, Charles. *History of the Huguenot Emigration to America.* New York: Dodd, Mead, 1885. Reprint, Baltimore: Genealogical Publishing, 1998.

Balmer, Randall. *Mine Eyes Have Seen the Glory: A Journey into the Evangelical Subculture in America.* 4th ed. New York: Oxford University Press, 2006.

———. *A Perfect Babel of Confusion: Dutch Religion and English Culture in the Middle Colonies.* New York: Oxford University Press, 1989.

———. *Thy Kingdom Come: How the Religious Right Distorts the Faith and Threatens America; An Evangelical's Lament.* New York: Basic Books, 2006.

Bamford, Paul. "The Procurement of Oarsmen for French Galleys, 1660–1748." *American Historical Review* 65 (1959): 31–48.

Barnes, Robert, and Catherine Barnes, indexers. *Genealogies of Rhode Island Families: From Rhode Island Periodicals.* Vol. 2: *Bates–Smith.* Baltimore: Genealogical Publications, 1983.

Barthélemy, E., ed. *Mémoire et Journal des Camisards.* Montpellier, 1974.

Bartlett, John Russell, ed. *Records of the Colony of Rhode Island and Providence Plantations in New England.* Vol. 4: 1707–1740. Providence: Knowles, Anthony, State Printers, 1859. Reprint, New York: AMS Press.

Baum, Johann, ed. *Mémoires de Pierre Carrière dit Corteiz, pasteur du Désert.* Strasbourg, 1871.

Beik, William. *Absolutism and Society in Seventeenth-Century France: State Power and Provincial Aristocracy in Languedoc.* Cambridge: Cambridge University Press, 1985.

Benoît, Daniel, ed. *Durand, Marie, prisonnière à la tour de Constance (1730–1768) sa famille et ses compagnes de captivité et ses compagnes de captivité d'après des documents inédits.* Toulouse: Société des livres religieux, 1884.

Bercé, Yves-Marie. *Croquants et nu-pieds: Les soulèvements paysans en France du XVIe au XIXe siècle.* Folio, 1974.

Bernard, M. "Journal de voyage aux Indies de Thomas-Simon Berard, 1712." *Bulletin de la société de l'histoire du protestantisme français* 90 (1941): 239–62.

Bernon, Gabriel. Bernon Papers. Rhode Island Historical Society, Providence.

Blaikie, Alexander. *A History of Presbyterianism in New England: Its Introduction, Growth, Decay, Revival, and Present Mission*. Boston: Moore, 1881.

Blanc, Cilette. "Genève et les origines du mouvement prophétique en Dauphiné dans les Cévennes." *Revue d'histoire suisse*, 1943: 33–54.

Boas, Ralph, and Louise Boas. *Cotton Mather, Keeper of the Puritan Conscience*. New York: Harper, 1928.

Bonbonnoux, Jacques. *Mémoires de Bonbonnoux, chef Camisard et pasteur du Désert*. Rept., Cévennes, 1883.

Bonnemère, Eugène. *Histoire des Camisards*. Paris: Cerf, 1869.

Bosc, Henri. *La Guerre des Cévennes: 1702–1710*. 5 vols. Montpellier, 1985–1990.

Bost, Charles, ed. *Mémoires inédits d'Abraham Mazel et d'Elie Marion*. Paris, 1931.

Bost, Henri. *Pierre Bayle et la religion*. Paris: PUF, 1994.

Briggs, Robin. *Communities of Belief: Cultural and Social Tension in Early Modern France*. Oxford: Clarendon, 1969.

Brodin, Pierre. *Les Quakers en Amérique du Nord au XVIIe siècle et au début du XVIIIe*. Paris: Dervy-livres, 1985.

Brousson, Claude. *La manne mystique du Désert*. Amsterdam, 1695.

Brueys, David-Augustin de. *Histoire du fanatisme de notre temps*. 3 vols. Utrecht, 1737.

Bunyan, John. *Grace Abounding to the Chief of Sinners*. London: Larkin, 1666.

Butler, Jon. "The Huguenots and the American Immigrant Experience." In Van Ruymbreke and Sparks, *Memory and Identity*, 194–207.

———. *The Huguenots in America: A Refugee People in New World Society*. Cambridge, Mass.: Harvard University Press, 1983.

———. "Les 'Hymnes ou cantiques sacrez' d'Elie Neau: Un nouveau manuscrit du 'grand mystique des galères.'" *Bulletin de la société de l'histoire du protestantisme français* 124 (1978): 416–32.

Cabanel, Patrick, and Philippe Joutard, eds. *Les Camisards et leur mémoire, 1702–2002*. Montpellier: Les Presses du Languedoc, 2002.

Caldwell, Patricia. *The Puritan Conversion Narrative: The Beginnings of American Expression*. Cambridge Studies in American Literature and Culture. Cambridge: Cambridge University Press, 1983.

Calvin, John. *Commentary on the Epistles of Paul the Apostle to the Corinthians*. Translated by J. Pringle. Grand Rapids, Mich.: Eerdmans, 1979.

———. *The Institutes of the Christian Religion*. Translated by Henry Beveridge. Edited by Tony Lane and Hilary Osbourne. Grand Rapids, Mich.: Baker Book House, 1993.

Carpenter, Esther Bernon, and Oliver Wendell Holmes. *South County Studies of Some Eighteenth Century Persons: Places and Conditions in That Part of Rhode Island Called Narragansett*. Boston, 1924. Reprint, New York: Ayer, 1971.

Carré, Ezéchiel. *The Charitable Samaritan*. Translated by Nehemiah Walter. Boston, 1689.

——. *Echantillon: De la doctrine que les Jésuites enségnent aus sauvages du Nouveau Monde.* Boston: Samuel Green, 1690.

The Case of the Poor French Refugees. N.p., n.d. [1697].

Cerny, Gerald. *Theology, Politics, and Letters at the Crossroads of European Civilization: Jacques Basnage and the Baylean Huguenot Refugees in the Dutch Republic.* Dordrecht: Nijhoff, 1987.

Chabrol, Jean-Pierre. *Les fous de Dieu.* Paris: Gallimard, 1961.

Chaumier, Adrian C., ed. *Les Actes des colloques des églises françaises et des synodes des églises étrangères réfugiées en Angleterre: 1581–1654.* MSS coll., Huguenot Society of London.

Chilcote, Paul Wesley. *She Offered Them Christ: The Legacy of Women Preachers in Early Methodism.* Nashville: Abingdon, 1993.

Chinard, Gilbert. *Les Réfugiés huguenots en Amérique.* Paris: Société Edition des Belles-Lettres, 1925.

Claude, Jean. *An account of the persecutions and oppression of the Protestants in France.* London, 1686.

——. *Les plaintes des protestans, cruellement opprimez dans le royaume de France.* Cologne: Pierre Marteau, 1686.

Coats, Catharine Randall. *(Em)bodying the Word: Textual Resurrections in the Martyrological Narratives of Crespin, Foxe, de Bèze and d'Aubigné.* Renaissance and Baroque Studies and Texts 4. New York: Lang, 1992.

——. *Subverting the System: D'Aubigné and Calvinism.* Kirksville, Mo.: Sixteenth-Century Journal, 1991.

Cohen, Sheldon S. "Elias Neau, Instructor to New York's Slaves." *New York Historical Society Quarterly* 55 (1971): 7–21.

Cosmos, Georgia. *Huguenot Prophecy and Clandestine Worship in the Eighteenth Century: The Sacred Theatre of the Cévennes.* Burlington, Vt.: Ashgate, 2006.

——. Response to the review by W. Gregory Monahan of *Huguenot Prophecy and Clandestine Worship in the Eighteenth Century, H-France Review* 6 (May 2006).

Court, Antoine. *Claude Brousson, avocate, pasteur, martyr.* Reprint, Paris: Librairie Protestante, 1961.

——. *L'Histoire des troubles des Cévennes.* Marseille: Laffitte Reprints, 1760.

Crété, Liliane. *Les Camisards.* Paris: Perrin, 1992.

Cruson, Cees. *Huguenot Refugees in Seventeenth-Century Amsterdam.* Working Paper 2. Rotterdam: Erasmus University, 1985.

D'Auborn, A. *The French Convert . . . To which is added, A Brief Account of the present Severe Persecutions of the French Protestants.* 2nd. ed., 1699.

Dedieu, Joseph. *Le rôle politique des protestants français, 1685–1715.* Paris, 1920.

Delafosse, M. "La Rochelle et les îles au XVIIe siècle." *Revue d'histoire des colonies* 36 (1949): 238–81.

De la fureur du calvinisme excitée dans la province du Languedoc. Manuscrit Gaiffe.

Demerez. *Journal des Camisards par Barthélemy: Chronique du Languedoc.* Montpellier, 1874.

Les Désirs de Philothée ou le Jubilée des Captifs. Amsterdam, 1701.

Deyon, Solange. "La Résistance protestante et la symbolique du desert." *Revue d'histoire moderne et contemporaine* 17 (1968): 33–52.

"Document sur le prophétisme en Dauphiné." *Bulletin de la société de l'histoire du protestantisme français* 56 (1902): 112–91.

Domson, Charles A. *Nicolas Fatio de Duillier and the Prophets of London: An Essay in the Historical Interaction of Natural Philosophy and Millennial Belief in the Age of Newton.* New York: Arno, 1981.

Doumergue, Albert. *Nos garrigues et les assemblées au désert: Église de Nîmes sous la croix, 1685–1792.* Nîmes: Musée du désert, 1924.

Ducasse, André. *La guerre des Camisards: La résistance huguenote sous Louis XIV.* Paris: Plon, 1962.

Ducommun, Marie-Jeanne. *Le Refuge protestant dans le Pays de Vaud: Fin XVIIe–début XVIIIe siècle, aspects d'une migration.* Geneva: Droz, 1991.

Dumas, André. *Le désert cévenol.* Paris: Renaissance du livre, 1932.

Dutton, Thomas. *Warnings of the eternal spirit, to the city of Edinburgh, in Scotland.* London, 1710.

The English and French Prophets mad or bewitcht, at their assemblies in Baldwin-gardens, on Wednesday the 12th, at Barbican, with an account of their tryal, 1707. London: Applebee, 1707.

Examen du Théâtre sacré des Cévennes, traduit en Anglois sous le titre "A Crie from the Desart." London, 1708.

A Faithful account of the cruelties done to the protestants on board the French king's galleries on the account of the reformed religion. 2nd. ed. London: Nutt, 1700.

Fatio, Olivier, ed. *Jacques Flournoy: Journal, 1675–1692.* Publications de l'Association suisse pour l'histoire du refuge huguenot 3. Geneva: Droz, 1994.

Fléchier, Esprit. *Lettres choisies de M Fléchier, évêque de Nîmes.* 2 vols. Paris, 1715.

Fontaine, James. *Memoirs of a Huguenot Family.* New York: Putnam, 1872.

Fosdick, Lucian J. *The French Blood in America.* New York: Revell, 1906. Reprint, Baltimore: Genealogical Publishing, 2007.

Fournier, G. *Les galères de France.* Editions du désert, 1943.

Fraissinet, Justin. "Le Camp des enfants de Dieu: Relation par Tobie Rocayrol." *Bulletin de la société de l'histoire du protestantisme français* 16 (1867): 273–91.

Frijhoff, Willem. "Uncertain Brotherhood: The Huguenots in the Dutch Republic." In Van Ruymbeke and Sparks, *Memory and Identity,* 129–171.

Garrett, Clarke. *Spirit Possession and Popular Religion from the Camisards to the Shakers.* Baltimore: Johns Hopkins University Press, 1987.

Garrison, Janine. *L'Edit de Nantes.* Paris: Seuil, 1985.

———. *L'Homme protestant.* Paris: Complexe, 2000.

Gerlan. *Abrégé de l'histoire de la bergère de Saou, près de Crest en Dauphiné.* Amsterdam, 1688.

Godbeer, Richard. *Escaping Salem: The Other Witch Hunt of 1692.* New York: Oxford University Press, 2005.

Goldgar, Anne. *Impolite Learning: Conduct and Community in the Republic of Letters, 1680–1750*. New Haven, Conn.: Yale University Press, 1995.

Goodbar, Richard, ed. *Edict of Nantes: Five Essays and a New Translation*. Bloomington, Minn.: National Huguenot Society, 2000.

Grey, Zachary. *A serious Address to Lay-Methodists, to Beware of the False Pretenses of their Teachers*. London, 1745.

Gwynn, Robin D. "The Arrival of the Huguenot Refugees in England, 1680–1705." *Proceedings of the Huguenot Society of London* 21 (1965–1970): 25–32.

———. *Huguenot Heritage: The History and Contribution of the Huguenots in Britain*. London: Routledge, 1985.

Haefeli, Evan, and Owen Stanwood. "Jesuits, Huguenots, and the Apocalypse: The Origins of America's First French Book." *Proceedings of the American Antiquarian Society* 116, part 1 (2006): 59–120.

Hall, David. *Worlds of Wonder, Days of Judgment: Popular Religious Belief in Early New England*. New York: Knopf, 1989.

Hallie, Philip Paul. *Lest Innocent Blood Be Shed: The Story of the Village of Le Chambon, and How Goodness Happened There*. New York: Harper and Row, 1979.

Hewitt, John H. "New York's Black Episcopalians: In the Beginning, 1704–1722." *Afro-Americans in New York Life and History* 3 (1979): 9–22.

Hirsch, Arthur Henry. *The Huguenots of Colonial South Carolina*. Durham, N.C.: Duke University Press, 1928. Reprint, London: Archon, 1962.

The History of the persecutions of the reformed churches in France, Orange and Piedmont, from the year 1655 to this time: shewing by what steps, artifices, and perfidious practices they were destroyed: with a short account of the present condition of the Protestants in France and elsewhere, wherein are many remarkable passages never before printed, 2nd. ed. London: Thomas Newborough and John Nicholson, 1699.

Holmes, Abiel. "Memoir of the French Protestants who settled at Oxford, Mass., a.d. 1686." *Massachusetts Historical Society Collections*, 3rd series, 2 (1830): 61.

Hughson, David D. *A Copious Account of the French and English Prophets, who infected London during 1707, and the following years; the exposure of some of them on the pillery; and a complete exposure of their infamous practices*. London: Oddy, 1814.

Huguenot Society of London. Pamphlets on the French Prophets.

Joutard, Philippe. *Les Camisards présentés par Philippe Joutard*. Paris: Gallimard-Julliard, 1976.

———. "La Cévenne camisarde." *L'Histoire* 1 (May 1978): 54–63.

Jurieu, Pierre. *L'Accomplissement des prophéties*. 2 vols. Rotterdam, 1687.

———. *Lettres pastorales*. 3 vols. Rotterdam, 1686–1689.

Jurieu, Pierre, and Michel Le Vassor. *The Signs of France in Slavery, breathing after liberty: By way of memorial*. London: Newman, 1689.

Kamil, Neil. *Fortress of the Soul: Violence, Metaphysics, and Material Life in the Huguenots' New World, 1517–1751*. Baltimore: Johns Hopkins University Press, 2005.

Kaufman, Peter Iver. *Redeeming Politics*. Princeton, N.J.: Princeton University Press, 1993.

Keizer, Gerrit. *François Turretini: Sa vie et ses oeuvres et le consensus.* Lausanne: Bridel, 1900.

Kidd, Thomas. *The Great Awakening: The Roots of Evangelical Christianity.* New Haven, Conn.: Yale University Press, 2002.

———. *The Protestant Interest: New England after Puritanism.* New Haven, Conn.: Yale University Press, 2004.

Kingdon, Robert. "Pourquoi les réfugiés huguenots aux colonies américaines sont-ils devenus épiscopaliens?" *Bulletin de la société de l'histoire du protestantisme français* 115 (1969): 487–509.

Klauber, Martin I. "Jean Alphonse Turretini (1671–1737) on Natural Theology: The Triumph of Reason over Revelation at the Academy of Geneva." *Scottish Journal of Theology* 47 (1994): 301–26.

Knox, Ronald. *Enthusiasm: A Chapter in the History of Religion.* Notre Dame, Ind.: University of Notre Dame Press, 1950.

Labrousse, Elisabeth. "Calvinism in France, 1598–1685." In *International Calvinism, 1541–1715,* edited by Menna Prestwich, 304–10. Oxford: Clarendon Press, 1985.

———. *Pierre Bayle.* Dordrecht and Boston: Nijhoff, 1985.

Laursen, John Christian, ed. *New Essays on the Political Thought of the Huguenots of the Refuge.* Leiden: Brill, 1995.

Le Mercier, Andrew. *The Church History of Geneva.* 2 vols. Boston, 1732.

Léonard, Emile-G. "La piété de l' 'Église des galères' sous Louis XIV." In *Mélanges offerts à M. Paul-E. Martin par ses amis, ses collègues, ses élèves,* 97–111. Geneva: Société d'histoire et d'archéologie de Genève, 1961.

Le Roy Ladurie, Emmanuel. *Les paysans de Languedoc.* Paris: Flammarion, Champs, 1969.

A Letter of a French Protestant, concerning the late miracle reported to have been done near the town of Saumur. London, A.M., 1668.

Levin, David. *Cotton Mather: The Young Life of the Lord's Remembrancer, 1663–1703.* Cambridge, Mass.: Harvard University Press, 1978.

Littleton, Charles. "Acculturation and the French Church of London, 1600–circa 1640." In Van Ruymbreke and Sparks, *Memory and Identity,* 90–109.

Lovelace, Richard. *The American Pietism of Cotton Mather: Origins of American Evangelicalism.* Washington, D.C.: Christian College Consortium, 1979.

Lucas, Paul R. *Valley of Discord: Church and Society along the Connecticut River, 1636–1725.* Hanover, N.H.: University Press of New England, 1976.

Lutz, Norma Jean. *Cotton Mather: Author, Clergyman, and Scholar.* Philadelphia: Chelsea, 2000.

Manigault, Judith Giton. "Early Manigault Records," *Huguenot Society of South Carolina Transactions* 59 (1954): 25–27.

Manuel, Frank E., and Fritzie P. Manuel. *James Bowdoin and the Patriot Philosophers.* Philadelphia: American Philosophical Society, 2003.

Marteilhe, Jean. *Mémoires d'un galérien du Roi-Soleil.* Rotterdam, 1757. Reprint, Paris: Le Mercure, 1989.

Mather, Cotton. *The Grounds and Ends of the Baptisme of the Children of the Faithfull.* London, 1647.

———. *Memorable Providences, Relating to Witchcraft and Possessions: A Faithful Account of the Many wonderful and Surprising Things, that have Befallen Several Bewitched and Possessed Persons in New England.* Boston: Pierce, 1689.

———. *Suspiria vinctorum.* Boston: Fleet, 1726.

Mather, Cotton, and Elias Neau. *A Present from a Farr Countrie, to the people of New England.* Boston: Green, 1698.

Maynard, John A. *The Huguenot Church of New York: A History of the French Church of Saint Esprit.* New York: French Church of Saint Esprit, 1938.

Mémoires envoiés de Londres à M* par M* au sujet de l'établissement d'un conseil pour veiller sur la conduite des protestans François refugiés en Angleterre. Cologne, 1699.

Mentzer, Raymond A. "Sociability and Culpability: Conventions of Mediation and Reconciliation within the Sixteenth-Century Huguenot Community." In Van Ruymbeke and Sparks, *Memory and Identity,* 45–57.

Merritt, Percival. "The French Church in Boston." *Proceedings of the Colonial Society of Massachusetts* 26 (1926): 323–48.

Meschinet, M. L. *Les Protestants rochelais depuis la Révocation de l'Edit de Nantes jusqu'au Concordat.* Paris: Plon, 1989.

Meyer, Judith Pugh. *Reformation in La Rochelle: Tradition and Change in Early Modern France, 1500–1568.* Geneva: Droz, 1996.

Michelet, Jules. *De La Révocation de l'Edit de Nantes à la guerre des Cévennes.* Montpellier: Presses du Languedoc, 1985.

Middlekauff, Robert. *The Mathers: Three Generations of Puritan Intellectuals, 1596–1728.* New York: Oxford University Press, 1971.

Misson, François-Maximilien. *Meslange de littérature historique et critique sur tout ce qui regarde l'état extraordinaire des Cévenols, appellez Camisards.* London, 1708.

———. *Le Théâtre sacré des cévennes.* London: Roger, 1707.

———. *Le Théâtre sacré des cévennes.* Edited by Jean-Pierre Richardot. Montpellier: Presses du Languedoc, 1978.

Moorman, John. *The Anglican Spiritual Tradition.* Springfield, Ill.: Templegate, 1983.

Morin, J., and J. Jacobi. *A Short Account of the Life and Sufferings of Elie Neau.* London, 1749.

Mours, Samuel. "Notes sur les galériens protestants." *Bulletin de la société de l'histoire du protestantisme français* 116 (1970): 184.

Mouysset, Henry. *Les Premiers Camisards, juillet 1702.* Montpellier: Presses du Languedoc, 2002.

Mullin, Robert Bruce. *Miracles and the Modern Religious Imagination.* New Haven, Conn.: Yale University Press, 1996.

Mursell, Gordon. *The Story of Christian Spirituality: Two Thousand Years, from East to West.* Minneapolis: Fortress, 2001.

Neau, Elie. *An Address to Persons who Complain they have no time to Prepare for Eternity: with an interesting account of a galley slave.* London, 1810.

———. *Histoire abbregée des souffrances du sieur Elie Neau, sur les galères, et dans les Cachots de Marseille.* Rotterdam: Abraham Archer, 1701.

———. *A Treasury of consolations, divine and human, or a treatise in which the Christian can learn how to vanquish and surmount the afflictions and miseries of this life.* New York: William Bradford, 1696.

Night, Janice. *Orthodoxies in Massachusetts: Rereading American Puritanism.* Cambridge, Mass.: Harvard University Press, 1997.

Noll, Mark. *The Rise of Evangelicalism: The Age of Whitefield and the Wesleys.* Downers Grove, Ill.: InterVarsity, 2003.

Nouvelle relation de la Caroline, par un gentilhomme françois arrivé depuis un mois, de ce nouveau pais. The Hague, 1686.

Orcibal, Jean. *Louis XIV et les Protestants.* Paris: Vrin, 1951.

Petitjean-Rouget, Jacques. "Les protestants à la Martinique sous l'Ancien Régime." *Revue d'histoire des colonies* 42 (1955): 220–65.

Peyrat, Napoléon. *Histoire des pasteurs du Désert: Depuis la révocation de l'édit de Nantes jusqu'à la Révolution française, 1685–1789.* 2 vols. Paris: Librairie de Marc Aurel frères, 1842.

Pezet, Maurice. *L'Epopée des Camisards: Languedoc, Vivarais, Cévennes.* Paris: Seghers, 1978.

Philips, Edith. *The Good Quaker in French Legend.* Philadelphia: University of Pennsylvania Press, 1932.

Pin, Marcel. *Un chef camisard: Nicolas Jouany.* Montpellier: Librairie H. Barral, 1930.

Plainte, et censure des Caolomneuses Accusations Publiees par le Sr Claude Grosteste de la Mote. London, 1708.

Plard, Henri. "L'Apocalypse des Camisards: Prédicants et inspirés." *Problèmes d'histoire du Christianisme* 8 (1979): 45–79.

Porterfield, Amanda. *Feminine Spirituality in America: From Sarah Edwards to Martha Graham.* Philadelphia: Temple University Press, 1980.

Puaux, F. *Histoire populaire des Camisards.* Toulouse: Société des livres religieux, 1886.

Randall, Catharine. *Building Codes: The Calvinist Aesthetics of Early Modern Europe.* Philadelphia: University of Pennsylvania Press, 1999.

———. "'Loosening the Stays': Madame Guyon's Quietist Opposition to Absolutism." *Mystic Quarterly* 26, no. 1 (March 2000): 8–30.

———. "Reforming Calvinism? The Case of the Cévennes Camisards." *Fides et Historia* 36 no. 2 (2004): 51–65.

Reaman, G. Elmore. *The Trail of the Huguenots in Europe, the United States, South Africa, and Canada.* Baltimore: Genealogical Publishing, 1983.

Reece, R. *A Compendious Marytyrology, containing an account of the sufferings and constancy of Christians in the different persecutions which have raged against them under pagan and popish governments.* 3 vols. London, 1812–1815.

"Remarks on the New Account of Carolina by a French Gentleman, 1686." *Magnolia,* n.s., 1 (1842): 226–30.

Report of a French Protestant Refugee in Boston, 1687. Translated by E. T. Fisher. Brooklyn, N.Y.: Munsell, 1868.

Rice, Howard. "Cotton Mather Speaks to France: American Propaganda in the Age of Louis XIV." *New England Quarterly* 16, no. 2 (June 1943): 198–233.

Robbins, Kevin. *City on the Ocean Sea: La Rochelle, 1530–1650.* Leiden: Brill, 1997.

Rosengarten, J. G. *French Colonists and Exiles in the United States.* Philadelphia: Lippincott, 1907.

Sample, Christie Gay. "Failure and Success of the Revocation of the Edict of Nantes: The Experience of Loriol, 1650–1715." PhD diss., University of Texas at Austin, 1998.

Schmidt, Benjamin. *Innocence Abroad: The Dutch Imagination and the New World, 1570–1610.* New York: Cambridge University Press, 2001.

Schwartz, Hillel. *The French Prophets: The History of a Millenarian Group in Eighteenth-Century England.* Berkeley and Los Angeles: University of California Press, 1980.

———. "Knaves, Fools, Madmen and That Subtle Effluvium." PhD diss., University of Florida at Gainesville, 1978.

Seconde Lettre d'un Protestant a un de ses amis de la contree. London, 1706.

The Shortest Way with the French Prophets, or, an Impartial Relation . . . of Those Seducers who Attempted Lately to Pervert Several Inhabitants . . . of Birmingham in Warwickshire: in a Letter from Thence . . . to which is added a Letter from John Lacy. London, 1707.

Silverman, Kenneth. *The Life and Times of Cotton Mather.* New York: Columbia University Press, 1985.

Society for the Propagation of the Gospel. "An Account of the Money Collected by the Reverend Mr. John Sharp and Mr. Elias Neau, 1711–12." *Letters,* series B, volume 8 (1701): 260–62.

Spini, Giorgio. "Remarques sur la réforme française dans l'historiographie puritaine de la Nouvelle-Angleterre." In *Historiographie de la Réforme,* edited by Philippe Joutard. Paris: Delachaux & Niestlé, 1977.

Stein, Stephen J. *The Shaker Experience in America: A History of the United Society of Believers.* New Haven, Conn.: Yale University Press, 1992.

Stevenson, Robert Louis. "The Country of the Camisards." In *Travels with a Donkey in the Cévennes.* 1879. Reprint, London: Dent, 1984.

Strayer, Brian. *Huguenots and Camisards as Aliens in France, 1598–1789: The Struggle for Religious Toleration.* Lewiston, N.Y.: Mellen, 2001.

Thomas, Eugène. *Un agent des alliés chez les Camisards.* Montpellier, 1859.

Tournier, Gaston, ed. *Le Baron de Salgas: Gentilhomme Cévenol et forçat pour la foi.* Musée du Désert, 1941.

———. *Les galères de France et les galériens protestants des XVIIe et XVIIIe siècles.* 1943–1949. Reprint, Montpellier: Presses du Languedoc, 1984.

———, ed. *Histoire des souffrances et de la mort du fidèle confesseur et martyr, M. Isaac Lefebvre* [1703]. Musée du Désert, 1940.

———, ed. *Vingt complaintes sur les prédicants des Cévennes martyrisés au XVIIIe siècle.* Musée du Désert, 1932.

Townsend, Craig D. *Faith in Their Own Color: Black Episcopalians in Antebellum New York City*. Religion and American Culture Series. New York: Columbia University Press, 2005.

Updike, Wilkins. *A History of the Episcopal Church in Narragansett, Rhode Island, including a History of Other Episcopal Churches in the State*. Boston: Merrymount, 1907.

Utt, Walter C., and Brian E. Strayer. *The Bellicose Dove: Claude Brousson and Protestant Resistance to Louis XIV, 1647–1698*. Brighton, UK: Sussex Academic Press, 2003.

Van Ruymbeke, Bertrand. *From New Babylon to Eden: The Huguenots and Their Migration to Colonial South Carolina*. Columbia: University of South Carolina Press, 2006.

Van Ruymbeke, Bertrand, and Randy Sparks, ed. *Memory and Identity: The Huguenots in France and the Atlantic Diaspora*. Columbia: University of South Carolina Press, 2003.

Vauban, Sébastien Le Prestre. *Mémoire pour le Rappel des Huguenots*. Paris, 1689. Reprint, Carrieres-sous-Poissy: La Cause, 1985.

Vic, Claude de, and Joseph Vaissete, eds. *Histoire générale du Languedoc avec des notes and les pieces justificatives*. Toulouse: Édouard Privat, 1873.

Vidal, Daniel. *Le Malheur et son prophète: Inspirés et sectaires en Languedoc calviniste*. Paris: Payot, 1983.

Vielles, Jules, ed. *Mémoires de Bonbonnoux, chef camisard et pasteur du Désert en Cévennes*. Anduze: Castagnier, 1883.

Vigne, Randolph, and Charles Littleton, eds. *From Strangers to Citizens: Integration of Immigrant Communities in Britain, Ireland, and Colonial America, 1550–1750*. Portland, Oregon: Sussex Academic Press, 2001.

Voorhees, David William. Review of *Innocence Abroad: The Dutch Imagination and the New World, 1570–1610*, by Benjamin Schmidt. *Journal of Interdisciplinary History* 33, no 4 (Spring 2003): 650–51.

Weber, Eugène. *Apocalypses: Prophecies, Cults and Millennial Beliefs through the Ages*. Cambridge, Mass.: Harvard University Press, 1999.

Weddle, Meredith Baldwin. *Walking in the Way of Peace: Quaker Pacifism in the Seventeenth Century*. New York: Oxford University Press, 2001.

Weeden, William. *Early Rhode Island: A Social History of the People*. New York: Grafton, 1910.

Weiss, Charles. *History of the French Protestant Refugees, from the Revocation of the Edict of Nantes to Our Own Days*. 2 vols. Translated by Henry W. Herbert. New York: Stringer and Townsend, 1854.

Weiss, N. "Précisions sur l'histoire des Camisards." *Bulletin de la société de l'histoire du protestantisme français* 1 (1909): 117–28.

Wendell, Barrett. *Cotton Mather*. New York: Barnes and Noble, 1992.

White, Anna, and Leila S. Taylor. *Shakerism: Its Meaning and Message*. Columbus, Ohio: Heer, 1904.

Wiley, Thomas. *A Brief History of the French Church of Saint-Esprit*. New York: French Church of Saint-Esprit, 1986.

Wilson, Katharina, ed. *Women Writers of the Renaissance and Reformation*. Athens: University of Georgia Press, 1987.

Wilson, Robert. *Prophecy and Society in Ancient Israel*. Philadelphia: Fortress, 1980.

A Wonderful Instance of God's Appearance for, and Presence with His People in a Day of Suffering; or a Narrative of the Most holy Life, and Triumphant Death of Mr. Fulcian Rey. London, 1688.

Yardeni, Miriam. "Conversions et reconversions dans le Refuge Huguenot." *Dimensioni e problemi della ricerca storica* 1996, no. 2: 239–46.

———. "Problèmes de fidélité chez les protestants français à l'époque de la Révocation." In *Hommage à Roland Mousnier: Clientèles et fidélités en Europe à l'époque moderne*, edited by Yves Durand, 297–314. Paris: Presses Universitaires de France, 1981.

Zakai, Avihu. *Exile and Kingdom: History and Apocalypse in the Puritan Migration to America*. Cambridge: Cambridge University Press, 2002.

Zysberg, André. *Les Galériens: Vie et destinées de 60,000 forçats français sur les galères de France, 1680–1748*. Paris: Seuil, 1987.

INDEX

CPSIA information can be obtained at www.ICGtesting.com
Printed in the USA
267501BV00001B/6/P